# Edible SPOTS & POTS

Small-Space Gardens for Growing
**VEGETABLES** *and* **HERBS**
in Containers, Raised Beds, and More

## STACEY HIRVELA

RODALE

Rodale books may be purchased for business or promotional use or for special sales. For information, please write to: Special Markets Department, Rodale Inc., 733 Third Avenue, New York, NY 10017.

Printed in the United States of America

Rodale Inc. makes every effort to use acid-free ♾, recycled paper ♲.

Book design by Christina Gaugler

Illustrations by Lindsey Spinks

Photography credits can be found on page 293.

Cover and page 4: Hanging salad garden photographed at Chanticleer Garden, Wayne, Pennsylvania

Library of Congress Cataloging-in-Publication Data is on file with the publisher.

ISBN-13: 978-1-60961-959-6   paperback

Distributed to the trade by Macmillan

2   4   6   8   10   9   7   5   3   1   paperback

We inspire and enable people to improve their lives and the world around them.

rodalebooks.com

To Adam,
my partner in the garden and in life

# contents

INTRODUCTION viii

CHAPTER 1: EDIBLE POTS: GROWING VEGETABLES IN CONTAINERS 1

CHAPTER 2: EDIBLE SPOTS: RAISING CROPS IN RAISED BEDS 43

CHAPTER 3: SPOTS & POTS GARDENING SCHOOL 73

CHAPTER 4: SPOTS & POTS PROJECTS 113

CHAPTER 5: THRILLER, FILLER, & SPILLER COMBINATIONS 163

CHAPTER 6: PLANT ENCYCLOPEDIA 217

RESOURCES 286

ACKNOWLEDGMENTS 290

ABOUT THE AUTHOR 292

PHOTO CREDITS 293

INDEX 294

# introduction

## Are you ready for a new way to grow your own food?

An easier way that *works,* no matter how much space or time you have?

A way that combines both beauty *and* bounty, enhancing your outdoor space while nourishing your loved ones with healthy, homegrown produce?

It's time to throw off the cloak of convention and grow down a different path with edible spots and pots. This new approach to vegetable gardening combines the sound, proven practices of the past with new ways, new ideas, and a new look for how and where you grow. It's a welcome departure from tradition that acknowledges that you live in the real world where you might not have as much time or space for your garden as you'd like, and that the privilege of saying "I grew that!" never loses its appeal.

## EDIBLE SPOTS, EDIBLE POTS

Growing edibles in spots and pots is a way to "think outside the plot," or the inground places where vegetables have traditionally been grown. Edible spots—or raised beds—let you garden just about anywhere in your yard, no matter what the soil is like. Pots—or containers—are familiar to most garden- ers as a place for flowers, but they are perfect for growing edibles, too. They let you transform any sunny spot on your property (including walkways, patios, decks, even your driveway) into a vegetable garden.

Gardening in spots and pots is more fun and less work than conventional garden plots, and you'll save precious time and resources. Just look at these advantages:

- Spots and pots take less time to plant and maintain—no heavy digging or cultivating.

- You can provide the perfect soil, light, and water conditions for every crop you grow.

- Rocky soil, clay soil, or compacted soil? No problem! Just grow on top of it.

- Fewer pests and diseases will impact your garden, and any that do appear will be far easier to manage quickly, effectively, and without chemicals.

- Raised beds and containers eliminate the need to kneel, stoop, or bend, saving your back and your knees.

- Fewer weeds appear in raised beds and containers, but those that do are easy to pull, even by hand.

- Spots and pots are more convenient to tend and harvest because they can be placed near the house, where it will be easy to pick a handful of fragrant herbs, a newly ripened vegetable, or the fixings for a super-fresh salad.

- Extend the season earlier in spring and later into autumn to enjoy a longer growing season and more produce compared to those folks who garden conventionally.

- Grow up instead of just out, utilizing walls, balconies, eaves, and window frames as potential garden spaces.

- You don't get as dirty working in raised beds and containers, so you can sneak in a few minutes of gardening whenever you have time.

When you grow your own food, the harvest is its own reward. And growing in edible spots and pots does it one better by making it super-convenient and easier on you. When a garden is as beautiful as it is productive, it's an inspiring and refreshing place to spend your time—whether you're at work or at play.

# PERSONALIZE WITH PROJECTS

There are dozens of ways to make edible spots and pots uniquely your own: You can choose the size and materials for your raised beds and containers, position them almost anywhere you like, and grow nearly any crop you like in them. This book features 16 do-it-yourself projects that give you even more possibilities for customizing your garden, helping you create new places to hold pots and space savers for your raised beds. Save money (and make good use of the off-season) by whipping up a bunch of grow bags or by building your own handsome-yet-sturdy dolly for moving your containers around effortlessly. These projects are based on components that are easy to find at hardware stores and garden centers and draw only on basic household skills to create them. You probably already have materials on hand for many of them, so you can get started right away! These projects are not just beautiful and useful, they are durable and designed for professional looking results, so you know that your time and money are being invested wisely in making your garden more efficient, more productive, and more uniquely your own.

There are projects here for every skill level and budget, all of them designed specifically to work as edible spots and pots. You'll delight in saying not just "I grew that!" but also, "I made that!"

# THRILLER + FILLER + SPILLER PLANT COMBINATIONS

A garden is full of life and color, a veritable stage for interplays of interesting plants, and this book brings a fresh approach—the thriller-filler-spiller scheme—to combining vegetables and herbs in spots and pots. Simply choose a thriller (a dramatic focal-point plant), a filler (a spreading, bushy plant), and a spiller (a vine or twining plant) to create beautiful and botanically sound edible gardens. And there's no guesswork needed—you'll find all of the information you need to combine beautiful, delicious edibles successfully using this method. Each crop has been labeled as a filler, spiller, or thriller, so all you'll need to do is decide which crops you and your family will enjoy most, follow the formula, and enjoy the results. It's a feast for the eyes as well as the palate! Long popular as a way to combine summer flowers, this simple, foolproof planting guideline will give you the same lush, appealing results with vegetables, herbs, and edible flowers that it does with ornamental flowers and foliage.

The thriller-filler-spiller formula helps you:

✛ Create stunning plant combinations with familiar vegetables and herbs, turning the idea of a boring or messy vegetable garden on its ear.

✛ Get more produce from a small space by combining plants with complementary growth habits and harvest times.

✛ Surround yourself with bountiful, beautiful vegetable, herb, and edible flower plants by decorating your patio or deck with varieties that are as pretty as flowers. After all, when you have a choice, wouldn't you prefer something pretty *and* useful instead of merely one or the other?

✛ Encourage optimal growth and production because you'll learn to evaluate the size and form of the plants you most want to grow and combine.

✛ Achieve consistently excellent results because you'll understand the varying nutritional needs and soil requirements for different crops and combine those that have the same preferences in the same pot or raised bed.

With *Edible Spots and Pots,* you'll discover lots of fresh ideas and reliable advice for creating a garden that's easy care, beautiful, bountiful, and cultivated with safe, nontoxic techniques. Even if you have an established inground vegetable plot, you can transform your large plots into raised beds and add containers to your garden space. And if you are a first-time gardener who hasn't yet broken sod to put in a plot, you'll be saving yourself time and effort by creating a manageable and an equally productive garden. Anytime is the perfect time to start, whether you'll be planning or planting.

I have been growing edibles in spots and pots for more than 20 years, and though it was originally out of the necessity created by being a garden- and food-obsessed renter living in the city, I wouldn't do it any other way now. When space, time, and resources are limited (and perhaps even if they're not), I'll take a pot of pretty peppers over a pot of petunias any day. If you feel the same, get ready to dig in.

# A NOTE FROM THE AUTHOR

We live in an age of misinformation—the Internet, though one of the most useful inventions mankind has ever produced, is a veritable minefield of bad ideas and unreliable statements and opinions that are too frequently taken as fact. If a myth or a lie gets spread by enough people, it is given preference by the search engines and will appear higher up in the results, furthering the guise of authority. Books like this one undergo a lengthy process of vetting and are read by dozens of people—editors, horticulturists, laymen, art directors—before they reach you. As such, most books (especially when put out by a venerable institution like Rodale!) can serve as a beacon of credibility, a voice of reason among the widespread chatter of conjecture that makes up far too much of our primary sources of information these days.

Still, a book is ultimately the work of the author and as such, does consist of his or her particular point of view. In this book, I discuss some rather contentious contemporary issues. I have done my best to present scientifically valid information in a way that allows you, the reader who has so graciously invited me into your gardening life, to take the information I provide and make your own decisions about what they mean to you and how you will act on them. When I first met Ethne Clarke, whose kindness and warmth made this book a reality,

I told her—warned her, really—that I teach, I don't preach. My goal in this book is not to tell you what to think and do, but to provide the information and knowledge that you need to make informed decisions and do what is best for your own personal reality and conscience.

When you talk about the environment, about organic food and organic gardening, about compost and the soil, and about water conservation, you enter an arena where strong opinions and powerful voices prevail. But as they say, we are all entitled to our own opinions, but not our own facts.

My personal agenda in this book is twofold, but both aspects are very simple. One, to present science-based information as impartially and sensibly as possible, and in a way that empowers gardeners to make the best possible choices in light of their own personal realities and beliefs; and two, to inspire people to garden—to get them as excited as I feel when I walk out to the garden on a summer morning and see my plants bursting with color, when I swear I can hear the cells multiplying and the bees buzzing and I feel and hear and see the power of nature everywhere I look.

I believe that the world would be a better place if more people were gardeners. How could it not be? Gardening teaches care, patience, hopefulness, and the value of physical work. It rewards with beauty, nutrition, entertainment, and a funny sort of humble pride that comes from few other practices. It strengthens relationships between neighbors and improves community. A house with a garden sends a powerfully positive message to passersby. I know this because growing things has been a central part of my life for 20+ years and I feel these things more keenly every season.

 chapter one

# EDIBLE POTS: GROWING VEGETABLES IN CONTAINERS

**Container gardening is now more popular than ever,** but for some reason, the trend hasn't progressed much beyond ornamental flowers and foliage. That's a shame, because containers offer so much potential for growing edible plants as well. The practical benefits are obvious, after all. Instead of being limited to sunny yard space, you can grow veggies and herbs anywhere: on a deck, porch, or patio; on your front steps; even right next to your kitchen door. Placing the containers close to your living area makes it much easier to keep an eye on them, so you can catch any problems before they get serious and immediately provide any care the plants need. And when harvesttime comes, you'll know it: no need to traipse out to a far corner of your yard to see what's ready to pick. When the plants are a few steps away from your house, you can pick them at the peak of readiness and chop or cook them just seconds later. You can't get any fresher than that! Edible containers

1

provide the perfect opportunity to exercise your creativity as well. It's just as easy to create fun and exuberant combinations with edibles as it is with annuals and tropical plants.

The basics of growing veggies and herbs are pretty much the same no matter where you plant them, but there are some tricks to getting the best out of edibles grown this way. In this chapter, you'll learn some professional secrets for choosing among the amazing array of available containers, putting them in the right place, and filling them with the perfect growing medium to get your crops off to a strong start.

## CONSIDER YOUR CONTAINER OPTIONS

If you haven't been container shopping for a while, you'll be astounded by the diversity of shapes, sizes, and materials to choose from! No longer is the selection at your garden center limited to plastic swan planters and those funny black cauldron pots. Plus, there are many other unique items that you can plant and grow your edibles in beyond those available at your local garden center, to create container displays that are both unexpected and easy to care for.

### Classic Pots and Planters

The containers that usually come to mind first are the four traditional favorites: pots, planters, window boxes, and hanging baskets. All of these can work just as well for edibles as they do for ornamental plants.

### Pots

The familiar, cylindrical "flowerpot" is a fine place to start your edible container plantings. You can use pots that you already own, provided they are big enough: Veggies and herbs usually do best in pots that are on the larger side (at least 10 inches in diameter). There's a wide range of materials to choose from.

⚜ **Terra-cotta** ("cooked earth") is another name for the material used for the classic clay pot. Terra-cotta containers are easy to find and affordable; they are offered in a range of appealing warm shades, from orange to brown. They are somewhat fragile, though, and suffer severe damage if exposed to freezing temperatures.

⚜ **Ceramic pots** are made of clay, then fired with a glaze painted on the surface, giving them a glossy sheen. They are often colorful and may offer multiple hues in a single pot. Though they are heavy and expensive, ceramic pots can make a striking aesthetic statement around your home. Some ceramic pots are weatherproof and can be left out all year; these are typically more expensive than nonweatherproof vessels, but you're saved from having to protect them from freezing temperatures.

⚜ **Concrete pots** are very heavy but also very durable. They're available in various shapes and often contribute an artistic, handmade look.

- ⚜ **Fiberglass** is a synthetic material that is lightweight and long lasting. Fiberglass pots often mimic traditional terra-cotta pots in color, shape, and form but also come in other styles and colors.
- ⚜ **Resin** is a type of plastic. Like fiberglass, resin pots are often designed to look like real terra-cotta in color and shape, but they are much lighter and extremely durable. Resin (also sold as polyresin or poly) is generally the lowest cost type of pot.

## Planter Boxes

Usually bigger than typical pots, rectangular or square planter boxes are great for large vegetable plants like tomatoes or zucchini and for combinations of several different smaller edibles. You may find planters made of metal, wood, vinyl, or composite, a rot-resistant material made to look like wood.

# STRAIGHT TALK ON SAUCERS

Terra-cotta, ceramic, and resin are the types of pots most likely to have matching saucers available. A saucer adds a finished look to a pot and helps protect the surface the pot sits on. Saucers are not imperative, however, and purchasing them for all of your pots can become quite expensive, since they are typically sold separately from the pot. Further, because saucers by design do not have drainage holes, they can hold water for long periods, creating a breeding ground for mosquitoes or simply becoming algae-laden and stagnant. I actually prefer to use the saucers I have upside down, with the bottom side up, as a low pedestal for a pot. This trick accentuates the shape of a container and gives it a little height boost while still providing some protection for the surface below.

## Window Boxes

Window boxes are scaled-down planter boxes that are usually hung below an exterior window. They also work well on deck or balcony railings. Though they tend to be on the shallow side, they can accommodate herbs, salad greens, edible flowers, and even strawberries for a charming, unusual departure from tradition.

## Hanging Baskets

Like window boxes, hanging baskets give you the opportunity for a harvest without taking up valuable ground-level space. Most hanging baskets are too small to accommodate large, deeply rooted vegetables (for my thoughts on the upside-down tomato hanging baskets, see opposite page), but they can work for herbs, edible flowers (especially pansies and nasturtiums, which will trail over the sides), and quick-growing crops like salad greens. Most metal hanging baskets meant to be used with coco liners are very ornamental. Plastic baskets aren't as attractive, but they are lightweight, inexpensive, and tend to need less frequent watering. You can also make simple plant hangers to transform any terra-cotta or plastic pot into a unique hanging basket; see the Hanging Basket Sling on page 128.

## Beyond the Ordinary

If you look beyond the container selection at your local garden center, you'll see lots of potential material for unique and affordable pots for your edible plants. In fact, looking beyond the garden center to hardware stores and agricultural suppliers will reveal even more interesting and inexpensive nontraditional options.

**Grow bags.** These have long been popular in Europe but are just coming on the scene here in North America. They are flowerpot-like

# ONE GARDENER'S CANTANKEROUS OPINION OF THE UPSIDE-DOWN TOMATO PLANTER

The upside-down tomato planter stormed onto the scene a decade or so ago, popping up in hardware stores and garden centers and even sold on television infomercials. In theory, it's a great idea: As a kind of outlandish hanging basket, it can be placed in an otherwise unused space, and it eliminates the need for staking tomatoes, which become notoriously heavy when bearing fruit. Because the plant doesn't make contact with soil, fruits are kept clean and there's no risk of picking up a beautiful-looking tomato off the ground only to find that the slugs have gotten to it first.

In reality, however, the upside-down tomato planter is far from qualified to meet the needs of tomato plants. First, the interior volume of one of these planters is not even three-quarters of a cubic foot, and the root volume of a typical tomato is dozens or even hundreds of cubic feet, depending on the variety. It isn't that a tomato plant won't grow in one of these planters—it will, to a certain point—but its roots will fill that volume rapidly, and once its roots have taken up all of the available space, they cannot support further topgrowth of the plant, effectively ending tomato season.

Second, with such limited volume for soil, an upside-down tomato planter quickly becomes a watering nightmare, requiring at least daily watering to even have a chance of bearing well. Try setting one on the ground as if it were a conventional pot: Would you ever think something that size was appropriate for growing a tomato plant?

So while I certainly commend the makers of the upside-down tomato planter for their unconventional approach to bringing edible spots and pots to the masses, I resent that they offer a gimmicky product that sets the buyer up for failure. Stick to large pots, planters, or raised beds for your tomatoes, and you'll be much happier with the results!

---

containers made out of industrial felt or heavy but flexible plastic (like a tarpaulin). Because these are designed primarily to grow vegetables, they come in sizes that easily accommodate large plants like tomatoes. Potatoes are especially easy and successful in grow bags. Large "raised bed" grow bags are even available! Grow bags are one of the lowest-cost ways to start a garden of edible pots. You can make your own following the pattern on page 125.

**Grow rings and grow towers.** These are simple, do-it-yourself types of containers formed out of wire mesh or chicken wire and filled with soil. They're best for use on the ground unless you fashion some sort of bottom for them to prevent the soil from staining your concrete or deck. Grow rings and grow towers are an inexpensive and easy way to grow potatoes, in particular, though they work well for other crops, too. You can learn more about them and how to make them on pages 137–145.

**Livestock equipment.** Farm-supply stores and catalogs can be a gold mine of durable and relatively inexpensive container possibilities, particularly if you look into items that are used for watering or feeding farm animals. Stock tanks, for instance, are large plastic or galvanized metal tubs that provide water to livestock in pastures. They are as large as bathtubs but relatively lightweight and lend a modern aesthetic. They often have a single plug to release the water for cleaning, so you may need to drill more holes in the bottom to provide proper drainage for your crops.

**Hayracks.** These are heavy wire structures that hold hay for grazing animals. They make such good garden planters that there are window boxes based on the same style that are also called hayracks. There are freestanding models (be careful to find one that is meant to be used on its own—some are designed to work with watering or feed troughs) and wall-mounted models that work fabulously as a vertical garden element. In either case, you will need to fashion some sort of liner out of moss or coco fiber to prevent the soil from spilling out of the openings. Once that is installed, however, you can cut into the liner to make additional planting pockets in the sides.

## Upcycled Containers

Many everyday items can be recycled (or upcycled, which means made even better) as garden containers. Look for generously sized items that hold plenty of soil and to which you can easily add drainage holes if needed. Most important, they *must* be food safe: not treated with toxic preservatives nor ever used to store

potentially harmful products. Plants take up chemicals through their roots and may store them in their tissues, where the chemicals can be passed on to you when you eat your harvest, so you don't want to take any chances. A number of common items can have a new life as containers, if you know how to choose them carefully.

**Old kitchenware.** Check out garage sales, thrift stores, and even your own cupboards for cooking pots, serving dishes, and utensils that can hold enough potting soil for edible plants. Stainless steel colanders, in particular, make for a playful take on the hanging basket, and they already have plenty of drainage holes. Since these items were originally intended for food use, you know that they are safe for growing edible plants, too.

**Plastic buckets.** Five-gallon buckets are the perfect size to hold one large tomato plant, two or three small peppers, or a selection of herbs. They're easy to drill for drainage and are often free or very inexpensive. Just make sure that the buckets you find have been used for shipping food-grade materials, not toxic materials like detergents or other cleaning supplies. Pizzerias, restaurants, and bakeries are good sources for food-safe 5-gallon buckets.

**Whiskey barrels.** Wooden barrels used to age and ship wine or whiskey make excellent garden containers, and gardeners have been using them for years. If you live in an area wine or spirits are produced, you may be able to find these barrels at a bargain rate. The rest of us might have to pay a bit more, but it's worth the price for containers that are long lasting and food safe and that feature a fun, rustic charm.

## Other Fabulous Finds

Once you start looking for unusual containers, you can find potential pots just about anywhere. Online garden-idea sites, especially, can be a great source of inspiration. Be aware, though, that these sites often show containers that look pretty in pictures but that aren't particularly safe or practical. It's important to do a bit of research before trying some of the more unexpected container ideas, such as the following:

**Metal food cans.** Large metal cans, such as those imported tomatoes are sold in, aren't a good choice for edible pots. They will rust quickly, and there are some concerns about the possible toxicity of BPA, a plastic coating applied inside the can to prevent the metal from reacting with the food it contains. If you have a big food can you'd like to use, enjoy it as a cachepot or as a temporary decoration for a party. It isn't a good long-term choice.

**Shoe organizers.** Cloth or plastic pocketed hanging bags meant for storing shoes are inexpensive and easy to place on a wall. However, their pockets are too small to allow for continued vigorous growth, and they will soon become stained from regular watering. They also become quite heavy when loaded down with water and soil, a weight they are not designed to bear. For a more practical take on

# WHAT'S A CACHEPOT?

*Cachepot* (pronounced kash-po) is from French words that translate to "hide pot." Cachepots are basically decorative pots that hide more serviceable but less attractive container, like plastic nursery pots. With a combination like this, you can use a much wider variety of items for the outer containers: even those that do not have any drainage holes. If you get a heavy rain, simply lift out the inner container, dump the water out of the cachepot, and replace the inner container. (If the inner pot is very heavy and wet, let it drain for a few days before returning it to the cachepot to give it a chance to recover from the flooding.)

this idea, check out the pocketed planter pattern on page 130.

**Gutters.** Rain gutters can do more than carry water away from your roof: Mounted on walls, they make interesting containers. Their safety is definitely questionable, however, since they typically incorporate lower-quality metals and may contain lead, and their surfaces may be treated with a sealant or coating to discourage corrosion and staining; you can use them for ornamental plants, but for your edibles, you're better off investing your money in more versatile, safer containers.

**Wine boxes.** Inexpensive (usually free from your local wine shop) and charming, wooden wine shipping boxes seem like a fantastic recycled container at first glance. However, my experience with them was a rather hilarious failure. I filled them with potting mix, sowed neat rows of lettuce seeds, and watered them thoroughly. I returned an hour later to find that the water had dissolved all the glue holding the sides together, and the tiny brad nails had popped right out, leaving me with piles of potting mix and no boxes! You will no doubt see photos on the Internet of adorable wine-box gardens; perhaps some brands or countries make higher-quality boxes than others. If you can get free wine boxes, go ahead and give them a try, but water the potting soil to ensure the sides will hold together *before* you waste seeds or plants.

**Wood pallets.** "Pallet gardens" have become increasingly popular, rising along with the vertical gardening craze. The basic idea is to take a wooden shipping pallet, staple some landscape fabric to the back to keep the soil in, lean it up against a wall on one of its short (or open) ends, and heap potting mix into the openings. You then plant small transplants or seedlings into the soil, and as the plants grow, they form a picturelike mosaic.

Pallet gardens are popular because they have such a small footprint—they take up almost no ground space—and can even hang on a wall. From a safety standpoint, however, I do not recommend pallet gardens for growing edibles. Wood pallets usually come from abroad and are made of the cheapest, roughest wood that cannot be used for anything else. It was in wood pallets that two notoriously invasive insect pests—the emerald ash borer and Asian long-horned beetle—arrived here and came to be such a threat to our trees. These days, all pallets shipped to the United States must be treated to kill pests. Though heat treating is the most commonly used method, some pallets have been fumigated or treated with toxins to kill any insects lurking within, and these are extremely dangerous for growing edibles. If the idea of a pallet garden really appeals to you, my advice is to make one and use it strictly for annuals and ornamentals, and enjoy it that way.

## Self-Watering Containers

Self-watering containers are a relatively new innovation, at least in mainstream gardening. These types of containers include a large reservoir for water in the bottom part of the container and some kind of wicking system to draw the water from the reservoir up into the root zone. You can buy specially designed self-watering containers or make your own out of a plastic storage bin (several different Web sites show you how). You can also find kits that allow you to convert many kinds of ordinary containers into self-watering ones.

Gardeners all over the world have enjoyed tremendous success with self-watering systems, cutting their watering chores dramatically. Because the reservoir is almost completely enclosed within the container, there are no worries about the water evaporating into the air. Self-watering containers need filling only every few days in most conditions (perhaps more often, depending on the crop and how hot the weather is). And the do-it-yourself versions are extremely cost effective: With materials readily available at most hardware stores and a drill, you can make your own self-watering container for around $25.

# Self-Watering Container Concerns

As wonderful as these containers can be, there are issues with self-watering containers. One concern is the possibility of salts building up in the potting soil. Salts are present in fertilizers, even in compost and compost-based fertilizers. Some water sources also have naturally high levels of salts. Watering a regular container from the top down results in excess water draining out the bottom, and salts, which readily leach out from the soil, go with it. In a self-watering container, however, you'll never get that flushing effect. Salts can accumulate and harm sensitive plant roots.

Another potential problem is that self-watering containers may readily flood during heavy rains, and it's very difficult to get the excess water out. Some of them are designed with an overflow hole, but even this may not be sufficient in the major thunderstorms that summer brings to many parts of the country. You can minimize this problem by keeping containers under the overhang of a roof or other sheltered spot. Depending on the design and material of the planter, you may also be able to drill a hole well above the reservoir to allow excess water to escape.

Some gardeners report problems with mosquitoes breeding in the reservoir. As self-watering container designs differ so much, this may never be an issue for you. However, a pool of standing water is exactly what mosquitoes seek out for breeding, and no one wants any more of these pests than they already get, so you may wish to cover any holes or entrances into the reservoir with a bit of screening or light fabric.

Finally, though the do-it-yourself self-watering containers are a fantastic, cost-effective idea, I have reservations about the long-term safety of growing food in the plastic storage bins that make up the containers. Sunlight degrades plastic, releasing many of the chemical compounds that comprise the walls of the containers; plants readily take up chemicals that leach into the soil and/or the irrigation water they grow in. Whether or not the plants take them up and store them long term in the same form—and what chemicals are in your specific container in the first place—is difficult to ascertain. So if you are committed to avoiding plastics in your day-to-day diet, self-watering containers made of plastic storage bins may not be the best choice for you.

Keep in mind that self-watering containers will not be self-watering right after planting. Whether you're using seeds or transplants, the roots first need to grow deep enough to begin taking up water. So no matter what the directions on your container say, plan to provide supplemental water the conventional way for several weeks before relying on the self-watering mechanism.

The hardest part of dealing with "self-watering" containers may be remembering that you *do* need to add water to the reservoir. It's easy to forget a task when you have to do it only occasionally, rather than every day. If you are the forgetful type, you may want to come up with some kind of reminder to fill, or at least check, your containers every few days so they don't dry out completely.

# CHOOSE YOUR CONTAINERS

While cost and aesthetics are probably the two biggest factors contributing to the types of containers you choose, you need to take into account several additional considerations when expanding your container collection.

## Design Details

Combining a variety of container materials makes for a fun, personal, and varied garden. To keep it from looking too busy and mismatched (unless, of course, that's the look you're going for!), you can try a couple of approaches to give a more unified look.

**Work with one color.** If you have several dramatic glazed ceramic containers that you love, continue that theme by purchasing more containers in that color family or by painting other containers you already have to match or harmonize with them. Never paint the interior of a container you'll be growing in—just the outside.

**Stick with one shape.** The classic tapered cylinder shape of terra-cotta pots can be found in all sorts of containers at all price levels. Square planters, too, are easy to find in various sizes and materials. Simply by selecting variations on one shape, you attain a more cohesive overall look for your container collection.

## NO-DRAINAGE CONTAINER OPTIONS

If you have a container with no drainage holes that you would prefer not to risk drilling into yourself (such as with a glazed ceramic container), it can still serve a purpose. Simply use it as a cachepot (see "What's a Cachepot?" on page 7), or turn it upside down and employ it as a pedestal to vary the heights of containers in your garden. Or put a piece of wood or a slab of stone over the top to create a side table (with bonus storage for tools and gear inside the pot). Or experiment with growing an edible that enjoys wet soil, like celery, water chestnuts, or taro.

## Drainage Decisions

Drainage is imperative in any container that holds a growing plant. There *must* be holes for excess water to escape. This keeps the soil from getting waterlogged; that is, it prevents all of the space between the soil particles from filling with water and thus effectively suffocat-

# How to Drill into a Container

| CONTAINER TYPE | DRILL BIT TYPE | NOTES |
|---|---|---|
| **TERRA-COTTA** | Masonry bit | Work slowly and do not push too hard or the pot will crack. Drill only on flat, not curved, surfaces. Pour water over the area frequently to cool down the material and bit. |
| **GLAZED CERAMIC** | Not recommended | Glazes can make drilling difficult, as can the usually very thick walls; given the expense of glazed ceramic pots, it is not worth risking the damage. |
| **CONCRETE** | Not recommended | The thick walls of concrete make drilling difficult and noisy. A hammer drill with a strong masonry bit could work, but this is not recommended. |
| **FIBERGLASS** | Glass and tile bit | Do not apply too much pressure when drilling—let the bit do the work. And work slowly; don't rush. |
| **RESIN** | Standard drill bit | Avoid the temptation to start with a very large bit. It's better to start small (½") and enlarge the hole gradually, or simply create more holes. |
| **WOOD** | Standard drill bit | Wood is the easiest material to drill. |
| **PLASTIC (BUCKETS, STORAGE BINS)** | Standard drill bit | Plastic is generally easy to drill; work slowly to avoid melting the plastic with the heat generated by the drilling friction. |
| **METAL** | Extrastrong titanium or cobalt bit | Metal can be slippery, so use a hammer and nail, a punch, or an awl to make an indentation at the drilling point to avoid the drill "walking" off your piece. |

ing the plant because the oxygen is displaced by water. Good drainage also prevents salts, which are present in irrigation water in many areas and in fertilizers, from building up in the soil and becoming toxic to the plant or preventing the uptake of crucial nutrients.

It would seem obvious that containers sold for gardening come with drainage holes, but that's not always the case. Many plastic containers, for example, are not predrilled. They have indentations on the bottom that indicate where the holes should go, but the manufacturers rely on the buyer to actually make the holes. Many beautiful ceramic pots are made without drainage—perhaps because they are intended for use as cachepots or for fountains or water gardens. If you plan on repurposing other materials, like 5-gallon buckets, or making self-watering containers, you will be creating drainage yourself. Adding drainage holes to plastic containers is easy, but doing it on other materials is a bit tougher. Use the chart above to help you decide the best course of action for adding drainage to your containers.

## Climate Considerations

Spending year after year outdoors can be tough on containers. Bright sunlight, constant watering, and winter temperature swings are

(continued on page 14)

# Choosing the Perfect Containers

| CONTAINER TYPE | SIZE RANGE | WEATHERPROOF? | DURABILITY | COST |
|---|---|---|---|---|
| **TERRA-COTTA** | 4"–26"+ | Only in special cases | Fragile but long lasting | $–$$$$ (for large weatherproof options) |
| **GLAZED CERAMIC** | 8"–26"+ | Only if indicated on the pot | Somewhat fragile but long lasting if properly cared for | $–$$$ |
| **CONCRETE** | 14"–32"+ | Not usually | Very rugged | $–$$$ |
| **FIBERGLASS** | 12"–32"+ | Yes | Easily cracked or punctured | $$–$$$ |
| **RESIN** | 8"–32"+ | Yes | Long lasting | $–$$ |
| **PLANTER AND WINDOW BOX** | 4" x 12"– 36" x 36"+ | Yes | Depends on material; usually very long lasting | $–$$$$ |
| **HANGING BASKET** | 6"–24"+ in diameter | Yes | Long lasting | $–$$$ |
| **GROW BAG** | 12"–50" | Usually | Relatively short-term use | $ |
| **STOCK TANK** | 2' x 4'+ | Yes | Long lasting | $$–$$$ |
| **HAYRACK** | Varies; 12"–18" high | Yes | Long lasting | $$ |
| **5-GALLON BUCKET** | Approximately 14" in diameter | Yes | Long lasting | $ |
| **GROW TOWER** | Varies; 15"–36" wide | Yes | Relatively short | $ |
| **WHISKEY BARREL** | 24" diameter | Yes | Long lasting | $$ |
| **SELF-WATERING CONTAINER** | Wide range; 14"–32"+ | Yes | Long lasting | $–$$$ |

| EASE OF MAINTENANCE | WEIGHT (WITHOUT SOIL) | DIY OPTION | PAINTABLE?* | NOTES |
|---|---|---|---|---|
| Must be stored for winter | Moderate to heavy | No, purchase only | Yes, with acrylic craft paint | |
| Low maintenance; may require winter storage | Heavy | No, purchase only | No | Check for drainage holes—some glazed pieces are intended for fountains or decorative uses |
| May require periodic repair | Very heavy | Yes | No, but can be stained or tinted when made | Easy to make at home, but homemade pots may be more prone to cracking and will be much heavier than commercial options |
| Low to no maintenance | | No, purchase only | Yes, with out-door spray paint | |
| No maintenance | Light | No, purchase only | Yes, with out-door spray paint | May fade with prolonged sun exposure |
| Little to none for most materials; low to moderate for wood | Moderate to heavy | Yes, wood only | Depends on the material. Wood can be painted, as can other materials as described here | |
| Liner may require annual replacement | Light | Yes | Depends on material | |
| No maintenance | Light | Yes | No | Plastic/synthetic materials are less durable than natural materials |
| No maintenance | Moderate | No | No | Many sizes are available; 2' x 4' best for edible-pot gardening and most affordable. Drainage must be added |
| Requires liner, which will need replacement | Moderate | No | Yes, with out-door spray paint | Many models and configurations available; wall-mounted racks best for edible-pot gardening |
| No maintenance | Light | No | No | Use food-safe buckets only; drill several holes for drainage |
| May require frequent maintenance | Light | DIY only | No | Flexible and easy to make from common, inexpensive materials; must be well made to hold up to growth all season |
| No maintenance | Heavy | No, purchase only | Yes, though not usually painted | Check for drainage holes; some barrels are sold for decorative uses |
| Low maintenance | Light to moderate | Yes | No | Self-watering containers range from very fancy ready-made models to plans to adapt a plastic storage bin to planter use |

*Avoid painting the inside of any pot used for growing edibles.

capable of causing damage to all common containers materials. As you plan your collection of edible-plant pots, you must consider what you'll do with your containers between growing seasons, unless you live in a frost-free area where you're able to grow something nearly year-round.

Clay and ceramic containers are the most likely to be severely damaged in the off-season. Terra-cotta is especially notorious for its inability to survive winter weather: Moisture in the porous clay freezes and thaws along with temperature changes, and the pressure of expanding (freezing) water causes the clay to

flake off in sheets. With both terra-cotta and ceramic containers, the entire pot may crack, breaking out large pieces or even splitting in two. Whether full of potting soil or completely empty, any clay container left outdoors in winter in cold climates is liable to suffer damage or destruction.

To protect your investment, store your clay and ceramic containers in a dry, protected area over winter. They can be in cold temperatures as long as they're not exposed to snow and rain; a barn, garage, or other outbuilding is okay, as are basements. Moving a large number of containers can be quite a chore (and a huge strain on your back!), so it's best to have your storage needs worked out before you invest large amounts into clay and ceramic containers. They may take up a great deal of room, even if you're able to stack them to save floor space.

If you love these types of containers but don't want to have to move them for storage, look for those that have been fired at extremely high temperatures, making them impervious to the moisture that causes breakage. They should be prominently labeled as "weatherproof." These are much more expensive than conventional clay and ceramic containers, but they can be worth the investment when you consider the time and effort you'll save not having to haul them indoors in winter.

Plastic and fiberglass containers usually don't break from winter weather, but continued exposure to sunlight eventually fades their color and degrades their chemical bonds, making them brittle and more susceptible to breakage. While it is not strictly necessary to tuck these types away for winter,

# PICKING POTS FOR OVERWINTERED CROPS

If you plan to grow perennial edibles in your containers, pay attention to the materials the containers are made from. Perennial vegetables and herbs, such as oregano, mint, rosemary, and horse-radish, won't survive the winter in a container that needs to be stored completely dry, such as clay or ceramic. The same goes for annual crops that you plant in fall for an early-spring harvest, like chervil, spinach, and parsley. Even though the plants are not actively growing, they still need some moisture, and that can be a problem for frost-sensitive pots.

To keep both plants and pots in good shape, give these crops weatherproof containers if you plan to leave them outside for the winter. Otherwise, remove them from their pots in early to mid-fall and plant the winter-hardy ones in the ground for the off-season. I'll move crops like chervil (which overwinters in my climate) to weatherproof pots like these composite window boxes so I can enjoy an early spring harvest instead of tossing these crops in the compost pile. Some warm-climate woody herbs, like rosemary, bay laurel, and lemon verbena, can grow indoors over winter. Keep these herbs in individual pots (of any material) and carry them inside before frost hits.

you may wish to group them together in a more shaded location or cover them with a tarp to prevent unnecessary exposure to sunlight and to prolong their life.

With their fabriclike materials and soft, flexible sides, grow bags are not likely to be damaged during winter, but summer sun takes a significant toll, fading colors and weakening the fibers. Grow bags are not nearly as big a

financial investment as other types of containers, yet you still want to get maximum life out of them, so store them out of direct sunlight when not in use.

Wood planter boxes may warp or split over winter, especially if filled with soil. Metal planters tend to be the most weather resistant, though their appearance may dull after many seasons outdoors.

## Container Sizes

Matching the size of the container to the crop you want to grow is both an art and a science. Plants are amazingly adaptable, so there's a fair amount of flexibility, but they'll grow most vigorously and produce most generously when you choose containers that are in proportion to their natural height, width, and root mass.

**Consider the width.** Containers are generally sold by the diameter of their top opening, usually in even numbers (10 inches, 12 inches, 14 inches, and so on). Aim to acquire a mix of container sizes, but focus on a nice selection of large pots and planters. Wide containers—those 14 inches and larger in diameter—are a particularly important and versatile component for container-grown edibles. Not only can they readily accommodate a large plant like a tomato or zucchini, they can also house nearly a whole conventional row's worth of peas, salad greens, or radishes. From a safety standpoint, these also tend to be more stable than narrow pots in windy sites.

If you are putting together your edible combinations based on the thriller-filler-spiller method described in Chapter 5, larger containers expand your options considerably, because you can fit more plants into them. However, smaller containers are useful, too, playing a role in creating a varied, visually appealing garden and lending themselves well to single specimens of woody herbs or dramatic plants like kale or eggplant.

Wide containers do have one potential drawback: Their large surface area means a lot more soil is exposed to the sun and wind, causing greater surface evaporation of water. Wide containers with a lot of soil exposed will require watering more frequently, but you can use a mulch and/or an underplanting (a compact crop planted below the main plant, or thriller) to shield the soil from the sun.

**Get the right height.** Unlike the width measurements, height (or depth) is not standardized and can vary wildly among commercially available containers. It's an important factor to consider, though, because it makes a big difference in what type of edibles you can grow in a given container. For example, a 14-inch-wide standard clay pot will be roughly proportional in its height and width and be perfect for a

tomato plant. However, there are plenty of 14-inch-wide pots out there that are just a few inches tall and are more suited to growing salad crops, strawberries, or edible flowers. The rule of thumb is to grow taller plants in tall, wide pots and shorter plants in short pots.

Keep in mind, though, that deeper pots are not always better. While plant roots need oxygen as much as their leaves do, oxygen only penetrates the soil to a depth of about 18 inches, so using a container deeper than that isn't helpful.

# SELECTING THE RIGHT SITE

To truly enjoy your edible container garden as the less-work solution it is, you need to place your containers in the best possible site. Your plants will produce to their full potential, and you'll find it much more convenient to care for them, too.

## Light Levels

Light is the most important factor to consider when deciding where to place your pots. Most edibles need at least 6, and preferably 8 or more, hours of bright sunlight daily to thrive. A traditional inground vegetable garden limits your options, but when you use containers, you can place your plants anywhere there's the optimum amount of light.

Another benefit of containers is that they allow you to take advantage of the reflected light around your home. Porches, patios, decks, and balconies are often brighter than they may appear to the eye because the light that reaches them is also bounced off nearby walls.

While this will not magically make a shady porch into a sunny one, it may open up an area that you thought unsuitable for growing.

Although few edibles will grow in all-day shade, you can produce something useful and tasty in spaces that get less than full sun. Salad greens, for instance, don't mind just a few hours of direct sunlight each day, especially in summer when it is hot. If an area is shady because of deciduous trees, it may be possible to plant a container of quick-maturing cool-weather vegetables, such as radishes or spinach, before the leaves on the trees expand and block the sunlight. One of the best things about growing vegetables in containers is that you can move the container to another spot if you feel that it isn't doing well in its initial location.

## Access to Water

When you're deciding where to place your container garden, put it close to an outdoor water source, if possible. Containers (especially clay pots and hanging baskets) in sunny spots can dry out quickly in hot weather, so you may need to water them at least once a day. That can be a hassle if you have to carry water from some distance. Even if you use self-watering containers, refilling them should be an easy task. The less of a chore watering is, logistically, the less likely you are to skip it at times when it is too hot or when you are too tired or busy.

## Convenience for Care

Forget about having to trek out to a far corner of your yard to look after your vegetable

# THE MYTH OF SPACE FILLERS

With the rise of container gardening has come a whole slew of products designed to take up space in the bottom of a container, designed to reduce the need for potting soil and even claiming to increase drainage. A simple Internet search reveals lots of do-it-yourself solutions as well, including Styrofoam peanuts, old plastic pots, bricks, rocks, and plastic milk cartons. While these space fillers sound good in theory, they can actually be harmful to your crops.

You see, in a container, the lowermost portion of soil will *always* remain wet. Since moisture drains downward, this area becomes saturated within the first few times you water the container, and it stays that way since it is never exposed to the evaporative forces of sun or wind, and there are few roots growing in that area to take up the water. If you take up space by installing a false bottom or by throwing in a bunch of old plastic pots, you push this constantly wet layer of soil closer to the area where healthy roots are growing, limiting the room in which they can spread out.

So what's a thrifty gardener to do? I have ideas for bulking up your potting soil to make it go further; look for them in the "Bulking Up" sidebar on page 33. Try these instead, and you'll have much happier and healthier plants!

Is it ever okay to use space fillers? It may be, if you have an extremely large, municipal style planter. Since sufficient oxygen only penetrates soil to a depth of approximately 18 inches, roots of annual crops grow very little past the 20-inch point. If your container is 24 inches or deeper, you may want to use a space filler—but be sure you are giving your roots at least 20 inches of soil depth to grow in. However, in these cases, I do recommend something heavy and firm, like rocks, rather than something lightweight, like Styrofoam peanuts, as you don't want the bottom to be lighter in weight than the top.

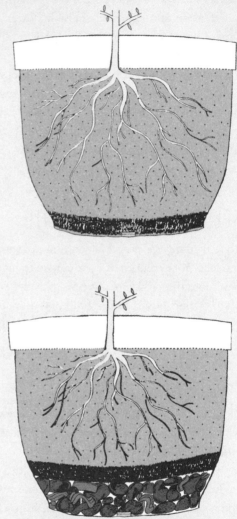

The top drawing shows healthy root growth in a pot entirely filled with soil. In contrast, you can clearly see how the space filler in the lower drawing has limited the space for the roots to grow and has pushed the zone of saturation closer to the delicate root tips.

garden. Take advantage of the flexibility you have in placing and moving containers, and put them where it's convenient for you to tend and harvest from them. Siting your edible container garden close to your house lets you take advantage of artificial lighting, too, so you can even plant or harvest after dark. When you can pop out to your garden at any hour to harvest some herbs, edible flowers, and cherry tomatoes and confidently leave dinner still simmering on the stove, you'll know why gardening in containers is much better than gardening in plots way out in your yard!

## Surface Thoughts

Most of us have many different types of surfaces to choose from for our edible container garden: paving, decking, grass, and so on. While you may need to utilize all of them to take full advantage of your space and sunlight, it is best to know how these surfaces may be affected in the long term by a container garden. Frequent watering, for instance, can pose problems for many surfaces, leading to rot or a change in the integrity of the surface. The water that drains from a container carries with it small particles of soil and may also collect salts and minerals as it travels through the growing media. When these leave the container, they can accumulate on the surface below and may stain it permanently.

**Paving is great.** Concrete surfaces, such as driveways, sidewalks, and patios, are ideal for containers because they won't rot or stain and they provide a firm, level surface. Most properties have an abundance of paved surfaces, and these areas are often unused, so turning them

into a pretty and productive garden with a collection of pots and planters just makes sense.

**Hit the deck.** Wood surfaces like decks are prime real estate for containers, since they're usually an integral part of your outdoor living space. However, wood can be stained by water draining out of containers, and it may rot or warp over time as well. Because spaces in between the slats of wood decking will allow water to drip through, it's important to consider the effect dripping water might have on the area below—especially underneath balconies!

**On the lawn.** Placing your containers on the lawn is usually okay, but be aware that they will kill the grass beneath them. (Fortunately, it's easy to repair this damage by sowing grass seed over the patch when you move the containers.) Keep in mind that you will also have to trim frequently around the containers to keep them looking tidy, which means more maintenance work.

## THINK ABOUT DESIGN

You've chosen your containers and decided where to put them. Now you can start planning how your container garden is going to look. This is where it really gets fun, as you exercise your creativity, making your edible-plant pots uniquely you. The best part is that you can never truly get it wrong: If you don't like the

# NEAT FEET

Sometimes, a simple solution—like lifting your containers an inch or so off the ground—can make a big difference. Raising pots and planters just this little bit gives your whole collection a nicer, lighter visual effect. It also minimizes or eliminates staining or rotting underneath each pot, because water that drains out can evaporate instead of simply sitting on the surface or pooling up in a saucer.

Garden centers that offer a good selection of container gardening supplies often sell terra-cotta "pot feet" specifically for this purpose. These fancy feet look good—some are elegant, and some are quirky—but they can be expensive. Fortunately, there are less costly options that accomplish the same thing, such as:

✺ Small ceramic tiles, stacked three or so high

✺ Wood shims, cut ends of lumber, or even slices made by cutting widthwise across small logs

✺ PVC or metal pipe cut into 1-inch slices with a pipe cutter

Once you start thinking about pot feet, you'll probably find many other fun and inexpensive things to use when you visit your favorite hardware store or rummage through your garage or basement.

way your garden of edible pots looks, you can easily move, rearrange, or replant the pots whenever you wish!

It's fine to start small if you are limited by space, budget, or time. If you live in an area where water is carefully rationed, you may want to begin with just a few containers to get an idea of how much moisture they'll require so you don't unexpectedly end up with an enormous water bill (or a summons!).

Because your container garden is more likely to be closer to, and even within, your living space than a conventional vegetable garden, you should make it as attractive as possible. Vegetables are inherently beautiful plants—they offer intriguing textures, vibrant colors, tons of flowers, and delightful fragrances—so they can be just as pretty as flower gardens. In fact, I encourage you to think of them that way. Forget about the boring "straight row" mind-set of a traditional vegetable garden and go wild exploring the exciting options for arranging your containers.

**Think in three dimensions.** Instead of placing pots and planters in a straight line along the edge of an area, create groupings with tall plants and lower-growing plants in each.

**Use odd numbers.** Using odd numbers of

(continued on page 24)

# Tom and Carol's Vegetable Library
## BUFFALO, NEW YORK
### the space makers

On the tiny 33 × 151-foot lot around their 1902 home, Tom Palamuso and Carol Siracuse have artfully accommodated a wisteria arbor, a sitting pergola, a fish pond, a waterfall, several flower beds, and a potting bench. For most gardeners, the idea of incorporating a vegetable garden into this efficient Eden would have been laughable, but Tom, a former technology teacher and interior designer who designed and built their fountain and engineered an elaborate rainwater collection system, is not most gardeners. Tom looked at their flat, sun-drenched garage roof and saw opportunity. He devised a plan to place self-watering containers along the front edge of the garage roof, accessed with a rolling library ladder installed above the garage doors. "It came to me all at once," he says. "I saw the library ladder for harvesting the crops, and once I got that in my head, there was no stopping it."

Carol, a retired architect, determined that their garage roof was structurally sound and strong enough to support the weight of the crops, containers, soil, and water, so they were clear to pursue Tom's vision. They first priced ready-made self-watering systems, but for the number of boxes they required, they instead opted to build homemade boxes that not only saved them hundreds of dollars but work just about perfectly. "We've had so much success with these boxes that even if we had room to do a conventional garden, we'd use these again," Carol says. The boxes are made from two sizes

(30 inches and 36 inches) of plastic storage bins—highly functional but not exactly attractive. For maximum aesthetics, Tom built a handsome wood fascia on the front and a serviceable plywood one on the back. These not only make their rooftop vegetable garden look more cohesive, they protect the plastic bins from the sun so the containers remain in perfect condition even after 3 years. "Our vegetable garden is as much about style as it is about substance," he says. To wit: the large ornamental hanging baskets that flank the crop boxes, and the strategically placed colorful flowers cascading over the edge.

The first year, they hauled bales of potting soil onto the roof by means of a rope and an old metal utility shelf. The second year, Tom installed an attic hatch with a ladder for direct roof access to make more involved maintenance like planting and cleanup easier. They have been reusing the same soil each growing season, amending it liberally with lime and granular fertilizer in spring. However, an infestation of squash vine borers their second year required the complete removal and replacement of 6 inches of soil in two boxes to eliminate pupae.

Watering is accomplished completely by means of a pipe incorporated into these simple but effective self-contained systems. The plastic sheeting over the top of the containers eliminates the risk of flooding during heavy rains, and an overflow hole in the side helps Tom ensure that the holes remain unclogged and that the containers drain well. The couple has enjoyed great success with most crops they've tried: tomatoes, summer squash (with the exception of the nefarious vine borers), eggplant, peppers, bush beans, and, most recently, tomatillos and husk cherries. Leafy greens and beets have not been as productive in their containers, Carol says, but the bountiful harvests of beans, peppers, and tomatoes more than make up for it. In fact, green beans are so productive that they plant them at the front edge of their containers so they can be quickly harvested each day during summer.

Tom and Carol's creative solutions aren't limited to their vegetable library: Containers of herbs are placed in sunny spots between the garage bays, and several years ago, Tom built shelves with routed-out spaces to accommodate large window boxes. These were installed on the property's wood privacy fence and host a bounty of annual and perennial herbs. Despite their compact lot, the couple enjoys an array of productive edibles for Tom to include in his recipes and a lively, dynamic, and colorful bounty from which Carol, an accomplished watercolorist, draws daily inspiration.

pots within each group gives you a more surprising, energetic arrangement and keeps the design from looking too dull and predictable.

**Layer your plants.** Place smaller pots in front of larger pots so you see the plants more than the pots. This also helps you to maximize the sunlight in the space.

**Vary heights.** If you have several pots of the same size, vary the look by placing them on top of makeshift pedestals—logs, scraps of wood, cinder blocks, or upside-down saucers or pots—of different heights.

**Look up.** With containers, you're not limited to ground-level growing. Hanging baskets, wall-mounted planters, and window boxes let you take advantage of additional growing space and add lots of visual interest as well. They also help create a sense of enclosure and privacy for your outdoor living spaces.

**Mix 'em up.** Combining different crops within the same pot makes your containers more interesting. One easy way to make sure each combination offers maximum impact is to use the thriller-filler-spiller method that has become so popular for ornamental plants. This surefire approach is described in detail in Chapter 5.

**Unify with plants.** Choosing one distinctive plant and using it in most or all of your containers helps create a more cohesive appearance overall. Just make sure that the plant is dramatic enough to stand out from the rest of the crowd, and, of course, it ought to be something that you enjoy using in your cooking! Some good choices include purple fennel, red shiso, variegated 'Pesto Perpetuo' basil, or a brightly colored, medium-large fruited pepper, such as 'Lemon Drop' hot pepper.

# CHOOSE YOUR CROPS

They say that variety is the spice of life, and it's a key to getting the very best from your garden, too. With so many great edibles to choose from, though, how can you ever decide which ones to try? To start out, I recommend dreaming big: Grab a bunch of seed catalogs and make a list of everything you'd like to grow if you had unlimited time, money, and planting space. Then ask yourself these questions to pin down which crops should get priority and which you could do without:

⚜ *How much do I enjoy eating this vegetable, herb, or fruit?* It's fun to try new or unusual edibles, but when space is limited, those that you know you'll eat should get priority. Put a star next to the crops that you're sure you and your family will enjoy.

⚜ *How important is it that this crop be at peak ripeness to truly enjoy?* Soft, juicy fruits like tomatoes and strawberries are shipped slightly underripe to prevent damage, which is why people often complain that they are flavorless. That makes delicate fruits like these excellent candidates for home growing, so if they're on your list, give them a star.

⚜ *Is the crop available in my area at a good quality and a good price?* Onions, for instance, are easy to find at any grocery store, so they're not a high-priority crop for gardens with limited space. But if you enjoy ethnic food, for example, and have no ethnic markets around you, an unusual crop like bok choy or Thai eggplant might be a good choice to grow. Give these specialty crops a star.

❧ *Will the edible earn its keep—that is, will it return enough in harvests for the length of time it takes to mature and the amount of space it takes up?* Sweet corn, for example, usually gives just a couple of ears per plant and takes quite a while to grow for that one harvest, while tomatoes keep producing fruits over a period of weeks or months. You can find more details about the space-to-yield ratios for the most suitable crops for containers in the plant encyclopedia in Chapter 6. Crops on your list that you can pick from multiple times, or that produce a generous harvest for the amount of space they occupy, get at least one star.

❧ *If the crop doesn't need a whole season to reach harvest size, is its season short enough that I can use that same space before and/or after its planting to grow something else?* Summer crops such as beans, for instance, leave time for a spring or fall sowing of quick crops like spinach and radishes, so you'll get two different harvests from the same amount of space. This approach is known as succession planting; you'll find more information about it in "Succeed with Succession Plantings" on page 78. These fast-growing crops earn a star, too.

Once you've answered these questions, you can see at a glance which crops on your list deserve the highest priority, which to consider if you have space left over, and which probably aren't worth trying. Then you can start evaluating each one for how well it is likely to perform in your garden (this information is in Chapter 6).

When you're ready to get growing, it's time to pin down the specifics of the crops you

selected. Choosing the right varieties can help you get an even bigger harvest in less space and with less maintenance. Look for those with traits that make them particularly good for container gardens. For example:

**Dwarf habit.** For the most part, full-size plants will grow fine in containers of an appropriate dimension. However, varieties that are selected for a more compact habit can grow in smaller containers than their full-size kin. Dwarf or miniature varieties will be described as such on the seed packet or pot tag. Look for cues in the variety name (words like *mini, tiny,* or *baby*) as well.

**Self-fruitful varieties.** Also known as "parthenocarpic" (a Greek word meaning "virgin

*(continued on page 28)*

# YOUR CONTAINER GARDEN TOOL KIT

If you've been gardening for a long time, you probably have most of the tools you'll need to plant and maintain edible pots. However, you may want to organize a section of your tool arsenal to make a special "container garden tool kit" so the tools are easy to find when you're ready to plant or care for your container crops.

- ✹ **Hand tools.** An ordinary, short-handled trowel (for digging and planting) and cultivator (for making rows for seed sowing and breaking up any crust on the soil surface) are best for regular maintenance of your container vegetable garden. Or try some of the new hybrid tools with telescoping handles that extend their reach.

- ✹ **Shovel or spade.** The only full-size tool you'll need is a shovel or spade for mixing soil, turning in amendments, and filling your containers.

- ✹ **Cutting tools.** I recommend both a pair of classic hand pruners and a pair of fine snips. Hand pruners are nice for heavier work, like pruning and harvesting eggplants, peppers, and other thick-stemmed crops, while snips are perfect for thinning seedbeds and harvesting herbs, lettuce, and edible flowers. A pruner holster is a handy accessory for keeping your pruners easily accessible.

- ✹ **Watering tools.** A good-quality watering wand offers many benefits to the container gardener. It extends your reach so you don't have to bend or strain your back. It is easy to maneuver in between plants and containers, allowing you to water everything well. And its slightly crooked neck gives it the perfect angle for watering hanging baskets and reaching over the rim of containers.

- ✹ **A tarp.** It takes up practically no storage space but is invaluable for many container-gardening tasks, including carrying weeds, leaves, and trimmings to the compost pile and keeping surfaces clean when you're filling containers or dividing or transplanting your crops. A tarp is handy for mixing and amending potting soil, too, and for kneeling on when the grass is wet or muddy. Opt for a small, heavy-duty type (typically brown on one side and silver on the other).

☀ **Stakes.** Bamboo stakes are great because you can cut them to size. Check out other options for staking, tying, and training your plants in "Staking and Pruning" on page 96. And be sure to browse the bamboo projects, such as the Bamboo Ladder Trellis (page 116) and the Bean Archway and Arbor (page 118), to see if either might work for your garden.

☀ **Wire.** Thin wire can be useful in your container garden for creating a bean tepee, for wiring up hanging baskets, or for improvising all sorts of solutions, so I suggest keeping 24-gauge paddle wire close at hand in your tool bag. You should be able to purchase it from a local florist or a craft store that sells floral arranging supplies.

☀ **PotLifter.** While not a crucial part of your container garden tool kit, the PotLifter is a nifty invention from a couple in Washington State: a sling that allows you to easily lift and carry very large or very heavy pots, even if they are full of soil and plants. Two people are required to use it, but they need not be unusually strong. The way the PotLifter distributes the weight makes the container surprisingly light. A PotLifter is especially useful with large glazed ceramic pots, which are slippery and difficult to grasp, or if you have concrete or stone pots and urns.

☀ **Something to keep it all in.** Storing all of your small container-gardening tools and equipment in one carryall is smart and efficient. A reusable shopping bag, a 5-gallon bucket (perhaps one of those rejects that contained laundry soap or drywall compound and is thus unsuitable for growing plants in), and even a regular toolbox are good candidates, as are the numerous bags made especially for gardeners.

☀ **Digital camera.** While you won't find it in the tool section at your garden center, a digital camera is very useful to gardeners. Sometimes, simply taking a photo of your garden and looking at it on the computer gives you the perspective you need to make changes to the arrangement of your containers for a bolder, more beautiful presentation. Photos of your garden are especially valuable in winter, when you begin planning for the new season.

fruit"), self-fruitful crops do not need a pollinator to bear fruit, so you can get a harvest from a single plant. That saves a lot of space. You'll learn about self-fruitful varieties in Chapter 6.

**Disease resistance.** A number of edible crops have been developed especially for resistance to common diseases.

**Unusual colors.** Not only does choosing an unconventionally colored variety add interest and surprise to your garden, it also often means a more nutritious vegetable, too.

It's possible to grow nearly any popular edible in a container. The trick is choosing the right variety of the crop as well as the right container. However, there are a few edibles—including corn, large-fruited squash and melons, and most perennial vegetables—that simply won't be as successful—that is, not as productive or as attractive as they ought to be—when grown in a pot or planter.

# Crop Substitutions

| CROP | REASON TO SELECT A SUBSTITUTE | ALTERNATIVE/SUGGESTION |
|---|---|---|
| **BRUSSELS SPROUTS** | 100+ days to maturity, large | Kale or collard greens |
| **CABBAGE** | Takes too much space, inexpensive and high quality at market | Kale or collard greens |
| **CAULIFLOWER** | High maintenance, high inputs, needs lots of space, low yield | Orange or purple varieties are lower maintenance and more interesting to grow than white varieties |
| **CELERY/ CELERY ROOT** | Difficult to start from seed, requires specific conditions, very long time until harvest, low yield | Chinese cutting celery and lovage are herbs that taste like celery and are more productive and easy to grow. Alternatively, start celery from the base of a bunch purchased at the store. It will still be a high-maintenance crop, but this overcomes the seed-starting difficulty |
| **FLORENCE FENNEL** | Low yield, needs high inputs | Leaf fennel, a self-sowing herb, provides the same flavor and is higher yielding and easier to grow |
| **LEEK** | High maintenance, 100+ days to maturity | Chives or scallions |
| **MELON AND WATERMELON** | Very low yield (1 or 2 per plant), needs a lot of space | If you must have melons, opt for small-fruited, parthenocarpic types |
| **ONION** | High maintenance, low yield, inexpensive and high quality at market | Chives or scallions |
| **PARSNIP** | Low yield, takes all season to mature a single root | Carrot |
| **PUMPKIN AND WINTER SQUASH** | Low yield, long season | Small-fruited varieties, like 'Munchkin' pumpkin and 'Speckled Hound' winter squash, are best suited to pots and raised beds |
| **TURNIP AND RUTABAGA** | Low yield, long season | Fast-maturing salad turnips like 'Hakurei' are most productive but are best enjoyed fresh, not cooked. The greens are also edible. |

## PICK THE POTTING SOIL

Choosing the crops you'll grow is the most fun part of the process, but selecting the growing medium you'll plant them in is easily the most important. Deciding on a material that is cost effective; promotes healthy, vigorous growth; and has a minimal impact on the environment is vital for having an enjoyable and successful experience with growing crops in containers.

First of all, you don't want to fill your containers with regular soil. True soil—the stuff under the grass in your backyard—is created over thousands of years through various geological processes. It doesn't just happen, and it cannot be created by man; it is a crucial natural resource.

Naturally occurring soil does not perform in the same way in a container as it does in the ground. It is heavy in weight, for one: a serious issue with the good-size pots you need for successful container crops. Soil is made up of three different types of particles—sand, silt, and clay—and depending on how much there is of each type, it may end up draining poorly, turning so hard that it can't easily absorb water, or being so loose that water and nutrients drain away before your plants can use them.

So what *will* you be growing in? If you've ever grown anything in a container before—even a houseplant—you've no doubt purchased a bag of stuff that was labeled "potting soil." However, the majority of bagged potting soil does not contain any actual soil and should be more appropriately sold as "potting medium" or "soilless mix." What these bags contain is mostly organic matter—such as peat moss, coco fiber or coir, tree bark, sawdust, and/or compost—along with

## COCO VERSUS COCOA

The words *coco* and *cocoa* look and sound similar, but in the gardening world, they refer to two different things. Coco refers to products that contain coconut fiber (the hairy brown stuff from the outside of a coconut). You may find it sold loose, for use as a soil amendment, or formed into mats for lining wire planters and baskets. It is increasingly popular as a substitute for peat in making small biodegradable pots for sowing seeds. Cocoa, on the other hand, refers to cocoa hulls, a product generally used as a garden mulch. It is a by-product of chocolate processing and smells distinctly like chocolate. Now that you know the difference, you can be sure that you're getting the right thing when you're shopping for gardening supplies!

a mineral material such as perlite or vermiculite (or both). Some may also include special horticultural grades of charcoal or sand.

### Peat-Based Potting Mixes

There are five primary qualities that describe a desirable potting mix:

1. Lightweight, so you can easily fill, move, and maintain your containers

2. Fast draining, so that water does not collect in the pot and suffocate the plant roots

3. Convenient to purchase, mix, use, and store

4. Affordable from a financial standpoint
5. Minimal environmental impact

Numbers 1 through 4 have been easy to fulfill for many years now through the use of peat moss. Peat moss, often shortened to just "peat," is also known as sphagnum, the botanical name of this moss that grows in wet areas. The majority of commercially available potting mixes are composed primarily of milled peat—the dustlike, rich brown stuff that readily sticks to your hands and arms when you work with the mix.

Ninety percent of the world's peat is found in cold-climate wetlands. Over the centuries, huge peat bogs have formed in parts of Canada, Scandinavia, and the United Kingdom; the United States, too, has millions of acres of peat bogs. Under ideal conditions, sphagnum moss plants flourish and reproduce more quickly than they

# UNDERSTANDING "ORGANIC"

The term *organic* gets thrown around a lot these days, which can make discussions about gardening techniques and materials kind of confusing. It's best to start with the old, original definition of organic: something made from the element carbon. Carbon is the building block for everything on earth that is alive or has ever lived. So when we talk about "organic matter" in the garden, we mean substances that are made from or by living (or once-living) things, like compost, manure, peat moss, and cocoa hulls. Organic matter helps a growing medium retain moisture and hold on to the nutrients and minerals applied in the form of fertilizers.

The "organic" in "organic gardening" basically means using natural products and processes to grow plants without the use of synthetic (nonnatural) materials. It does not necessarily mean nontoxic, though. Rotenone, for instance, is a pesticide derived from a plant, so it is technically organic, but it has been banned for home use because it is toxic to fish and aquatic life.

Organic matter is not necessarily organically produced, nor is it always suitable for organic gardening. For example, coir is a type of organic matter because it is made from coconut husks, an all-natural material. However, if the husks were harvested from a coconut plantation that was maintained with the use of synthetic pesticides and fertilizers, it can not be sold in the United States as "organic coir."

So if you want to grow your containers organically, it's vital to shop with care when you are choosing a growing medium. Look at all of the contents listed on the label to make sure that no synthetic materials are included. Also, check for the logo of OMRI (Organic Materials Research Institute)—the only organization to certify horticultural and agricultural materials as safe for organic growing. For more information, visit omri.org.

more, the harvest and processing of peat releases sequestered carbon and creates a significant carbon footprint through the running of enormous machinery and the packing and shipping of products over thousands of miles. Though peat producers have funded research to reestablish and conserve peatlands, and though they actively replant harvested areas, the unavoidable truth is that peat is a natural resource, as valuable and precious as water or soil.

decompose, creating thick layers of this spongy, lightweight, extremely water-retentive material.

Demand for peat has increased dramatically over the last few decades. It is very effective at retaining moisture and is an inexpensive bulk ingredient for commercial potting soils. And because it is so lightweight and can be heavily compressed without compacting, it is efficient to pack, ship, and store. However, peat resources are being used up rapidly, and the environmental impact of their harvest and processing is becoming impossible to ignore.

Peat producers argue that peat is an abundant, renewable resource and that it can be managed and harvested responsibly without presenting a threat to the environment. This is partly true—peat is a "slowly renewable resource." *Slowly* is the operative word—it renews at just about $1/4$ inch per year under ideal conditions. Present levels of harvest and use far exceed peat's ability to regrow. Further-

Environmental concerns aside, peat has some inherent disadvantages when it comes to container gardening. Peat and water just don't mix—not easily, anyway. Once you do get peat wet, it stays wet, but it is extremely difficult to get it to absorb moisture at first. (It helps to use warm water rather than cold.)

Peat's hydrophobia is not just inconvenient; it can be detrimental to plants. If you've ever used peat as a mulch or top-dressing (which many gardeners like for its neat, uniform appearance and rich color—and which these gardeners will hopefully stop doing once they learn about peat's environmental costs), or if you've ever left a filled but unplanted container exposed to the sun and wind, you've probably seen how peat can form a hard crust that makes water roll right off instead of soak in. Peat-based potting soils also tend to pull away from the walls of the container if they dry out, so when you try to rewet them, the water runs right down the sides and out the drainage hole—a sad waste of another important resource.

Ultimately, all gardeners have a responsibility to reduce, if not completely eliminate, their use of peat products; acknowledging peat's origins and its importance to wetlands and the environment, understanding how it grows and how peat bogs are formed, and rightfully recognizing peat as a finite resource, not a manufactured product, are important first steps. At present, however, most home gardeners will find that they have few affordable alternatives to peat, so if you use peat, conserve it: Save it from year to year by using the recharging techniques described in "Recycled Potting Soil" on the opposite page. Fill your containers on days with little wind and wet the potting soil after filling to prevent any peat from blowing away. Store your peat in a dry space and use it wisely. Let your garden center or agricultural supplier know that you are interested in the peat alternatives described next. Hopefully, within the next few years, we can all significantly reduce our reliance on this natural resource.

## Peat Alternatives

One way to reduce or eliminate the reliance on peat-based potting mixes is to use an alternative growing medium. Many of these show tremendous potential for commercial horticulture and home gardeners alike.

- **Coir (coconut fiber).** Coir—the brown, fibrous outer layer of coconuts—shows the most promise as a peat replacement. It is relatively inexpensive and shares peat's weed-free and moisture-holding properties.

- **Wood products.** Bark and composted sawdust have also shown some promise. They are lightweight and moisture retentive while still allowing for the excellent drainage that is so important in container growing. Because North America has an established lumber industry, bark and sawdust are relatively local by-products (certainly more local than coir, which must be shipped in from the tropical areas where coconut palms grow).

- **Compost with sand.** Compost is an easy-to-find, inexpensive peat alternative that works very well for container crops. Mix well-rotted garden compost or composted manure with an equal amount of coarse builder's sand (not beach or play sand). The compost contributes nutrients and moisture-retaining properties; the sand contributes bulk and drainage.

These and other peat alternatives aren't yet as easy to find as peat-based potting mixes, so you may need to hunt a bit for them. Start by looking locally for garden centers that pride themselves on their selection of products for organic gardeners. You can also visit farm-supply stores, which often stock large packages of horticultural products. No matter where you shop, don't neglect the power of simply asking the owner or manager to order a product for you. Perhaps the reason garden centers don't stock a product is because they don't think there is an interest in it. The best time to request a special order is winter or no later than early spring, before they get their deliveries and become busy with the rush of gardening season.

## Homemade Potting Mixes

If you can't afford to buy all the commercial potting mix you need to fill your containers, if you can't find an all-organic mix locally, or if you're seriously looking to cut down on how much peat you use, you can create your own custom blend. Use coir, wood products, or a compost-with-sand mix as the primary ingredient (at least 50 percent), then add one or more of the materials listed in the sidebar "Bulking Up" (at right) for the rest. Keep track of what you use and how much, so you can easily replicate the mix in following years if it works well or try different amounts or ingredients if you want to adjust your formula.

To mix up your potting soil recipe, spread a tarp on the ground and place the ingredient you have most of in the center. (If you have roughly equal amounts of main ingredients, place the heaviest ingredient in the center.) Then add the remaining ingredients and turn the pile repeatedly with a shovel or spade. You may find it easier to mix in lightweight elements, like bark or perlite, gradually, sprinkling them over the main pile, mixing thoroughly, and then adding more. Make sure each component is thoroughly mixed in before placing your custom-made potting medium in your containers.

## Recycled Potting Soil

One of the best ways to conserve peat and other natural resources—and to save money, too—is to reuse your potting soil year after year. There are two issues you need to consider,

# BULKING UP

No matter what you use as a growing medium in your containers, it's likely to be one of your biggest expenses. Whether you use a traditional peat-based potting soil or an alternative commercial mix, there are other, less-expensive ingredients that you can blend into it to make it go much further, allowing you to fill more containers.

- Biochar
- Compost
- Perlite
- Rice hulls
- Sand
- Topsoil
- Vermiculite

though: the fertility of the growing medium and the potential for disease problems.

**Necessary nutrients.** Peat and coir, on their own, have essentially no nutrient value. This is why the majority of potting mixes you find in garden centers are blended and sold under the labels of big fertilizer brands. Without the addition of some type of fertilizer to provide vital plant nutrients (including nitrogen, potassium, and phosphorus), plants in containers will not grow vigorously.

By the end of one growing season, your container crops will have used most or all of the nutrients in commercially blended or home-blended mixes. So if you want to reuse your potting soil, you need to "recharge" it with nutrient-rich amendments such as compost (traditional plant compost or composted manure)

*(continued on page 36)*

# Potting Soil Components

| POTTING SOIL COMPONENT | OTHER NAMES | DURABILITY | DESCRIPTION |
|---|---|---|---|
| **BARK** | Wood chips, fir bark, coarse bark | Medium to long lasting, depending on type of bark and climate | Hard, flaky chunks |
| **CHARCOAL** | Biochar, horticultural charcoal | Long lasting | Shimmering gray black flakes or chunks |
| **COCO FIBER** | Coir, coconut hulls | Long lasting | Rich brown in color, hairy/fibrous, can be dusty or stringy depending on processing |
| **COMPOST** | | Short—continuously breaking down | Dark brown, crumbly, rich looking, fresh smelling |
| **MANURE** | Composted manure; chicken, horse, or cow manure | Short to medium | Dark brown, crumbly, rich looking, no pungent odor |
| **PEAT MOSS** | Peat, sphagnum, sphagnum moss | Long lasting | Light brown, dustlike; repels water when dry |
| **PERLITE** | | Long lasting | White, irregularly shaped, spongy yet rocklike |
| **RICE HULLS** | Rice husks | Very long lasting | Straw colored, very lightweight, oblong, and concave |
| **SAND** | | Long lasting | Coarse, varied grains, usually roughly cubic |
| **SAWDUST** | Wood shavings, sawmill waste | Short to medium, depending on particle size | Curls of light-colored, fresh wood, or pale tan yellow dust |
| **STYROFOAM** | | Indefinite | White, spongy, very lightweight |
| **VERMICULITE** | | Long lasting | Silvery, rough-edged flakes or layered nuggets |
| **WATER RETAINING CRYSTALS** | Hydrogel, moisture crystals, absorbing crystals | Short | Opaque white, resembles coarse salt |

| PURPOSE/BENEFITS | DISADVANTAGES | COST |
|---|---|---|
| Adds bulk to mix without weight | Does not contribute much nutrition, nor does it hold on to fertilizers | $ |
| Holds onto nutrients, provides lightweight bulk, absorbs excess water | Expensive, usually only sold in small packages | $$ |
| Retains moisture, lightweight, fast draining, does not readily compress | Produced only in distant tropical areas | $–$$ |
| Adds nutritious organic matter, retains water | Good, homemade compost usually is in scarce supply; purchased or municipal compost varies in quality | Free–$$ |
| Adds organic matter, powerful nitrogen-rich amendment, helps retain moisture | May be difficult to procure, depending on location; weed seeds prsent | Free–$$ |
| Retains moisture well once wet, lightweight and fast draining | Devoid of nutrients, jeopardizes a natural resource | $–$$ |
| Adds bulk without weight, holds onto nutrients in fertilizers for later plant use | May be difficult to find in anything but large packages, questionably sustainable | $$ |
| Supplies excellent drainage and aeration while adding little weight | Must be used with a rich compost or regular fertilizer program | $–$$ |
| Adds heft and structure | Heavy; appropriate types of sand may be difficult to find—saltwater beach or playbox sand cannot be used | $–$$ |
| Adds bulk and organic matter | Can rob nitrogen from plants if not allowed to break down before mixing with soil | $ |
| Adds bulk | Does not contribute to the nutrition or health of soil; easily rinses away or floats to top of soil; can become a litter issue, as it is so lightweight and does not degrade | Free–$ |
| Adds bulk without weight, retains nutrients, fosters abundant air space for roots to get oxygen | May be difficult to find; a mined mineral, hence questionably sustainable | $$ |
| Supposedly absorbs water and holds it for later plant use | Effective only in the short term; certain types release toxins as they degrade, posing a threat to humans, pets, and wildlife | $$ |

job a bit easier on your back and shoulders.

**Disease issues.** Those of you who have grown vegetables before are probably familiar with the concept of crop rotation—changing the location of your crops within the garden from year to year to prevent pests and pathogens (disease-causing organisms) from building up in the soil. Fortunately, the risk of pathogens accumulating in potting soil is much smaller than in garden soil.

If do you suspect that a soilborne disease has taken hold in one of your containers, you're best off replacing the growing medium with fresh potting mix. Spread the old mix in an unused corner of your yard, or put the soil in a bag and dispose of it through your municipal trash system.

# FILL 'EM UP

You've put a good deal of thought into choosing the perfect containers, the perfect plants, and the perfect potting soil. Finally, it's time to put your pots and potting soil together so you can plant your crops and get the season under way.

## Before the Soil

It's natural to want to cover the drainage holes in your containers to ensure your precious potting soil doesn't fall out when you fill or water them. While it's not absolutely necessary to do that, large holes *will* allow some potting soil to wash out: not enough to make a significant difference in the soil level, but enough to make a mess. A traditional solution is to put a single piece of broken pottery over each hole, but

and/or slow-release granular fertilizers.

At the beginning of the season, just as you get ready to start gardening, I recommend that you dump the contents of your previously used containers on a tarp. Spread out the pile, picking out any tough root clumps or insect larvae. Then refresh the mix by adding a commercial organic fertilizer according to the directions on the label and adding enough compost to equal at least a quarter of the total volume of the pile. (If you started with enough mix to fill four 5-gallon buckets, for example, then add one 5-gallon bucket of compost.) Do this recharging step in several batches if you have a lot of containers or if you wish to make the those sharp bits could be dangerous when you dump the used soil into your compost pile or out onto a tarp to freshen up the mix next spring.

A much safer solution is to place a piece of newspaper over the bottom of the pot. This forms a barrier to keep soil in while still allowing free drainage. By the time the newspaper decomposes, the soil in the pot will have settled enough to stay together. A single, small piece is enough. A square of landscape fabric also works.

Open basket-type containers, such as hayracks, wrought-iron window boxes, and wire hanging baskets, may require a more effective liner to keep the potting soil from falling out. You may be able to find a coco fiber liner made especially for the job, or purchase a roll of coco liner (available at hardware stores and garden centers) that you cut into pieces to make a custom liner. Or look for sheet moss at your florist or craft supply store. This fresh or dried moss creates a lush green lining. It may not keep its color all summer, but it will look especially attractive as it holds the soil and moisture in your hanging basket or window box.

## Add the Growing Medium

To make this step easy on yourself, pile the potting soil on a tarp instead of trying to dump it directly into each container. If the potting mix is very dry, mist it with a hose to moisten it a bit, so that you're not breathing in a lot of the dust. Use a plastic pot or large, curved trowel as a scoop to fill smaller containers. A regular garden shovel makes the job go quicker for larger pots and planters.

*(continued on page 40)*

# WHAT IS "SLOW-RELEASE FERTILIZER"?

This is a term that gets thrown around an awful lot without much explanation. If you've visited a garden center and stared at their fertilizer section looking for that term on a package, you've probably been miffed as to why these specific words appear on few—if any—of labels. Slow-release fertilizer essentially just means a fertilizer that is not available to the plant all in one go. The fertilizer requires weathering (chemical reactions with surrounding particles of soil or potting mix) to become available to the plant, and so it provides its nutrient load over a longer period. Most granular fertilizers are slow release, though many also contain a good measure of "instantly available" nutrients as well. Do not confuse slow-release fertilizer with time-release fertilizer, which is a different type altogether. In time-release fertilizers, the nutrients are encapsulated in a plastic shell known as a prill. The plastic is engineered to allow different amounts of nutrients seep out based on temperature changes. I prefer slow release to time release, and if organic gardening matters to you, you'll have much better luck finding an organic slow-release fertilizer than an organic time-release version.

# Deciding How Much Potting Soil to Buy

Figuring out how much potting soil you'll need to fill all your containers is an important step in creating your container garden. This calculation will help you determine how much money you'll be investing in your garden of edible pots. And it will save you from having to make multiple trips to the garden center to buy more bags to finish filling your pots.

## DETERMINE THE VOLUME OF A CONTAINER

Potting soil is sold by volume, not weight. If you buy a new container with a label telling you its volume, your job is easy: You know exactly how much potting soil to purchase. Otherwise, you'll need to do a bit of math—a simple volume equation—to figure it out for yourself.

Write down all of the measurements and volumes of your containers in a safe place so you can refer to the numbers in future years instead having to go through the process all over again.

**Square and rectangular containers.** For square or rectangular planters, this is quite simple. First, measure the height, length, and depth. (Measuring the outer edges instead of the inner edges not only makes the process easier, it also allows for a slightly more generous result.) Then multiply these three numbers together to find out the volume of the container, expressed in cubic inches.

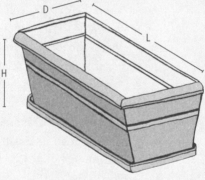

**Cylindrical containers.** Figuring out the volume of a round container is a touch trickier but still pretty straightforward. You just need to use the formula for determining the volume of a cylinder, which is $3.142 \times r^2 \times h$.

☀ *3.142* is the numerical value of ⅓, or pi. It represents the relationship between a circle's radius and diameter and exists in this equation because of the circle portions of the cylinder.

☀ *$r^2$* is the radius squared, or multiplied by itself. The radius is half the diameter, so to find out this figure, measure across the entire container, divide this number in half, and then multiply it by itself.

☀ *h* represents the height of the container, so just measure how tall it is from ground to top.

Chances are that your container will not be a true cylinder: It will taper downward, and the circle that makes the bottom will probably be smaller than the one that makes the top. Simplify the equation by measuring the container as a true cylinder and use only the largest circle in your calculations.

If you have an unusually shaped cylinder, like a footed urn, inspect the container before deciding where to measure. If the pedestal portion is hollow, you will need to include it in your calculation. If it is solid, do your best to measure just the receptacle portion.

**Hanging baskets.** For calculating the volume of a hanging basket, it is best to begin with the formula for the volume of a sphere: $4.19 \times r^3$.

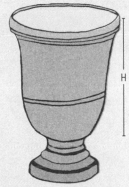
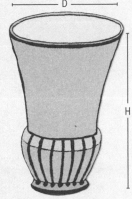

Simply measure across the hanging basket's surface, divide this number in half to get the radius (r), and multiply it by itself three times. Multiply that result by 4.19. Then divide it by 2, since the hanging basket is only half of a sphere.

**Other containers.** If you have an unusually shaped container, do your best to simplify its lines into an easily recognizable shape, always erring on the side of a larger container than a smaller one.

## CONVERT THE RESULTS

You probably measured all of your pots in inches or centimeters, which is fine, except that potting soil is not sold by the cubic inch or cubic centimeter. It is sold by dry volumes, like quarts or gallons, or in cubic feet or even cubic yards for very large amounts.

So determining that your pot holds 453 cubic inches still doesn't tell you how much potting soil you'll need. You have to convert those inches to a more usable figure. You can easily do this online—there are many online converters that allow you to simply plug in your number, select the unit you figured it in, select the unit you'd like it in, and then get your answer. There are even smartphone and tablet apps that you can download for the job. Just type "converter" into your search engine or app store.

Converting cubic inches to cubic feet the old-fashioned way isn't too difficult, either: Just divide a result in cubic inches by 1,728 (the number of cubic inches in a cubic foot). To get cubic yards, divide that result by 27.

If you convert the volume of each container to cubic feet separately, you'll probably end up with a lot of fractions to add up at the end. So it's best to figure out the volume of each of your containers in cubic inches, add up all of the volumes, and then convert your final result to both cubic feet and cubic yards. I recommend that you then add 5 to 10 percent of this figure on top for some leeway and to account for spillage and loss. While I have suggested that you figure all the volumes generously, the soil will settle over time, and it's better to have too much than too little.

It's important to strike the right balance between firming the potting soil and preserving its light, airy structure. If you don't tamp the soil down gently and periodically as you fill the container, it is likely to settle several inches within a few weeks. It is, however, possible to overfirm the potting mix, eliminating the space available for oxygen and water. So briefly firm the soil once when the container's about half full, again about three-quarters of the way up, and then again when you reach the top. As long as you don't spend a lot of time or effort really trying to push it down, you should get good results.

Fill your containers to within 1 to 2 inches of the very top. This leaves a "watering lip"—a sort of basin area where water can accumulate and drain through the growing medium. Even if you are using self-watering containers, it is important to leave this space to accommodate rainfall. You don't want to leave too much of a lip, though: Drastically underfilling containers causes the rim to cast a shadow on your sun-loving vegetable plants, and it gives a half-finished look.

There is an older school of thought that holds that anytime you are planting—whether it's a shrub in your yard or an annual in a container—you dig the hole, fill it with water, and then plant. I feel that this does little but slow you down and make a muddy mess; it does nothing that a thorough watering after the fact can't accomplish. I recommend that you wait until after planting to water, unless you will be sowing seeds in the container, in which case you should thoroughly wet the top several inches of potting soil, sow the seed, and water again gently.

# LET'S GET GROWING

From this point on, growing plants in containers is fairly similar to growing plants in other situations, but there are special maintenance tips and ideas that can help ensure success. You'll find all of the information you need about sowing seeds, growing plants, and maintaining your crops in Chapter 3, Spots and Pots Gardening School, and Chapter 6, Plant Encyclopedia.

# Eight Tips for Excellent Edible Pots

1. **Don't overcrowd.** It can be tempting to treat these pots like you do your summer flower pots, jamming in lots of material for an abundant show. If you treat edible crops like that, you'll end up with small plants and very little harvest. Generally speaking, the larger the plant, the more space it will want for itself. If your crops are performing poorly, it's probably a good indication that they are too close together. Thin them (remove selected individuals) or remove the least important crop entirely. You may be able to transplant it, depending on the crop and its maturity.

2. **Fertilize.** Remember that a container offers a finite amount of nutrients and as the plant uses them, they aren't replenished except through applications of fertilizer. A combination of granular fertilizer in the soil and liquid fertilizers applied through the season is best.

3. **Grow what you like.** You probably won't have room for everything you'd want to grow in an ideal world, so identify your favorite vegetables and herbs and give them priority.

4. **Color counts.** Because your edible pots are likely to spend their season right there in your living space, choose the most colorful varieties and mix and match them for a bold statement that is as pretty as any flower pot.

5. **Be proactive.** Sometimes, a crop may not be growing well—it may be because of the weather you're having that season, it may be the specific variety of crop, but don't waste your season with anything that isn't productive and beautiful. While you still have time, rip it out and replace it with a quick-growing, tried-and-true crop that you enjoy eating.

6. **Water, water, water.** Do not let plants dry out, as even a small amount of stress can seriously set back a crop. Repeated drought stress can take a crop out for a season. As long as your container has a drainage hole and the soil allows for the free flow of water (i.e., it never becomes or remains sodden and muddy), the threat of overwatering is minimal. Even if rain is in the forecast, water your pots thoroughly and regularly.

7. **Keep records.** Whether you keep a traditional garden journal or simply take photographs throughout the season, reviewing these each winter will help you significantly improve your garden in the coming season. Evernote (evernote.com) is an excellent smartphone app for storing photos and notes about your garden.

8. **Pull off a leaf.** In containers, the smallest tweak can sometimes make the biggest difference. Simply removing a leaf that may be blocking a fruit from receiving the sunshine it needs to reach ripeness can help you harvest sooner. Don't be afraid to primp and prune your plants to give each individual its best shot at maturity.

## chapter two

# EDIBLE SPOTS: RAISING CROPS IN RAISED BEDS

Raised-bed gardening—growing plants in spaces where the soil surface is higher than ground level—is fun, highly productive, and very rewarding. It combines the problem-solving flexibility of growing edibles in containers with the high yields, satisfying "working the soil" experience, and more expansive growing space of traditional inground vegetable plots. Raised beds are the ultimate edible spot.

You can start either by building one or more raised beds from scratch or by converting an existing ground-level plot into a raised bed. The method may be as simple as a mound of soil just a few inches tall or as elegant as a collection of geometric beds framed in brick or bluestone. While they're usually built on the ground, raised beds can include tall wooden growing tables that make gardening possible for those in wheelchairs or with other mobility issues. Whatever space, budget, and time you have available, there's an ideal raised-bed approach for you.

In the same way that raised-bed gardening combines the best of container growing and a regular vegetable garden, it also combines some of the challenges of each. As with containers, for example, beginning a raised-bed garden requires an investment in materials and soil. You can start small and expand the system as your budget allows, though, and you can be crafty about your methods and materials to get as much as possible for little or no money. Weeds will be a bit more of a problem than they are in containers, but managing them is easier than in a traditional plot since you don't have to spend hours on your knees removing them. When you consider the value of going the raised-bed route, you'll see that these few drawbacks are minor considerations in the long run.

# A SUREFIRE SOLUTION FOR PROBLEM SOIL

Forget about struggling for years to get poor soil into good shape for gardening! Raised beds are the answer for almost any troublesome soil condition, including:

- High clay content, where digging is difficult and drainage is poor

- Very rocky soil, which is almost impossible to dig and impedes the growth of root crops like carrots and potatoes

- Very sandy soils, which are too fast draining and low in nutrients

- Caliche, a soil condition primarily specific to arid regions where the soil bakes into a concrete-hard layer that cannot be dug and is nearly impervious to water as well

- Extreme pH levels, where the soil is either too acidic (below 6.0) or too alkaline (above 7.0)

- Yards where there are abundant black walnut (*Juglans nigra*) trees, which emit the chemical juglone and inhibit growth of many plants, especially edibles

- Sites where soilborne diseases or nematodes are abundant

# CONSIDER THE ADVANTAGES

While raised beds may appear to be similar to classic plot-based gardening, they offer an enormous range of benefits over traditional inground growing.

- **Maintenance made easy.** Raised beds are much less trouble to care for because they require less stooping and bending than ground-level gardens. You can even build them to heights that don't require kneeling. Every step of planting, maintaining, and harvesting becomes physically easier on you without sacrificing the productivity enjoyed by growing plants in the ground.

- **A head start in spring.** Raised beds warm up before ground-level soil in spring, giving your crops a jump start on the growing season. This is partly because of the better-than-average drainage and partly because the smaller volume of soil picks up the warmth of the sun more efficiently in spring. Stone- and brick-framed beds generally warm up the quickest of all materials. This early warming lets you start planting days or even weeks earlier, extending your growing season and increasing your harvests.

- **Simple soil improvement.** Building raised beds saves you the hassle of trying to work in or improve problem soils. You just place the bed right on top of a level surface, fill it with ideal soil, and start growing.

- **Keep critters out.** If ground-based pests like rabbits, voles, mice, woodchucks (groundhogs), or gophers are a problem in your area, you can exclude them from the garden entirely with the right materials and the right height of raised bed.

- **Easy to customize.** Raised beds easily allow for an array of additions, including connectors for covers, a cage for bird or deer netting, irrigation, and built-in trellising/staking systems.

- **Ample space for sizable crops.** Raised beds offer significantly more planting options than containers do. You can easily grow more permanent perennial vegetables, such as asparagus and rhubarb, as well as tall or wide-spreading crops like corn, melons, and pumpkins.

- **Grow almost anywhere.** You can even build raised beds directly on top of concrete, asphalt, or heavily compacted soil. The sides need to be at least 18 inches deep

*(continued on page 48)*

# The Untalan Family
## DEXTER, MICHIGAN
### the problem solvers

The 1891 farmhouse in Dexter, Michigan, that Chris and Katie Untalan purchased in 2009 had most everything they wanted when they moved there from Boston—old-fashioned charm and an idyllic 1-acre plot dotted with beautiful 100+-year-old trees. Their first summer in their new home, they dug four good-size plots behind their garage and set to growing their own food. "The tomatoes were doing great," Chris, a figurative sculptor and tattoo artist, recalls about that first season. "They had a ton of fruits and were just starting to ripen, when all of the sudden, the plants just kind of collapsed in on themselves." After a bit of research as to what may have caused such a dramatic decline, they discovered that the massive black walnut at the edge of their property was to blame, and that, in fact, their entire property had once been the site of a walnut farm.

Black walnut trees are one of the best-known examples of allelopathy, a natural phenomenon in which a plant emits chemicals from its leaves, fruits, and, most especially, roots, that interfere with the growth of nearby plants. Juglone, the chemical produced by walnut trees, is notoriously antagonistic to tomatoes and their relatives; it affects other edibles, as well, by inhibiting the respiratory process, resulting in stunted growth.

Undaunted, Chris and Katie resolved to build raised beds the following year so that they could continue growing their favorite crops—tomatoes, peppers, and potatoes—in this perfectly suited space. That winter, their plan was to transform the house's original sagging covered front porch into an office for Katie, a web designer who works from home. This project let them salvage several feet of old, dry, wide boards that were perfectly suited to upcycling into raised beds. They merely needed to buy 2 × 2 lumber to secure the corners to allow them to build two 4 × 8-foot raised beds. Now they grow tomatoes and peppers and root crops like carrots in the raised beds and juglone-tolerant crops like beans and corn in the areas between the raised beds, enjoying enormous harvests from their garden.

"I've learned you better grow things that you love, because you're always going to get more than you expect!" quips Katie, even as her daughter, Safia, age 8, prematurely digs baby carrots out of one of the beds.

They plan to add more raised beds in coming years and particularly want to build deeper raised beds, which will help keep root crops like potatoes well out of the walnut's root zone. Their biggest challenge now is keeping up with the weeding, since the raised beds provide a juglone-free environment for them to take hold as well. Fortunately, Chris and Katie's son Lio, age 5, is an enthusiastic weeder. But they've also put down cardboard and straw on the paths between the beds, which not only minimizes work but neatens the appearance of their garden. Now their vegetable garden is a peaceful and healthy spot in their large yard, and the century-old walnut tree is a beautiful backdrop to it all.

Just to the right of this garage, you can see the massive walnut tree that necessitated the use of raised beds. The three trees in the background of the photo on the opposite page are also large, mature walnut trees, evidence of the walnut farm that used to occupy their land. Juglone, the chemical that interferes with the growth of many plants (but especially tomatoes and their relatives), is present in all parts of the walnut tree, but the biggest problems for gardeners come from the juglone emitted by the roots of the tree and accumulating in the soil from leaves and nuts on the ground in autumn. Even if a walnut tree dies or is removed, the vast network of decaying roots continues to have an allelopathic effect for many years. While the effect dissipates over time, plants that are highly juglone intolerant will continue to struggle when even a small amount of the chemical is present.

(ideally more) to accommodate the length of the roots and still allow a few inches for drainage. Growing in a raised bed on concrete will probably result in a permanent stain on the concrete, should you ever wish to remove the bed, and the frequent watering your garden will need can lead to cracking and flaking of the surface, which will be a safety hazard and costly to repair. However, a raised bed is an excellent way to green up an otherwise desolate, concrete-covered area, like an unused part of a playground, driveway, or parking lot.

## INVESTIGATE YOUR OPTIONS

Ultimately, a raised bed is like a giant container. You get to decide on the size and materials, depending on the space and budget you have available. And as with containers, you can start small and simple and expand or upgrade as you go along.

### Basic Soil Beds

The simplest raised beds are just soil mounded a few inches higher than ground level. They take hardly any time to make, you can easily change their size and shape, and your financial investment is minimal. Over time, though, the unsupported sides are likely to crumble or erode with watering, so you'll need to rake them up again. The higher the bed, the quicker the sides will collapse, so it's best to keep them just 3 to 4 inches high.

If you're converting an existing ground-level garden to raised beds, simply stake out where you want the beds to be, rake the soil in the bed areas, and use the spaces between the beds as paths. If you want the beds to be higher, spread more soil on top.

Starting your soil beds from scratch is easy, too. First, spread cardboard or newspaper where you want the bed to be. (A single layer of cardboard or several sheets of newspapers is enough to smother the grass.) Water the area thoroughly, then pile soil on top, making sure to completely cover the cardboard or newspaper, as any exposed edges wick water away from the soil and create an impervious layer between the bed and the soil.

### Wood Boards and Timbers

Most gardeners sooner or later end up adding some sort of frame around their raised beds. This holds the soil in place, allowing them to build the sides higher for more rooting room and less stooping. Permanent sides also help keep weeds and grass from creeping into the beds, minimizing maintenance chores.

Wood is the most commonly used material for framing raised beds. It is attractive, long

# THE GREAT DEBATE ABOUT TREATED LUMBER

Like so many topics that pertain to human health and the environment, the safety of using treated lumber to create raised beds for edibles has generated a lot of controversy and disagreement. Chemical treatments to help lumber last longer outdoors have become less toxic over the years, not just because of concerns about human consumption but also because of the possibility of environmental pollution during the process of soaking the lumber in the treatment and, later, as the chemicals leach out of the wood and into the soil and eventually groundwater.

The fear of using treated lumber in raised beds goes back to the introduction of creosote, which was first used to make lumber rot and insect resistant in the 1840s. It is, in fact, still used today for railroad ties and utility poles (this is why you should not install railroad ties in your vegetable garden). That the material is carcinogenic to humans was essentially irrelevant, since most plants could not thrive in its presence.

In the 1940s, the lumber industry began treating lumber with chromated copper arsenic (CCA). CCA is responsible for the lumber's green tint. Though it was touted as safe for many years, it came under scrutiny in the 1990s when it was found to leach into the soil. Though research on CCA in gardens has shown that uptake by vegetables is minimal and always well within what is considered a "safe" dose of the respective toxins, it is generally not recommended for these applications. CCA has since been phased out of the North American lumber industry, so you probably won't come across it if you are using new lumber to construct your beds or buying a raised-bed kit.

A new chemical treatment, known as ACQ (alkaline copper quaternary), became available in the early 2000s. Though it contains five times as much copper as CCA did, it contains no compounds or ingredients that are classified as toxins by the EPA. Does this mean it is safe to use in raised beds? That's a difficult question to answer. At one point, CCA-treated wood was believed to be safe for use in gardens. Though subsequent research showed its risks to be minimal, they were risks nonetheless.

The EPA recommends taking some fairly serious safety precautions when working with ACQ-treated wood, including wearing a respirator and gloves and bathing thoroughly and washing clothes after work is completed for the day. Plus, the high copper content makes it so corrosive that you must assemble ACQ-treated wood only with stainless steel fasteners. While this does not necessarily mean that copper will leach into the soil, or that if it does, that plants will take it up and we will consume it when we eat our harvest, this points to a strong recommendation to avoid using ACQ-treated wood in raised-bed gardens.

An updated version of ACQ is called MCQ (micronized copper quaternary) and might be found as an alternative to ACQ at lumberyards. While this product has some improvements over ACQ, it is still a chemically treated product and should be avoided as a material in raised beds.

# THE DIRT ON STRAW-BALE GARDENING

We gardeners tend to be a thrifty bunch, doing our best to gain more growing space while doing the least damage to our bank accounts. As such, the idea of straw-bale gardening is initially appealing. Straw-bale gardening is essentially a form of raised-bed gardening: making a temporary bed by placing a layer of soil on top of a straw bale and planting directly in it. The layer of soil provides enough loose substrate to get the plant going, and then the roots grow down through the straw. This gives you many of the advantages of a raised bed without the work of building a frame to contain it or the expense of buying a lot of topsoil to fill it.

While the low-cost, low-work aspect of growing in a straw bale is appealing, this method also has some significant drawbacks.

☀ Straw bales only last one growing season, so you have to purchase new ones each year.

☀ This method requires a lot of water. You have to soak the bales thoroughly over the course of a few weeks before you plant, and they'll need frequent watering through the growing season as well.

☀ Straw in the bales is tightly packed, making it difficult to carve a pocket to set in started plants.

☀ Straw bales tend to be weedy. They contain numerous weed seeds that will be encouraged to sprout by the frequent watering, and the resulting weeds will take your time to control or else rob nutrients and water from your vegetable plants.

☀ Straw bales can't always support tall plants like corn, tomatoes, and okra. The maturing plants will simply fall over because they cannot form the strong, well-anchored roots needed to support their height, and it is extremely difficult to drive a stake into the straw bale itself to keep plants artificially upright.

☀ Root crops like potatoes and carrots are not their most productive when grown in straw bales. Though the tight bales do loosen up over the season, these early root crops will struggle to grow and may be difficult to harvest.

☀ At the end of the season, you're left with a fairly significant mess to clean up and dispose of. While the straw can, of course, be composted (see page 94), the volume of straw you'll have to handle will overwhelm most average-size compost piles.

There are many success stories of straw-bale gardening, and it does have merits. However, I would not recommend this method when there are so many longer-lasting alternatives that are comparable or superior in cost and benefits yet consume fewer resources, demand less of your time, and look much better than a decomposing straw bale.

lasting, and inexpensive; it requires little technical knowledge or specialized tools to work with; and it allows for lots of flexibility in bed size and configuration. It's strong enough to hold a significant amount of soil and porous enough to allow water to drain freely, preventing damage to the bed frame itself.

If you want to save money and are handy with basic tools, you can build your own raised-bed frames fairly easily. Look for complete instructions on page 153.

**DIY or kit-based beds?** There are countless ready-made kits that include all the materials you need—precut lumber, nails and screws, and instructions—to quickly assemble a raised bed at home. Don't immediately write these off as a gimmick or novelty that won't meet your requirements as a serious vegetable gardener. The economies of scale available to the makers of these kits usually result in high-quality materials conveniently precut to a precise, usable length, with all necessary hardware and other accoutrements selected, sorted, and packaged for quick and easy assembly.

A compromise option for creating wood-framed raised beds is to buy the lumber yourself and use a ready-made corner brace set. These specially designed brackets sturdily join boards at the corners. They allow for board lengths up to 8 or 10 feet, so the dimensions and shape (square or rectangle) are somewhat flexible. Some require no tools for assembly—you simply place the corner braces and slot your precut boards into them—while others may require a drill and screwdriver to secure the framework. Prices range from under $50 to well over $100, not including the cost of the wood sides. I recommend sturdy metal versions over plastic corner braces. The initial cost may be more, but the metal units will more than make up for it in their longevity in the garden.

**Choosing the wood.** Pine boards are readily available in many parts of the country. They are relatively inexpensive, but they also tend to rot, and you'll probably have to replace them fairly often.

The ideal wood for creating raised beds is naturally rot-resistant cedar. Recognizable by its distinctive red hue and delightful woodsy fragrance (especially when scratched), cedar boards tend to be more expensive than other types, but cedar is good-looking and longer lasting. Its natural rot resistance negates the need for chemical treatment, so almost any cedar you find is appropriate for use around edibles.

Other types of wood are frequently treated to last longer outdoors; some of these treatments can be toxic and must be avoided, as the chemicals can be taken up and stored by your plants. Look for a few clues to determine if lumber has been chemically treated or not. It may have a greenish or bluish hue, or it may have an incised pattern of hash marks over the surface. Newer chemical treatments for lumber, like micronized copper quaternary (MCQ) pressure-treated wood (an updated version of ACQ—see page 49), may not show any color at all, so when shopping for wood, look carefully at the labels on the displays; lumber is also stamped on one of its ends, indicating its grade and any treatments. Look for the initials "CCA" (for copper chromium arsenic, which has been phased out of the North American lumber system but which you may nonetheless encounter) or "UC" plus a number: These refer to chemical treatments the wood has received to resist rot.

Though levels of arsenic and other toxins have been reduced, and some research shows that any levels that do get taken up by your crops are still safe for consumption, it is best to avoid using chemically treated lumber around your edibles, period. For more details, check out "The Great Debate about Treated Lumber" on page 49.

There is another wood treatment that helps lumber resist rot and does not pose a threat to your garden or your health: heat treatment. In this case, the wood is placed into a kiln or furnace and dried to remove some of its inherent moisture, making it less likely to reabsorb moisture in the atmosphere (such as in humid climates) or, in a raised-bed situation, from the soil. The initials HT stand for "heat treated" and are used in lower grades of lumber. Look for the acronym S-DRY (surface dried) or MC15 (moisture content less than 15 percent) on higher-grade structural lumber. While these treatments don't make lumber rotproof, they will prolong the longevity of a raised bed made from them.

When shopping for lumber, whether cedar or another type of wood, choose boards that have the highest proportion of the darker-colored heartwood. Heartwood—that is, the center of the tree—is much more rot resistant than sapwood (the younger, outer part of the

## Raised-Bed Materials Comparison

| MATERIAL | COST | EASE OF USE (CUTTING, FASTENING) | DURABILITY |
| --- | --- | --- | --- |
| MASONRY (BRICK, STONE, AND CONCRETE CHUNKS) | $–$$$$ | Heavy and time consuming to construct; may require specialized knowledge and tools in some cases | Essentially permanent if well built |
| METAL | $$–$$$ | Difficult and possibly hazardous to cut if necessary; securing takes effort and may require special tools and experience | Long lasting; may eventually rust, depending on material |
| PLASTIC OR COMPOSITE LUMBER | $–$$ | Moderately difficult to cut accurately and fasten securely, especially when compared to wood | Very resistant to rotting; may bow if not built and supported properly |
| WOOD | $–$$ | Very easy and flexible to use; recommended for beginners and inexperienced builders | Low (2+ years) to moderate (7+ years), depending on climate, wood type, and thickness |

tree), so boards with a higher percentage of light-colored sapwood will be a bit more rot prone than boards with more dark heartwood.

**Reusing old lumber.** The visual cues that indicate chemical treatment of wood are most noticeable on new lumber; weathering fades colors and diminishes patterns. Therefore, it is not advisable to use recycled boards around edibles unless you are 100 percent certain that they were not treated.

Similarly, you should always avoid using railroad ties and old landscape timbers. While their bulky mass provides a sturdy frame and rustic charm, these were once chemically treated. Even if they are very old, it is impossible to say how much, or even precisely which, toxins they may contain. Though any of these can be reused for ornamental or landscape purposes, you should keep them away from raised beds and enclosures for edibles to be on the safe side. Your health is far more valuable than free lumber!

**Maintenance considerations.** Frequent rainfall and irrigation in your garden may shorten the life of your wood-framed raised beds. You can expect cedar to last 8 to 10 years, possibly well beyond. Untreated conventional lumber ought to last at least 5 years, though it will fade and soften as time takes its toll. Durability will depend on the climate—hot, humid climates are more conducive to wood decay than arid climates, and in extreme situations, conventional lumber may only last two or three growing seasons—but you can still expect a long-lasting payout for your investment in clean new lumber.

It's common to paint, stain, or seal furniture, decks, and other outdoor wood structures to prevent cracking, fading, and rotting, and it's tempting to translate this idea to a raised bed. However, conventional stains and sealants contain toxic compounds and are not recommended. Recent years have seen the introduction of a wide range of nontoxic sealers that are marketed as safe. While they well may be, none that I found was labeled as safe for treating lumber for raised beds or containers where edibles will be grown. As such, I do not recommend that you treat the lumber for your raised beds with any such products, even if you find one that bills itself as organic or nontoxic, since this applies only to the uses described on its label (typically, decks, furniture, or wood house siding).

## Plastic and Composite Lumber

Plastic and composite "boards" are made primarily of recycled plastic. Composite materials include actual wood fiber and often have a woodlike color and grainlike pattern for realistic effect. These products are sold in the same dimensions as natural wood lumber ($2 \times 4$, $2 \times 6$, and so on).

You may have seen plastic and composite materials advertised especially for decks and swimming-pool areas: They are rotproof, never splinter as wood does, and can be cut, attached, and built with in the same way as lumber. They do have a few disadvantages: They're more expensive than traditional lumber, and some people dislike their "fake" look, though aesthetics have improved. Also, though plastic or composite lumber is heavy in weight, it is not as strong as traditional lumber of comparable size, so it cannot be used for a long span with-

giving your raised-bed garden a completely unique style. Keeping an eye on construction or demolition sites and Web sites like the Freecycle Network and Craigslist could result in a bonanza of used brick, pavers, or concrete blocks at little or no cost. These items, along with chunks of concrete from demolition sites, are especially useful in urban areas or in regions where there is little natural bedrock.

Masonry beds require more site preparation than other materials do: The surface must be perfectly level, or any slope compensated for in the design of the beds. These also need a firm footing of crushed gravel or masonry sand to prevent shifting or crumbling later. Sides built up to about 6 inches tall can be free-stacked (which gives you the option of more easily moving or changing the size of the beds later, if needed), but taller sides should be mortared for stability. Considering these special requirements of masonry construction, you may wish to hire a professional to ensure that your beds will be long lasting and stable.

The additional warmth provided by masonry beds is an excellent season extender and may help plants like lavender, thyme,

out cross bracing. Still, these materials can be a good choice if you like the idea of using recycled materials in your garden or if you don't want to have to replace the frames of your raised beds every 5 to 10 years, as you may need to with wood lumber.

Because of the difficulty of cutting plastic lumber, your best bet for constructing raised beds out of this material is to buy it in a precut raised-bed kit. Several are available by mail order, and they are designed specifically to work with the material, saving you the trouble of engineering a plan to compensate for its shortcomings.

## Masonry Options

Raised beds made from materials like brick, concrete, and stone generally require a more substantial initial investment in money and labor to create, but they are the most permanent and have the most potential to be an attractive part of your outdoor living areas. They also offer plenty of opportunities to use recycled materials, holding the cost down and

and rosemary make it through winter more successfully. However, that microclimate may invite chipmunks or snakes to take up residence, especially in the case of unmortared flagstone or rocks, with their abundant nooks and crannies. While snakes provide superb rodent control, gardeners who don't particularly relish the sight of serpents (or those who live in areas with many venomous species) may wish to consider less snake-friendly materials.

## Metal Frames

Typically expensive and potentially difficult to work with, metal can nonetheless be a viable option for creating raised beds. Corrugated aluminum or steel roofing panels, for example, can be incorporated into raised beds, and they're probably the easiest and least expensive way to make a metal raised bed. Use them on their own, with one edge buried in the ground and the sides secured with rebar, or build them into wood frames to provide support. Cutting them is not advised, as it requires special tools and leaves a sharp edge that would be dangerous to work around; fortunately, they come ready-made in usable sizes for raised beds (6 or 8 feet long and 2 feet high).

Steel plating and the currently very chic Cor-Ten steel can also be adapted into raised beds. Again, cutting is an issue, but those with access to these heavy, pricey materials and the tools to cut them can create really interesting, contemporary raised beds. The natural rusting process is a design feature with steel, but heavy panels will last for decades. Similarly,

# STAY AWAY FROM SEPTIC SITES

While raised beds seem like the perfect answer to making use of a septic-system drain field, they do not, unfortunately, get around many of the dangers. First of all, there's the potential for expensive damage to the drain field as well as to your plantings (if repairs need to be done to the drain field and you have to remove the beds). Second, the drain field contains water that may be contaminated with bacteria and household chemicals, and if the roots of your edibles come in contact with it, or if it's close enough to the surface to splash up on leaves, then your crops, too, may be contaminated and unsafe to eat.

Theoretically, it is possible to build a raised bed deep enough that crop roots will not come in contact with any portion of the leach field. The more soil you dump on the site, though, the more potential for impeding the proper working of the drain field, so it's far preferable to seek another spot for your raised beds.

corrugated metal drainpipe or culvert pipe makes a nice-size, easy-to-install raised bed if you can find it in a usable dimension. These large, open cylinders are typically used for municipal projects and are sold to the trade in very long lengths; however, they are often found in community and city gardens.

Though not yet widely available, metal raised-bed kits exist and are becoming more

(continued on page 58)

# Lafayette Greens Garden
## DETROIT, MICHIGAN
### the bridge builders

No matter which direction you approach it from, Lafayette Greens garden in downtown Detroit comes as a complete surprise. This thriving, exuberant vegetable garden explodes off the street with lush crops, colorful zinnias, happy honeybees, and a throng of businesspeople, locals, and visitors who are almost magnetically drawn to this beautiful place. Situated on a funny triangular lot made vacant with the demolition of the Lafayette Building in 2010, Lafayette Greens was founded by Compuware Corporation in 2011 as a way to beautify the area and to provide a new type of community gathering space unlike any the neighborhood had seen before.

What visually and spatially defines this year-round garden is its dozens of chic galvanized steel raised beds neatly arrayed over two-thirds of the site. Designed by Beth Hagenbuch of Kenneth Weikel Landscape Architecture, the beds and their layout establish a theme of urban geometry, bringing order and unity to the hundreds of organically grown edible plants. "The metal beds reinforce the urban aspect of the garden," says Gwen Meyer, the garden coordinator. "With that in mind, along with the cost of cedar lumber, using steel was an obvious choice." The beds, built by a local steel fabricator, are constructed of corrugated steel panels, tied to the ground with cedar posts, and reinforced inside with strong threaded rod to prevent bowing. Not only did Hagenbuch design sturdy, permanent beds appropriate to the location, she also sited them within the lot to maximize sunlight, an important consideration when surrounded by tall buildings.

It would be easy to write off Lafayette Greens as a high-budget showplace until you actually visit the garden and see visitors' reactions as they walk though. "The space is open to everyone—its purpose is to be an open and safe space for people from all walks of life," says Megan Heeres, community art and garden program manager. The beds contribute significantly to the all-inclusive nature of the space, as their heights, ranging from 12 to 26 inches high, invite participation from all ages and abilities, which is important for this mostly volunteer-maintained garden. "Though the range in bed height was necessary because of the 4-foot overall slope of

the site," says Gwen, "this works to our advantage. Kids and folks who are able to bend work at the short end, and seniors, folks in wheelchairs, and those who need to pull over a chair to work help maintain the tall end."

Local residents and workers drop in for educational sessions on everything from seed saving to making art from the garden, and the busy urban site invites impromptu informative sessions as well, which was really the point of Lafayette Greens in the first place. "The edibles are curious and fascinating to some visitors, and recall personal histories in others," Gwen says. "We have had wonderful, meaningful interactions with drivers for nearby hotels and the federal court and the seniors who live downtown; we have engaging conversations with folks who've never been to Detroit. Lafayette Greens is an opportunity to demonstrate the plentiful positive things happening in Detroit." Everyone, from economists to urban planners, predict that urban agriculture is the future of Detroit these days, and Lafayette Greens, along with the growing contingent of farms in the city, is a bellwether for the city. Gwen sums it up best: "We are working to change some of the stigmas around vegetable gardening as messy, unsightly, and threatening by balancing form and function. Everyone who visits can appreciate the beauty of the space, and the edible element really allows folks to recognize that as humans, we're not that different at all."

popular with the rise of urban gardening. These are especially handy, as they save you the work of cutting and shaping metal panels. They also eliminate the potential issue of sharp or rough edges jutting out on home-cut metal. As with other types of raised-bed kits, ready-made metal bed kits generally cost less than buying new materials, and they offer pre-drilled holes and included hardware. What they lack in flexibility, they make up for in cost savings and convenience.

# SELECT THE RIGHT SITE

Where you put your raised beds is just as important as what you make them out of. You want them to be convenient to your house for easy planting, maintenance, and harvesting, of course, but for the best yields possible, the needs of your plants take priority.

## Light Levels

Plan to build and install your raised beds in the sunniest area available. Most edibles require at least 6, and ideally 8 or more, hours of direct sunlight each day to produce the vigorous leafy growth needed for healthy, high-yielding plants. The sun's warmth helps the plants take greater advantage of the soil-warming proper-ties inherent to raised beds, giving them a head start on the growing season and lengthening it into autumn. Sunny sites help reduce potential rot issues with wood-framed raised beds by drying out the wood surfaces quickly.

Keep in mind that a site you think is sunny might actually be shaded during parts of the day, due to nearby trees or buildings. To get a realistic idea of the light conditions, you may find it helpful to stick bamboo stakes in the corners of the site where you hope to place the beds and then watch the site over the course of a whole bright, sunny day to see if (or when) it's in sun or in shade. Shade patterns can change a surprising amount in different seasons—especially around deciduous trees, which may allow ample sunlight in spring but cast deep shade once they leaf out by early summer—so it's smart to evaluate your potential site in sum-mer, when most of your crops will be growing.

One way to take best advantage of sunlight is to orient your raised beds along a north–south axis. This little trick helps minimize shading so that the most light reaches all of your crops through the day. It isn't always possible on every property, and if orienting your beds this way would mean that a portion of them would be heavily shaded by nearby trees or structures, then adjust the beds so they get the most possible sun, even if they don't run north to south.

## Drainage Issues

Many yards have one or more natural low spots where water collects after a storm or areas that stay wet longer than others. Areas that flood only occasionally after very heavy rains may still be suitable for a raised-bed garden, but if a site regularly retains standing water 3 or 4 days after a heavy rain, this indicates a fairly serious drainage issue that could damage your beds and your crops. Stagnant water can exacerbate disease issues as high humidity and standing water favor fungal diseases like powdery mildew and anthracnose.

## Slope Considerations

The ideal site for raised beds is flat ground. It's easy to build a level bed there, and the soil will readily stay in place.

It's certainly possible to make a raised-bed garden on a sloping site, but the surface of each bed still needs to be level. That means you must construct a frame to keep the soil from washing away, and you'll have to compensate for the incline by increasing the height of the bed on the downslope side. A series of raised beds can turn an essentially useless, steeply sloping site into usable garden space, but a project like this requires a significant investment of time and money and a great deal of planning and building skill to accomplish. If you don't have a lot of building experience, call in a professional to provide advice and construction plans appropriate to your site.

On a sloped site, raised bed frames will necessarily increase in depth as they march down the hill; the short sides correspondingly increase in length as well, as shown at right. The more dramatic the slope, the more adaptations you'll have to make to construct durable raised beds that retain the soil.

## DECIDE ON THE SIZE

When you start with a commercial raised-bed kit, you're usually constrained by the proportions prescribed by the kit. Though ready-made kits are often a good workable size, and many of them are even expandable, making your own raised beds lets you adapt the dimensions to your space and your needs and preferences. There is a limit, however, and how big your raised beds can be depends on the overall amount of space you have available, the materials you're using for the frame, and your budget.

### The Right Height

From the perspective of your plants, the most important issue is how high the sides of the bed are, because that determines how much room the roots will have to spread out in. If you're converting a traditional vegetable garden where the drainage is good and you've been improving the soil for years, your crops will have plenty of rooting room below even if their raised beds are only 3 or 4 inches tall. An impervious surface like asphalt or concrete, on the other hand, calls for a much higher frame:

# CONSIDER CUSTOM FEATURES

If you're going the raised-bed route, then why not make the most of it by adding some custom features while you're at it? When you build your own raised beds (or if you're the type who likes to tinker with ready-made products), you can include several useful adaptations in the bed structure to make your garden even easier to maintain.

☼ Metal mesh to deter digging animals. Secured to the inner edges of wood-framed raised beds with a staple gun, hardware cloth or chicken wire can prevent digging animals like rabbits, squirrels, voles, and woodchucks from attacking your crops from below.

☼ Covers to protect from cold and pests. Using inexpensive plastic plumbing parts (pipes, elbows, T-connectors) and semicircular brackets, you can easily build an adjustable or removable frame to support a covering of heavy plastic for spring frost protection, screening for shade, or floating row cover to keep pests away.

☼ Built-in irrigation. Many raised-bed kits include irrigation features, like spigots that allow you to hook up a hose for easier watering or for a drip irrigation setup.

☼ Special supports. While this may limit your crop rotation potential somewhat, permanent trellising is an attractive, effective way to save space and maximize the yields from your crops.

To learn more about how to upgrade a basic raised bed into a custom growing system, see "Raised Bed Extras" on page 156.

at least 18 inches tall, and ideally more. A height somewhere between 3 and 18 inches is fine for beds built on unimproved soil or lawn.

For your own convenience, a high bed (one built at knee to hip level) is easier to care for than a low one, which will still require kneeling. Taller beds require a bigger investment to build and fill with soil. They may also require more water, depending on the material used to build them, though this is easily remedied through the use of a soaker hose or drip system. Furthermore, the taller the bed is, the shorter in length the sides should be, as increased soil volume brings with it extra weight than can cause sides to bow or bulge.

## Not Too Wide

One of the significant benefits of raised-bed gardening is that the soil never gets packed down because you don't walk on it. To take full advantage of that, though, you need to keep your beds narrow enough that you can easily reach into them without straining. A width of 3 to 4 feet is suitable for most adults. If you site a raised bed against a fence or wall, make it no more than 2 feet wide, since you'll only be able to access it from one side.

## Length Is Flexible

A 3 × 3-foot or a 4 × 4-foot square is a popular shape for a raised bed, but if space allows, you can easily extend the length to make a rectangular bed. It's not advisable to build a single raised bed over 8 feet long, though, if you are using wood or plastic lumber, because these flexible materials tend to sag or bow. The

instructions for building a raised bed in Chapter 4 outline the construction of a simple 2 × 4-foot bed that makes total use of one 12-foot-long board.

## Material Matters

Some raised-bed size decisions will be made for you based on the materials you're using to build the frame. For example, lumber is generally sold in even-numbered widths (2 × 6, 2 × 8, 2 × 10) and even-numbered lengths (4, 6, 8, 10, or 12 feet), so you may choose to stick with even-numbered dimensions to reduce or eliminate board cuts. Similarly, concrete blocks and paver stones are available only in prescribed proportions, so your bed size will be determined by how many you want to use. Concrete blocks are typically 8 inches high, 8 inches wide, and 16 inches long, meaning your bed length and width would end up as a multiple of 8 or 16 inches.

# THINK ABOUT DESIGN

Raised beds may not be as decorative as colorful, moveable containers, but that doesn't mean they have to be boring. There are several ways to create a uniquely personal raised-bed garden that is as pretty as it is productive.

## Ordered Chaos

With their vertical sides and 90-degree angles, classic raised beds tend to have a rather formal appearance. This can bring a welcome sense of order to a vegetable garden, which often tends to become a joyful tangle of growth and vigor as plants get larger and bend under the weight of ripe produce. The sharp geometry of raised beds gives you the freedom to experiment without fear of your garden looking too messy or visually confusing. This doesn't mean you have to stick with beds of all one shape and size arranged in rows like a regular vegetable garden, though. Mix square and rectangular beds in one space, or to arrange the beds in interesting patterns.

## Nonstandard Shapes

Rectangular or square beds are easiest to construct and make the most efficient use of space and materials, but it's possible to make other shapes, too, depending on what frame materials you use. Metal, especially, can be gently coaxed into more rounded forms, as evidenced by the classic three-tiered metal strawberry beds long sold in mail-order catalogs. It will need to be secured in place with tightly packed earth and/or long, strong rebar spikes.

Concrete, stone, and pavers can also be stacked into flowing curved and round beds. Though this free-form approach will give less surface area for planting relative to the amount of materials used (and, particularly in the case of rounds, may make the center of the bed difficult to reach without climbing in), it can be a fun way to create something unexpected.

## Made in Multiples

Raised beds are best in groups. Not only does having multiple raised beds give you more growing space, providing a larger harvest and the opportunity to plant crops in different spots from year to year, it's more visually appealing, too. A single raised bed can look lost and forlorn in a large yard, while a grouping of two, four, or more beds creates a landscape feature.

From a practical standpoint, you may find it more efficient to build multiple beds all at once, rather than just one a year. Even if you feel that a single bed is enough to meet your family's food needs, building two gives you room to rotate crops, grow a cover crop (see page 68), or plant some easy annual flowers for cutting.

## Access Paths

Even if you have only one raised bed, you will need some surface around it that's comfortable to walk or kneel on. And where there are two or more beds, the spaces between them will serve as pathways as well as access points for planting, maintenance, and harvesting. It is important to site your raised beds far enough apart for the path to be useful, easy to care for, and easy to access when you're carrying or using a wheelbarrow to take tools and materials to and from your garden: ideally about 24 inches apart. As

# GATHER YOUR TOOLS

Just as raised-bed gardening combines the advantages of both containers and traditional inground plots, it requires a combination of the tools best suited to each.

For grading the soil surface, spreading compost, digging in cover crops, harvesting potatoes, and similar chores, you'll need full-size, long-handled tools, like a traditional shovel and steel rake. For small-scale jobs like planting, seed sowing, and weeding, you'll need the same small hand tools that are so helpful for container gardening, like a trowel and cultivator.

There is also a happy medium worth considering: new midlength tools from California-based Corona Tools. Designed specifically for raised beds, these tools have a convenient 18-inch length, making them perfectly suited for reaching the middle of a bed from both sides, and they are telescoping, extending your reach another 12 inches. The business end is sturdy but light in weight, so the tools are easy to use without straining your arms or your back.

As your raised-bed garden will probably require more weeding than a container garden—though not nearly as

much as an inground garden—you may also want to have a bucket, a tip bag (a large, handled bag meant for garden debris), or a wheelbarrow to carry compostable material that you remove from the garden.

If your raised-bed garden is bordered by a lawn, consider purchasing a pair of grass shears. This rather old-fashioned tool, sadly supplanted by noisy, dangerous line trimmers, is an excellent companion for keeping a fastidiously neat edge where the bed meets the turf.

For ideas of other tools that you may find handy, check out "Your Container Garden Tool Kit" on page 26.

far as covering the paths, you have the option of keeping them strictly utilitarian or making them a vibrant part of your garden's setting.

### Grass

The simplest solution for a path is to keep whatever already exists on the site, which frequently is lawn grass. In this case, it's vital for the beds to be far enough apart that you can push a mower through them, or you'll be stuck with a whole lot of hand trimming. Measure your mower deck at the widest point, and make each path wide enough to cut with one or two passes with the mower.

### Bare Earth

Bare soil isn't the most elegant option for a path surface, but you can't beat the price. Bare-earth paths will be muddy in wet weather and may be uneven underfoot, especially for the first few seasons, until they get completely packed down. You can hasten the process with a sod roller or concrete compactor from a rental shop. Maintenance is mostly in the form of frequent weeding.

### Clover

If you start with bare earth and wish to plant a low-maintenance groundcover for your paths, you can sow them with white clover (*Trifolium repens*). Clover is highly beneficial to the soil, and its flowers attract bees, which will hang around to pollinate your crops. It is also a tough perennial that will quickly cover the area and can tolerate foot traffic. It grows thickly enough to keep most weeds out, but

# SELF-PLANTING EDIBLES

Self-sowing plants are those that drop their ripe seeds on the ground and pop up in different places from year to year without any help from you. They're a true delight if you love an informal or a cottage-garden look, creating beautiful plant combinations that you might not have considered but that literally just happen by chance. They save you money and time, too, because you don't have to buy new seeds or deal with planting them each year.

Just remember that the plants need to produce flowers to produce seeds, so you must leave flower heads in place so they can ripen and drop their seeds, even if they're past their useful harvest period. If the seedlings come up where you don't want them, simply transplant them or pull them out while they're still small.

A number of self-sowing edibles are eminently suited to raised-bed gardens, providing a useful harvest and attracting pollinators when they bloom. Some wonderful self-sowing vegetables, herbs, and edible flowers include arugula, lettuce, borage, calendula, cilantro, chervil, dill, fennel, Johnny-jump-up, and summer savory. You can find out more about these self-planting edibles in Chapter 6.

you'll need to mow it a few times during the growing season.

## Edible Groundcovers

To make the most of every square inch of garden space, you may choose to plant low-growing herbs and edible flowers, such as creeping thymes, wild strawberries, chamomile, or violets, in the paths. While these will do the job of keeping down mud and weeds, they do not tolerate being walked on as well as clover or grass does. As a compromise, you could place them along the edges of the paths and use stepping-stones in the middle so you're not stepping right on the plants.

## Gravel

Gravel makes an attractive groundcover that does a stellar job of keeping down weeds. There are no mud or flooding concerns, and it is essentially maintenance free once installed. However, it does have a few drawbacks: It may be expensive, depending on where you live, and installing it is very hard work indeed. A wheelbarrow can be difficult to maneuver on gravel, though a four-wheeled wagon can be pulled through most gravel easily, if the path is wide enough. And depending on your preferred gardening footwear, gravel can become a painful nuisance in your shoe! It is also worth bearing in mind the surroundings of your raised-bed area—gravel tends to get tracked onto adjacent surfaces and, if surrounded by lawn, can pose a hazard when mowing.

## Mulch

Shredded bark mulch is an inexpensive alternative to gravel, with many of the same advantages. It keeps down mud and weeds well, and it is much lighter in weight and easier to install. Mulch is easier to roll a wheelbarrow over than gravel (especially once it settles), and it contributes an organic, cohesive look to your raised-bed area. You'll need to refresh it every so often, though, because it decomposes over time.

## Paving

Stepping-stones and recycled brick are great ways to pave your paths, as are landscape pavers. While these solutions may be expensive, their permanence and classic look (especially in the case of traditional brick) merits the expense. They're easy to walk on or roll a wheelbarrow over, and they need essentially no maintenance.

## Wood Rounds

Wood rounds—thin cross sections cut across a branch or tree trunk—make a fun and low-cost alternative to purchased paving. They have a natural look and are a good way to recycle dead wood. Typically $1/2$ to $1^1/2$ inches thick, they need to be set level and tamped to stay in place. Sections of mature arborvitae (*Thuja occidentalis*) can be especially well suited to this, for both their diameter and their rot resistance.

# CONSIDER YOUR CROP OPTIONS

Unlike containers, raised beds pose essentially no physical restrictions on what you can grow. In fact, the only real issue is with tall crops such as sweet corn or okra growing in raised beds that are already 2 to 3 feet high: You may need a stepladder to harvest them! With so many crops to choose from, plan to do a bit of homework to narrow down your choices to fit your requirements and the space you have available. The same approach that works for container plantings works well for raised-bed gardens, too; see "Choose Your Crops" on page 24.

## Plant Placement

Once you've pinned down your plant list, think next about how you're going to arrange your crops. Raised beds lend themselves well to both traditional planting in rows and carefully composed thriller-filler-spiller schemes as described in Chapter 5. There are advantages and disadvantages to both, and some crops are easier to incorporate in one system over the other.

**Classic rows.** Planting in straight rows or solid blocks is a common approach in inground plot gardens, and it can have a place in raised-bed gardens, too. Some vegetables, for instance—like corn—need to grow close to one another to ensure pollination. If you have just a few corn plants scattered throughout your raised beds rather than in a concentrated block, their wind-dispersed pollen might be whisked away, never falling upon the silk of its neighbors to create the full, luscious ears of corn you planted them for in the first place.

Row planting keeps crops organized and easy to find and harvest within the garden. It also maximizes the amount of sun each plant can receive because you account for the plants' ultimate height and width when you sow seed or plant out transplants.

On the downside, many insect pests of edible plants have evolved to home in on row patterns while in flight, so very obvious rows act as a sort of "eat here now" sign to flag in the voracious critters. And from a design standpoint, row planting can increase the rigid appearance of tall, steep-sided raised beds, which may be too formal or severe looking for many gardeners.

**Free-form plantings.** The thriller-filler-spiller method of combining plants is another fine guideline for composing plantings in your raised beds. Because this method uses plants' natural habits to complement one another, allowing all of them to get their full share of sunshine, it is a useful and practical way to approach the layout of your garden. From an aesthetic standpoint, mixing up your crops gives your garden a unique, varied look—more like a flowerbed than a vegetable garden. There are lots more suggestions about incorporating thriller-filler-spiller techniques into your raised beds in Chapter 5.

## Perennial Edibles

Perennial herbs and vegetables—those that come back every year—are better suited to raised beds than they are to containers. For one thing, they'll have the room they need to spread their roots and get established enough to provide an abundant harvest. For another,

# CROPS ON THE MOVE

Because you'll be replanting the majority of your raised-bed garden each year, it's a good idea to plant each crop in a different place from season to season, a technique called crop rotation. That's because some soilborne pests and diseases are particularly tied to certain crops or crop families (such as club root on cabbage-family plants). If you grow the same crops in the same place year after year, you make it easy for pests and pathogens to build up and bother your plants. Different crops also have different nutrient needs, so moving them around each year gives them fresh soil each season (and gives you the chance to rebuild the soil fertility, too).

Serious vegetable gardeners put a lot of effort into planning multiyear rotation systems, which is fine if you have a lot of space available. If you have just a few raised beds, though, you probably won't be able to leave more than a year or two between the same crops. Every little bit helps, however, so do your best to avoid planting the same annual crops in the same spots over and over. If you have only two beds, for instance, grow your tomatoes in one bed one year and switch them to the second bed the following year.

raised-bed perennials will grow for a much longer time before they will need to be transplanted (if they ever do), compared to those growing in the more restrictive volume of a container. The notion of being weatherproof is irrelevant in raised beds, too.

# FOUR EASY COVER CROPS

There are lots of cover-crop options, but if you're looking for quick cover, these four fast growers are tough to beat.

| CROP NAME | PLANTING TIME | TILLING TIME | GROWTH RATE | HARDINESS | NOTES |
|---|---|---|---|---|---|
| RYEGRASS | Spring to fall (winter in warm climates) | Spring of the following year | Fast | USDA Zone 6; will protect soil over winter in any zone | In cold climates, plants can be tilled in as soon as soil is workable since plants will have died over winter |
| BUCKWHEAT | Spring to summer | 4 weeks after germination | Fast | Not hardy; use only during growing season | Fast growing, so good to squeeze in between growing seasons (for example, in early autumn, or after spring crops are done) |
| MAMMOTH RED CLOVER | Spring to fall | When flowering is complete | Fast | USDA Zone 4 | Replenishes nitrogen in soil; good for bees and other pollinators |
| MILLET | Summer | After flowering | Fast | Not hardy; grow only in summer | Tolerant of dry soils |

In a container, asparagus is a waste of time and resources, but you could conceivably devote an entire raised bed to a planting of asparagus (or artichokes, Jerusalem artichokes, or rhubarb) and reap the benefits for a decade or more. Similarly, you can devote an entire bed to perennial herbs, such as sage and oregano, or place them strategically in the corners or at the edges throughout your array of raised beds. For more details on these plant-and-forget crops, check out "Perennial Vegetables" and "Herbs and Edible Flowers" in Chapter 6.

## Cover Crops

Cover crops are a valuable tool in the arsenal of any organic gardener. Though they are most widely used in fields and traditional plots, they are just as simple to install and as beneficial in unconventional growing scenarios like raised beds. While cover crops are growing, they stabilize the soil, protecting it from erosion by wind, rain, and snow and preventing runoff water from carrying away valuable soil nutrients. Flowering cover crops can be magnets for pollinators and other beneficial insects, too. With their many benefits, it's definitely worth considering how you can work them into your planting plans at least every couple of years.

Cover crops also improve your soil when you dig the plants into the soil. Legume (bean family) cover crops, such as alfalfa and soybeans, take this a step further by pulling nitrogen out of the air and contributing it to the soil

through specially adapted nodules on their roots. When cover crops are used to build soil fertility, they're often called green manures. They add nutrients and organic matter to your soil just as animal manures do, but without the hassle, mess, or smell of hauling animal manures.

**Choosing a cover crop.** The best way to choose a cover crop for your raised beds is based on the timing you are faced with. Some crops are sown in summer or fall and left in place only until spring; others might be spring sown and left in place for a year until they are tilled under a year later. Some crops need to grow only a short time to be useful, while others need a long period in the ground. This gives you a lot of flexibility in planning out their season. For example, if you have one bed that you want to lie fallow for a year, you could sow just that one with the cover crop once it was freed up. If you wanted to recharge all of your raised beds with the help of a cover crop, you could choose a late-summer- or early-fall-sown crop, plant it, and then have your beds ready to plant again by your growing season.

Once you've determined the time frame for the cover crop, you need to look at growth rate and at hardiness if you intend to keep the crop in place over winter. Some plants used for cover crops, like barley and millet, are tender and will die at the first frost, not doing their job at all; others, like oats, will die when it gets cold, but their roots will persist strongly enough to stabilize the soil, decomposing by spring and contributing back their nutritive content.

A good seed company will explain how much seed you need to cover a given area and when best to sow it. Even if you buy only the minimum amount of seed, you'll probably have more than you need for one or two raised beds, but you can generally keep it for a few seasons as long as it is stored properly.

**Managing cover crops.** Planting a cover crop is about as simple as sowing any other seed: You rake the soil smooth, scatter the seed over the surface, rake it into the soil, and keep the area moist until seedlings appear.

Let the crop grow as long as you wish, or until the following spring, then cut the tops close to the ground with hand shears or a string trimmer and dig the cut tops into the soil. Let the whole bed sit for at least a week (preferably 2 to 3 weeks) before planting to give the cover crop a chance to decompose.

## SELECT THE SOIL

No matter where they're growing, edibles need good soil to produce vigorous, high-yielding plants. Raised beds are much like containers in that you aren't limited to working with the soil that's already on your site. You won't be using the light, fluffy potting mixes that work well in containers, though: You can buy high-quality topsoil, use compost, or create a custom blend to provide ideal conditions for great root growth.

## Straight Topsoil

The obvious choice for filling raised beds is topsoil. Topsoil—the richest, darkest part of a field soil—is usually a mix of organic matter, sand, silt, and clay. It tends to be heavy, and you need a good bit to fill even a small raised bed, so getting a bulk delivery is generally much more practical than buying topsoil in bags.

Before you begin your raised-bed project, call a couple of bulk yards or landscape suppliers and find out what their minimum delivery amount is. This can give you an idea of how many raised beds will be cost effective to start with. Many bulk yards will have at least a 2-yard minimum delivery requirement, which sounds like a lot and even looks like a lot when they are dumping it, but it fills a bed surprisingly quickly.

To estimate the volume of soil you'll need for each bed, multiply the length, width, and height (ideally using feet for all three). That will give you a result in cubic feet. For example, a bed that's 4 feet wide, 6 feet long, and $1/2$ (0.5) foot high will need 12 cubic feet of soil. Topsoil is usually sold in cubic yards, so to covert cubic feet to cubic yards, divide by 27. In this case, you'd need about $1/2$ cubic yard for each bed.

## PLAN AHEAD FOR AN EASY DELIVERY

Schedule your soil delivery well ahead of time, as landscape yards are typically extremely busy in spring. Plan a place for the delivery truck to dump your load of soil as close and as convenient as possible to your raised beds. When you call to book the delivery, give specific instructions as to where you would like the load to go—there's nothing more frustrating than finding a huge load of soil dumped in an area that makes the already rather arduous task of moving the soil even more difficult and time consuming! You may wish to place a tarp on the surface where the load will be deposited, which makes cleanup easier, minimizes soil waste, and clearly indicates to the driver where you'd like the soil to be dropped.

## Compost or Compost Mixes

To make purchased topsoil go further, you can mix it with compost. Use what you make at home, or, if you're lucky enough to have a municipality that offers free compost or leaf mold and have a way to haul it home, use that instead. You can add as much as 50 percent compost by volume; however, because compost continually breaks down, the more you use, the more you will have to add each year as the previous year's batch decomposes completely. A 2- to 3-inch top-dressing applied each year is easier to maintain from season to season while still conferring all the benefits of incorporated compost.

It's possible to use straight compost if you're filling a bed only a few inches deep, or if you're covering grass with cardboard or newspapers and topping it with 2 to 3 inches of compost. In deeper beds, though, the volume will decrease dramatically over time as the compost breaks down, so you'll have to add a significant amount of additional compost each year. Also, pure compost may be too wet and sticky to work well as the sole growing medium, but you can get around that by mixing it with an equal amount of coarse sand. (Never use beach or playbox sand in the garden.)

## FILLING YOUR BEDS

Now for the fun part: getting your raised-bed garden started. Clear the site you've chosen of any debris, and remove the grass and weeds, too, unless you plan to build your beds right on top of them. Use bamboo stakes to mark the corners of your beds-to-be, then make sure you are happy with every aspect: their shapes and sizes, the way they are arranged, and the widths of the paths between them. Once everything looks right to you, build the beds or assemble the kits right on-site.

Lining the bottom and sides of raised beds with weed barrier or landscape fabric is unnecessary and not recommended. Though some kits will come with a fabric liner you can install, it's a waste of time and materials. A deep raised bed (6 inches or taller) has more than enough soil depth to smother any grass or weeds below your installation site. In a shallower raised bed (which, when filled with soil, is still probably deep enough to smother most weeds), a fabric liner can hinder root growth and will quickly be destroyed with all the digging and other work you'll be doing to plant and maintain your garden. If you are concerned about turf and weeds coming up through the soil, lay down a single layer of cardboard or newspaper, wet it thoroughly, and build the bed over it. That will ensure that any plant life below is completely blocked from light, and it will decompose in a season or two.

It's easy to fill beds that are lower than the height of your wheelbarrow: Simply tip each load of soil or compost right over the sides and into the beds. Taller beds can be more challenging, because you will need to fashion some sort of ramp to be able to dump the soil into the bed. A wide, sturdy board laid on the top edge of the bed should be sufficient; plywood is not strong enough for the job, however. Use a long board to fashion a low angle; a steep incline gets exhausting to walk up and down and increases the risk of a spill, wasting energy and soil. Rake the soil to level the surface of the beds, and you're ready to plant!

## LET'S GET GROWING

Once your raised beds are in place, the basics of growing crops there are pretty much the same as for containers or regular ground-level gardens. You can find all the basics of planting and maintenance in Chapter 3, Spots and Pots Gardening School, and in Chapter 6, Plant Encyclopedia.

## chapter three

# SPOTS & POTS GARDENING SCHOOL

Whether you're just starting your gardening adventure or have years of experience with traditional inground gardening, there's always more to learn, especially when you transition to new materials and methods. Now that you know how to create the edible spots and pots, here you'll find everything you need to grow vigorous and productive crops from seed to harvest and every step in between. This chapter shares information on how to produce a healthy harvest the organic way, with earth-friendly techniques and materials that are safe for the people and pets that share your outdoor spaces.

## GROWING FROM SEEDS

With the increasing interest in vegetable gardening, garden centers now carry an amazing array of edibles as started seedlings. All you have to do is make your selections, take them home, and pop them in the ground to get your garden growing. With such convenience available, why would you even consider sowing seeds yourself?

**An excuse to get outdoors.** By late March, which is an excellent time to begin seed starting many crops, gardeners really start feeling the itch to get out and garden. Sowing peas and other cold-tolerant crops is a great reason to go outside and get your hands in the soil.

**A cure for spring fever.** After a long winter, nothing compares to the excitement of assembling your seed-starting supplies, nestling tiny seeds full of promise into their pots, flipping on the lights, and watching for the first sprouts.

**No transplant stress.** Many crops are more

# SMART SHOPPING FOR TRANSPLANTS

I encourage you to start as many of your crops from seed as you can; but sometimes it's not possible or practical. If you're beginning with a couple of containers, for example, it may be cheaper to purchase one plant of each kind than to buy a bunch of seed packets and seed-starting supplies. Buying transplants may also be the best (or only) way to go if you don't have the time, space, or interest in indoor sowing, or if you're getting a late start on the season.

When purchasing transplants, follow these cues to be sure you're getting the most for your money.

☀ Consider the size. When it comes to transplants, bigger is not always better. You want them to have several leaves, indicating that they're beyond the just-sprouted stage. But if they're much larger than their pot, their roots may be so crowded that they'll have trouble settling into your containers or raised beds.

☀ Peek underneath. When you lift up the pot, you should be able to see a few roots growing past the drainage holes. If they're crawling out, that's a clue that the seedling may already be past the peak point for transplanting. If there are no signs of roots, the seedling may be too young and not worth the money.

☀ Shop around. Raising healthy plants is a skill, and some growers are better at it than others. If the plants at one garden center or farmers' market aren't as healthy and vigorous as you'd like, it's worth taking the time now to visit another place to ensure a great harvest later.

vigorous and productive when they grow from seed started in the garden, right where you want them to grow. This includes popular crops such as salad greens, beans, squash, cucumbers, and melons, as well as those grown for their roots, like beets and radishes.

**Jump-start the growing season.** Sowing seeds indoors in late winter gives a head start to crops that mature later in the season, such as tomatoes, peppers, and eggplant. Broccoli, cabbage, kale, and cauliflower all do well started indoors, too.

## Seed-Buying Basics

A seed packet is more than a pretty envelope: It is like a little owner's manual for the seeds inside, covering the most important information you'll need to know to successfully plant and harvest your crop. The packets aren't large, though, so the information is often quite condensed, with terms that you may not recognize but that are important to know.

## Days to Germination

Most seed packets provide an estimate of how many days you can expect to pass between planting and sprouting. This helps you plan your sowing times and gives you a clue to how closely you'll need to monitor the planted area for signs of life.

## Special Germination Needs

Seed requirements vary widely, and some need special treatment to ensure germination. For example, shiso seed is best stored frozen and allowed to come to room temperature for 24 hours before sowing. Several types of seed

(most notably, lettuce) require light to germinate, a very important tip that ought to appear right on the packet. Still other seeds do best when soaked overnight before sowing or nicked with an emery board to help them absorb water more quickly. The seed packet should tell you if any special treatment is required.

## Days to Maturity

Generally speaking, days to maturity—the time from planting until the first harvest—is based on when the plant starts growing outdoors. For indoor sown seeds, use the transplant date as day 1. For seeds sown in the garden, count from the day that the first true leaves—that is, those that resemble the mature plant's actual foliage—develop to get a rough idea of when you can expect to harvest. Weather and the care you provide will be the most influential factors in how quickly your harvest develops, but the days to maturity are good for helping you plan what to sow and where and when to do it.

## Packed-For Date

Seed packets are dated, so you'll know you're buying fresh seeds packed for the current year, not those that have been lying around in a warehouse for a few years, losing their vigor.

## Germination Percentage

Even brand-new seed doesn't always exhibit 100 percent germination. Certain types of plants simply don't produce seeds that are all equally viable (able to sprout). Take note of the germination percentage indicated on the packet and sow accordingly. If the percentage is 90 percent or higher, you can sow just one or two seeds per pot. If it is lower (and some more unusual crops, like artichoke, can be as low as 70 percent even when fresh), sow three or more seeds in each spot. There's no problem if they do all sprout: Simply cut off or carefully transplant all but the strongest seedling on each site.

## Pelleted

Many types of tiny seeds, such as those of carrots and lettuce, are available in "pelleted" form. This means that the seeds have been enrobed with a clay mixture to make them easier to handle. Pelleted seed is a bit more expensive but is usually worth the expense since it makes sowing much easier and reduces or eliminates the need to do a lot of tedious thinning later. Generally speaking, pelleted seed will not last longer than a single season, so buy only as much as you need for the season ahead and try to use it all.

## Treated

Some seeds, such as those of corn, cucumbers, lettuce, and peas, are prone to rot when sown outdoors early in spring or in cool, wet soil. Many of these are treated with a chemical fungicide to help them withstand the less-than-ideal conditions until germination occurs and growth begins. Treated seed is often dyed a rather alarming blue or pink color. The packet should indicate that the seed has been treated.

## Organic Seed

Organic seed is harvested from plants grown with organic techniques on land managed according to USDA organic standards and is processed in a specially approved organic pro-

cessing facility. Organic seed can still be treated and/or pelleted, as there are versions of these processes that are approved for organic production.

Purchasing conventional seed does not preclude you from growing your crops organically all season long any more than purchasing organic seed would be of value if you applied synthetic pesticides and fertilizers all summer long. While it is always preferable to purchase any type of product from environmentally responsible producers over those that are held to no such standards, it is ultimately the way you treat the plants growing in your vegetable garden that best determines the healthfulness and safety of the crops produced.

## Sowing 101

Whether you'll be starting your seeds indoors or planting them right in a pot or raised bed, the basics of planting and aftercare are essentially the same.

**Deciding when to start.** Once you have your seeds gathered for the season, sort them into two piles: those you plan to start inside and those you'll sow right in the garden. Then, within each group, arrange the packets by when you need to sow them. Refer to the seed packet for this information, or consult the plant encyclopedia in Chapter 6. It's helpful to make yourself a list or calendar so you can see at a glance when (and where) you will sow each crop. You can also use a seed organizing system like the Seed Keeper (see Resources) to safely store your seeds and organize them by sowing date.

Frequently, you'll find sowing times given in relation to your "frost-free date" (also referred to as the "last frost date" or "after all danger of frost has passed"). The frost-free date is based on the average date of the last frost in your region, and it's a good general guideline for planning sowing dates for crops that are planted indoors and those that go directly into your container or bed. Your local garden center can tell you which date to use for your area. Keep in mind that this date is only an average, though: In any given year, the actual last frost might be several weeks before or after that, so you'll need to look at the actual temperatures and forecast when it comes to setting out indoor-grown seedlings.

**Planting depth.** Generally speaking, a seed should be covered with soil or some other growing medium by about three times its thickness. That doesn't have to be exact, but it's better to err on the side of less than more, because if you bury a seed too deep, it will use up its stored energy before it breaks the surface. After planting, gently firm the surface to get good contact between the seeds and the soil.

Some gardeners like to cover their seeds with sand (the kind sold for top-dressing succulent and cactus pots—not beach sand, which may contain salt) or chicken grit (available at farm stores). These are both handy options because they don't wash away readily when you water in the seed, and they make gauging the depth of the seed much more accurate. However, sprinkling a measure of the same soil or potting mix you are growing in is perfectly acceptable as well. Before you cover your seeds, though, double-check whether they need light to germinate (lettuce is one crop that usually does). If that's the case, then just press the seeds gently into the surface of the growing medium.

**Watering.** Watering is the step that sets the germination process in motion. You need to do it carefully, though, because it's very easy to push the seeds too deeply into the soil or to wash them away if you get overly enthusiastic. I like to water freshly sown seeds with a spray bottle on the mist setting, concentrating several sprays over the surface to be sure it is completely saturated without flooding it. A watering can or watering wand with a rose (a nozzle with many small holes to soften the flow) or a misting attachment for a standard garden hose can also work well. If you accidentally wash away some of the soil covering the seed when you water, gently replace it to the original intended sowing depth.

If you have sown seed directly in a self-watering container, or in a raised bed or container that is hooked up to drip irrigation, do not count on either of those methods to provide enough moisture to allow germination and good initial growth of a seedling. Water by hand with a hose or watering can fitted with a rose until the plant is strong and established, indicating that its root growth is extensive enough to take up water from below. This may take as long as 4 to 6 weeks, depending on the type of plant and the weather conditions.

**Keeping seedlings healthy.** Seedlings are

# SUCCEED WITH SUCCESSION PLANTINGS

Sowing seed is not a springtime-only practice. In fact, to keep your raised beds and containers as productive as possible during the growing season, you should create a strategic plan for succession sowing throughout the season. Succession sowing can mean that you plant more seed for a crop every 2 weeks or so, to keep a constant supply of it, or it can mean that you simply replace a spring crop with a summer crop.

Crops that lend themselves to multiple sowings through the season include:

- ☀ Arugula
- ☀ Beets
- ☀ Broccoli
- ☀ Carrots
- ☀ Cilantro
- ☀ Collard greens
- ☀ Dill
- ☀ Kale
- ☀ Lettuce
- ☀ Parsley
- ☀ Swiss chard
- ☀ Turnips

Crops that will need to be replaced with something else in summer due to poor performance in hot weather include:

- ☀ Peas
- ☀ Radishes
- ☀ Spinach

It's a good idea to mark dates on the calendar to remind yourself to sow if you aren't yet in the habit. I know from experience how frustrating it can be to have to buy something you would still have fresh from the garden if you'd only remembered to put in a few seeds!

delicate little plants when they first emerge. They are very susceptible to damage at this stage and may be afflicted with a fungal disease known as damping-off. This causes them to rot at the base and fall over, never to revive. Damping-off can happen indoors or out, as it is mostly caused by cool, wet conditions. To minimize the chance of problems, water carefully (try to keep the soil moist, but not soggy). Indoors, keep your seedlings in a warm environment (60° to 65°F is ideal for most crops). There's not much you can do to alter outdoor temperatures, but you can delay your sowing time a bit if the weather is cool and rainy. Good air circulation is also important to avoid fungal conditions including damping-off, so avoid crowding seeds when sowing.

Once seedlings have put on their first set of true leaves—the ones that look like those of an established plant—fertilize lightly with quarter-strength compost tea or a liquid commercial organic fertilizer to help them gain momentum and quickly outgrow the risk of damping-off.

## Start Right Outside

Planting seeds outside, right where you want them to grow, is known as direct sowing. Sowing seeds in edible spots and pots is easier than sowing in the ground. It's physically easier, in that you don't need to hunch over in the garden, hands in cold, wet soil, fumbling with tiny seeds. It's easier in that you can better monitor the seeds' progress, watching their water needs and making sure they don't dry out or get damaged by wind or animals. I recommend that you direct-sow as much as your climate will allow, sowing indoors or buying

plants of only the latest-cropping, most heat-loving plants, such as tomatoes and peppers.

## Indoor Sowing Secrets

Starting seeds indoors takes a bit more time and equipment, but it's a useful skill to have. And, let's face it, it's fun to be able to watch those tiny seeds sprout up close!

**Choosing containers.** If you are not sowing directly into your garden, you'll need to find small containers in which to start seeds. You can purchase an array of materials—plastic cell trays, small plastic pots, and biodegradable pots—or reuse the pots from plants you've purchased in the past. I like to keep things as fuss free as possible and start my seeds in 3- to 4-inch-wide pots straight away to avoid the need for moving them to a larger pot before planting them outside.

**Providing light.** To get the best results

from seeds started indoors, you should provide supplemental light once your seedlings emerge. Even very bright rooms won't furnish the direct, concentrated light that young plants require to grow well. There's no need to buy an expensive plant-light setup, though, because a standard two-tube fluorescent shop light works perfectly well for the job. The trick to achieving success with this standard fixture is placing the light source close to the plants: The light-bulbs should be no more than 4 inches above the plants from germination until the seedlings are ready to move outside. To make it easy to raise the bulbs as your seedlings grow, hang the fixture from a pair of S hooks attached to lengths of chain.

# SETTING OUT TRANSPLANTS

Planting day is the most exciting part of the process for many gardeners. It's tempting to move your carefully tended seedlings or purchased transplants outdoors during the first spell of mild spring weather, but before you give in to the urge, take a close look at the extended weather forecast for your area first, particularly the nighttime temperatures. For cool-season crops, such as broccoli, it's good enough if the nights are supposed to stay above 32°F. For heat-loving crops, such as peppers and tomatoes, wait until night temperatures are consistently in the mid-50s.

## Ease the Transition

"Hardening off" is the term gardeners use for the process of introducing indoor-grown plants to the outdoors. From a plant's point of view, the transition from indoors to out is enormous. The light is hundreds of times more intense outdoors, winds batter and draw water out of tender leaves, and temperatures are much warmer, too.

A plant makes several adaptations at the cellular level to adjust to life in the new environment, although these changes aren't apparent to the naked eye. Waxes are produced to protect the soft foliage, cells elongate and harden against the wind, and chlorophyll changes with exposure to the new light. Without a gradual introduction to these new conditions, the plant is forced to deal with them at once and must divert its energy into simply staying alive instead of growing and flourishing. When you introduce the new environment carefully, over a longer period, the plant is able to adapt slowly, and it can jump into new root and leaf growth once you get it in the ground.

Hardening off your seedlings doesn't need to be as much of an ordeal as some books make it out to be, but it is important. Aim for 10 to 14 days of hardening off if possible, counting back from the date that you decide you will plant your indoor-grown crops outside. Start them in a sheltered, shady site, and gradually move them to a sunnier, more exposed site until they can tolerate the conditions where you plan to plant them. Pay special attention to watering them during this period, because the small pots can dry out quickly.

## Get Them in the Ground

While the process of planting is fairly straightforward, there are tips that help make your planting days easier and more successful.

**Handle with care.** Try to handle only the leaves of the plant as you work. It's tempting to grab the stem instead, but if it gets damaged with even a minor bruise or bend, that can cause significant problems for the future growth of the seedling—or kill it altogether. If a leaf gets damaged, though, the plant can simply grow another.

**Check the level.** Most plants should be planted at the same soil level they have been in their growing pot. The exception to this is tomatoes, which can be set deeply, to their first set of healthy leaves. Tomatoes can root along their

# KEEPING SEEDS FROM SEASON TO SEASON

Most seed packets contain way more seeds than the typical gardener can use in one growing season. Fortunately, most vegetable seeds remain viable for several years if you store them properly, so a $3 investment in a seed packet can pay off for a long time. Keep the seeds dry and at a consistent temperature; avoid direct sunlight and drafty areas. If you live in a humid region, you may wish to place desiccant packets, like the ones that come with new shoes, in your seed storage area. You do not need to put the desiccant in your seed packets; simply tuck a few inside the jar or box that holds your seeds.

The shortest-lived seeds are onions, parsnips, and parsley; these don't last much longer than a year. The longest-lived seeds are beets, cucumbers, melons, and tomatoes, which remain vital for 4 years or more. You can safely rely on most seeds lasting for three growing seasons if properly stored.

There is a simple way to test if your seeds are still "good" or not. Wet and wring out a paper towel, carefully place 10 seeds on the surface, and roll it up like a jelly roll. Stick it in a resealable plastic bag and put in a warm place, such as on the top of your refrigerator.

After 3 days, unroll the paper towel and check for tiny roots or shoots emerging from the seeds. Some species naturally take much longer to germinate, so if you don't see any action, recheck daily for up to 10 days or so for signs of roots or topgrowth.

Once you see evidence of germination, count the number of seeds that are alive. Since you started with 10, you can easily calculate that if 7 seeds germinated, you're looking at a 70 percent germination rate. You can then sow accordingly, placing extra seeds in each sowing site to compensate for those that are no longer viable or replacing the entire batch if germination is 10 percent or less.

Perform germination tests around the time that you plan to sow each crop. If you wish, you can transfer the germinated seeds into your pot or garden soil to continue growing them.

stems—you may have already seen this happen in the garden—and by burying any surplus stem, the plant can better anchor itself in the soil. Besides, the bare stem won't produce any fruiting branches, so it may as well be buried.

**Work quickly.** Minimize the amount of time the roots are exposed to light and air. This is especially important if you are planting on a sunny and/or windy day—roots are designed to grow underground and are not equipped to withstand the stress of light and wind. If you can't put a plant in its site or back into its pot and you need to set it down for a few minutes,

cover the rootball with a cloth or, in a pinch, a tool (like the blade of a trowel) to minimize exposure.

**Give them a drink.** Watering is the crucial next step after planting. Even if rain is likely in the near future, it's worthwhile to give each seedling a drink as soon as possible after planting. Targeted irrigation helps settle the soil around the roots and minimizes the stress on the transplant.

**Supply some support.** Install the stake or cage at planting time for plants that will require support later. It may look a bit silly and out of proportion, but staking is a garden chore that is better done sooner than later, and you are far less likely to sever any roots by installing the support at planting time than later, once the plant is established and actually needs help staying upright.

# BE PREPARED WITH POTS

When you're planting, it's handy to have a few empty plastic pots nearby to hold the soil you remove when you dig a hole for each seedling. This is especially important if you are planting into a container where you already have something growing. For example, if you've sown a ring of spinach seed on the outer edge of the pot earlier in the season and you are planting a pepper plant in the center in May, you don't want to bury the spinach or get the leaves needlessly dirty. Use an extra pot to hold the soil you dig out, and draw from this reserve to backfill around your newly planted seedling.

## WATERING WISELY

The watering you give each crop at spring or planting time is just the first of many you'll provide through the growing season. Plump, succulent vegetables get that way thanks to ample soil moisture, and between summer's high temperatures, bright light, and storms with strong winds, regular watering is necessary. Spring is the perfect time to strategize on how to make all that watering as convenient, simple, and fast as possible.

### Timing Is Everything

The ideal time to water not just vegetables but nearly all plants is early in the morning. This gives the foliage all day to dry off, keeping down fungal diseases. It minimizes drought stress the plants might otherwise experience during the hottest part of the day, and it also reduces water loss through evaporation, since the sun is still weak and temperatures are low in the morning. The reality, though, is that morning watering doesn't always fit in with our busy lives. So really, it's fine to water whenever you have time. The important thing is to give your crops water when they need it, not to wait until the ideal time of day.

Schedule time every day in the growing season to check on your plants. If you're growing in

containers, plan on near-daily watering, especially when it is very hot and sunny, unless you have a drip system or self-watering containers.

Keep in mind that the more plants you put together in a container, or the more closely spaced you plant in a raised bed, the more water the area will require. When roots intermingle together in an area of finite space, only so much water can possibly be available for plant use. As a result, containers with several plants in them (or densely planted raised-bed areas) will need closer monitoring and more water than containers with single plants or raised beds where the crops are widely spaced. As a rule, the greater the number of fruit-bearing types of plants within a small space, the quicker the water will be used up.

When in doubt, give your plants a little additional water rather than less. As long as the soil is well drained, your plants will always appreciate a bit of extra $H_2O$, especially in summer when temperatures are high and evaporation from leaf and soil surfaces is abundant.

**Watch for wilting.** Wilting is not always an indication of a dire need for water. On very hot, very sunny days, some plants lose water out of their leaf surfaces faster than they can take it up with their roots. The result is wilting— leaves droop and look dull and grayish. However, as long as the garden has been thoroughly watered recently, more water will not correct the situation. This wilting is a physiological reaction that will only be reversed by a decrease in temperature and/or light levels.

If wilting persists on cooler days or plants do not recover later in the evening or by the next morning, this may indicate that you are not providing enough water when you irrigate.

*(continued on page 86)*

# Urban Roots Community Garden Center

## BUFFALO, NEW YORK

### the experimenters

Founded in 2007 as a local garden center for Buffalo's sizable population of enthusiastic gardeners, Urban Roots has become a beloved supplier of seeds, plants, and unique garden-themed goods and gifts located on the city's newly invigorated west side. Though plenty of garden centers create display gardens to show off their products, Urban Roots, one of the few cooperative garden centers in the nation, took this one step further and made their display gardens a community gathering place, vegetable growing laboratory, and classroom.

"We originally made a couple of raised beds in the sales yard to test varieties of vegetables not normally grown here that might interest the ethnic and refugee population in our community," says Patti Jablonski-Dopkin, Urban Roots' general manager. They constructed some of the beds with found materials familiar to urban residents, like cinder block and chunks of concrete, and some that incorporated ready-made products for making raised beds, like the M Brace brackets and the Frame-It-All System (see Resources, page 286), so customers could see how these items worked and looked in the garden before purchasing them.

Raised beds are an especially good choice for growing edibles in urban environments, where soil can contain high levels of lead and other toxins from decades of paint on nearby homes and a legacy of manufacturing pollution. In fact, after lead was found in the vegetable garden of a nearby elementary school, Urban Roots reached out to the teachers and students and invited them to make use of the garden center's raised

beds to continue their educational program. "Obviously, we wanted to provide a safe gardening experience for them," says Patti, "but our staff was also able to help the class's teacher, Mr. Haan, with his lessons on watering and feeding the plants, thinning rows, and weeding around the beds. During their summer break, we maintained the beds for them so when school was back in session, they could return to harvest their crops. It was wonderful to see the excitement they had when they actually took a bite of a carrot or tomato they had raised!" Though the school's lead issue was abated and their program restarted, the raised beds at Urban Roots weren't

vacant long. They now host an extracurricular garden program with a neighborhood organization called the WASH Project (thewashproject.org). This program for refugee families has brought the crops in Urban Roots' raised beds full circle, as they now are back to growing unusual ethnic vegetables right alongside more conventional crops like tomatoes and carrots. Barrett Gordon, the WASH Project coordinator (shown at left with Patti), and his program participants visit Urban Roots at least once a week during the growing season to help out and tend to the beds.

"Watering the beds is probably the most time-consuming aspect of having them in the garden center," Patti remarks. "But since we're out watering the plants that are for sale anyway, we've gotten used to it." The beds and their crops have also earned their keep by eliciting conversation from local residents, who are inspired to build their own raised beds after seeing them at Urban Roots. "When people come in and ask about building their own gardens, we can help them understand the importance of where to put it in their yard, deciding what they want to plant, and providing a water source. After that, anything goes! We review possible materials with them and encourage them to be creative with what they make and what they plant." Urban Roots is now drawing customers from the rural and suburban areas around Buffalo for their diverse and fascinating educational sessions (Urban Mushrooming, Living Roofs) and their off-season "Gardeners' Give and Take" open roundtable discussions, a true testament to the welcoming, laboratory/classroom nature of this unique garden center.

In hot climates, it may also signal that the area is too hot and sunny for those crops. If the plants are growing in containers, you can move them to a shadier spot or one that is shaded for part of the day (ideally only in the afternoon, the hottest part of the day). You need more creative shade solutions for crops in raised beds: Try positioning a patio umbrella to shade the plants in question during the afternoon, or perhaps attach a regular rain umbrella to a bamboo stake. A drape of cheesecloth or light-colored, lightweight cotton or linen, or a piece of floating row cover, can also be effective as a short-term solution.

**Vacation watering.** The main vegetable-growing season overlaps with the vacation season for many gardeners, but there are ways you can have a garden and enjoy your summer holiday as well. The best solution is to install a drip irrigation system, but there are other options: the time-honored tradition of asking a friend or neighbor to come over and water the garden, for example.

Self-watering containers can give you a few worry-free days away, but a trip longer than 2 or 3 days will necessitate supplemental watering. If you ask a neighbor to come by and refill your self-watering containers, be sure to explain how they work! There are many different models out there. Not only may your neighbor have no idea how your specific type works, he or she may never have heard of or seen a self-watering container before.

It is also possible to configure a soaker hose around your containers or garden and hook it up to a timer to water your plants while you are out of town. Just be certain to select a timer that you can program for multiple watering cycles, not one that merely allows you to run a single cycle and then requires resetting.

If you are going away for a short period and the weather is expected to be cool, you could try grouping containers together in a shady spot. If they are thoroughly saturated before you leave, this should be enough to hold them through a summer weekend.

## Where to Water

When watering, always concentrate your efforts at the soil, around the root zone of the

# A SIMPLE STICK TRICK

You can use a short length of a bamboo stake as a kind of dipstick to check how deeply water has penetrated into the soil or potting mix. Push it in a few inches deep at the edge of the container or on the outer perimeter of a plant (try to avoid severing any roots) and pull it out. If the soil is wet several inches down, the stake should feel cool and come out darkened, so you could wait at least another day to water. If the soil is dry, the stake will come out looking much like it went in, with perhaps a few clinging dustlike soil crumbs that fall off the stake easily. In that case, plan to water as soon as possible.

plants, not on the leaves. The oft-repeated old saw about water burning the leaves on a sunny day is a myth, but wetting the foliage is a waste of water. Plants do not absorb water through their leaves, and wet foliage, in fact, encourages fungal diseases to take hold or spread. Washing off your plants once in a while isn't terrible (dust settling on the leaves can cause the plant to put more energy into photosynthesis than it otherwise would have to), but do this only if rainfall has been scarce or if you're attempting to dislodge or drown insects like aphids or caterpillars.

## Watering Equipment

There are, of course, many ways to provide your plants with water. Garden centers and gardening catalogs offer a wide selection of equipment for both hand-watering and automatic watering. You can choose according to your time, budget, and energy, and on what and when you need to water. For example, when I must water everything, I'll use a hose and watering wand, but I also keep a nice big watering can by the hose in case one or two pots require water and I'm too rushed or tired to wind out 100 feet of hose.

**Hand-watering tools.** Since your containers or raised beds may be sited in an area of your yard that didn't previously call for water, make sure your hoses reach all parts of your raised bed or container collection. A watering wand can extend your reach and make it easier to deliver water all around the plant, though the very long types can be clumsy to use and potentially damage plants. A 16-inch-long wand, equipped with a breaker or spray head

# CONTAINER CONCERNS

Containers, in particular, can dry out quickly in summer. The relatively small volume of potting mix simply cannot hold enough water to sustain the plants over long periods. During hot, dry, and/or windy weather, you may need to water as often as every day, or even twice a day for smaller pots.

Water your containers gently and thoroughly, being sure that water saturates the actual root mass, not just the surface. Don't be fooled by seeing water come out the bottom of the pot. Potting mixes tend to pull away from the pot walls as they dry, making it look like the container has been totally drenched and excess water is draining away—when in fact the water is running straight down the sides and out the drainage hole. To prevent this, begin with a gentle flow directly on the surface. Once the top layer of soil is wet, the surface tension is broken and the water will begin to saturate the pot from the top down. You can also carefully break up any crust that forms on the surface with a trowel or hand cultivator, which will expose fresh soil that can more easily absorb water than the dried layer.

and a trigger or a ball valve on/off switch, is an excellent, versatile option.

Watering cans are equally indispensable: Not only can they give a thirsty plant a quick drink with minimal effort on your part, they're also handy for mixing and applying fertilizers.

A 1-gallon model makes mixing fertilizer especially easy, as instructions are typically rated for a quart or gallon. While prices run from just a few dollars to nearly $100, if you purchase a quality model that you like looking at and using, you'll get decades of enjoyment out of it.

**Soaker hoses.** A damaged, hole-ridden hose must have been the inspiration for the soaker hose. Soaker hoses are made from a porous material that allows water to seep out from all around the surface instead of channeling water toward a single opening at the end. Soaker hoses apply water slowly and gently and can be allowed to run for several hours. They are laid on the soil, close to the base of the plants, and left there for the entire season. You can use them in both containers and raised beds, though when you wind them through several containers, there will typically be some waste of water where the soaker hose bridges pots.

**Drip irrigation.** Vacations, hot weather, and immaculate produce are no challenge when you have a drip system. On top of that, drip systems are the most efficient way to water while still meeting a plant's moisture needs.

A drip system is constructed around a main feed tube that hooks up to a timer, which in turn connects to your water source. The main feed tube can supply other main feed tubes to link several garden areas together, if you wish. The feed tubes can be run along a wall or hidden along edge of a deck. They can even be buried to run them out farther in your yard. Don't bury them where you'll be digging frequently, though, or you'll probably be doing a lot of repairs.

Off the main feed line come "spaghetti tubes": thinner lines that supply water to a container or a specific garden area. At the end of each spaghetti tube is an emitter that regulates the water flow. Let these lines rest directly on

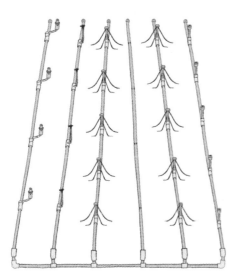

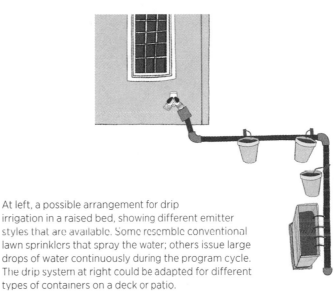

At left, a possible arrangement for drip irrigation in a raised bed, showing different emitter styles that are available. Some resemble conventional lawn sprinklers that spray the water; others issue large drops of water continuously during the program cycle. The drip system at right could be adapted for different types of containers on a deck or patio.

the ground, or attach them to stakes to hold them above the surface and keep soil from clogging them. You can run several spaghettis into a single container or garden area if needed, and you can install them all along the feed tube line to suit your specific configuration of containers or plants. The illustrations above show how a drip system might be set up to water both a raised bed and a container garden.

Drip systems are extremely flexible: They can turn corners, they can run up or down slopes for several feet, and they offer different emitter ends that bubble, mist, or spray. The programmable timer provides even more options. You can program your system to run for 15 minutes in the morning and 15 minutes in the afternoon, or for a set amount of time midday, or for whenever and whatever duration works best for your conditions.

You can install a drip system for well under $200. The biggest expense will typically be

the timer. (A simple one-zone timer will cost in the range of $50 to $70.) Timers are weatherproof and run on a regular battery. Once you've invested in a timer, your only remaining expenses are the tubing and your time. For most people who pay for city water, a drip system will pay for itself in water savings (not to mention time savings and how much more productive your garden will be) within the first season, especially in hot and dry climates.

Drip systems do have a few limitations and challenges.

⚜ They are not great for keeping seedbeds evenly moist, so you'll need to provide supplemental water when you are starting seeds right in your garden.

⚜ The consistent supply of water can encourage plants to grow too quickly, which may result in weak, floppy stems or aphid infestations (these tiny pests love lush, tender leaves and shoots). Both of these problems are fairly easy to deal with, though: Simply cut back a bit on the duration or frequency of watering, or remove an emitter or two from near the plants having issues. Floppy growth can be staked and will generally firm up properly with time; aphids can be rinsed off or squashed (if the infestation is small and concentrated, you may even consider pruning off the affected portion).

♣ Salts can build up in the soil in areas with saline or mineral-rich water or in containers or raised beds that are fertilized frequently and watered only by drip irrigation. This could be especially problematic in areas with dry summers. To deal with this, simply get in the habit of thoroughly watering your containers with a hose every 2 weeks or so throughout the growing season to wash the salts out of the root zone.

♣ Gardeners with well water may be unable to use drip systems if their water is high in particles or minerals, because these materials can clog the system in relatively short order. It's possible to install a simple filter at the hose bib, but you'll need to clean and empty it regularly to keep the system functioning.

## Water-Saving Strategies

We have good reason to want to conserve water in our edible gardens. Not only does watering become a tiresome chore, it is also expensive for those on city water. Most important, water is a natural resource. Though it does renew, there are no substitutes for this vital life force. There are several small things we can do as gardeners that add up to water savings for us and set a good example for our fellow citizens.

**Mulch around plants.** We think of mulch as an obvious companion to ornamental areas of our gardens and yet inexplicably neglect it in the vegetable garden. That's a shame, because it can be a big help in conserving water.

♣ Mulch keeps down weeds, which compete for water that crops could be using.

♣ It lowers soil temperatures, keeping roots cooler, which minimizes stress on the plants and helps the roots make more efficient use of soil moisture.

♣ It protects the soil surface from heat, light, and wind, minimizing evaporation so that water in the soil doesn't just vaporize into the air.

A 2- to 3-inch-thick layer of shredded bark mulch, compost, or other organic materials is sufficient to accomplish all of these things. Shredded bark and pine needles have the added benefit of helping keep your produce cleaner, as they keep soil from splashing up on the foliage and fruit.

**Use drip irrigation or self-watering containers.** For details, see "Drip Irrigation" on page 88 and "Self-Watering Containers" on page 8.

**Attach a ball valve or on/off switch to the hose.** That way, you can easily stop the flow of water when moving from place to place while hand-watering. It won't conserve all that much water in a single use, but over the course of the season, this can save several gallons.

**Collect rainwater.** Besides taking advantage of a free source of water, using rain barrels

# Don't Try This

The Internet is full of ideas for vacation watering your containers and beds. Many of these seem like viable solutions, but they simply don't work. Here are a few widespread, but fundamentally wrong, ideas you may encounter.

☀ Adding water-holding crystals or hydrogels. There are two major problems with these materials. First, those made out of acrylamides are toxic. Other types made from starches are nontoxic, but this is irrelevant since these products are completely ineffective. Water does not move through soil or potting mix in the way that the sellers of these gels pretend it does. Yes, the gels swell when watered and hold water, but they do not "give it up" to neighboring soil particles. They merely hold on to it and look and feel disgusting when you're working in the soil.

☀ Putting a kitchen sponge in the soil. Though the sponge becomes saturated through repeated watering, it does not release water to the surrounding soil or potting mix. If a plant root makes contact with the sponge, the root hairs can take water off its surface, which could be helpful in the short term but probably not any more effective than a volume of soil equal to that of the sponge would be if it was also thoroughly saturated.

☀ Burying a baby diaper in the container. This is so disturbing I can barely bring myself to discuss it here, but it is being touted on the Internet as a "brilliant idea" (especially for hanging baskets). The theory is that diapers contain hydrogels similar to those sold for incorporating into potting mixes, so that if you bury a diaper in a container, it will absorb and release water back to the soil. In reality, the diaper will just soak up water until it is saturated, but it cannot release it into the soil. As any young parent can tell you, these things are meant to *hold* moisture! All this "idea" accomplishes is to create a really awful mess cleanup at the end of the season and contribute to a significant problem for trash disposal and landfills.

☀ Cutting the bottom off a 2-liter soda bottle and burying the bottle, neck down, in the soil, leaving the open part exposed, and filling it with water. This seems like a good idea, but in practice, it won't work unless the potting mix or soil is already completely saturated. Under normal conditions, the water will drain right out into the soil instead of remaining as a reservoir for the plants to use later.

I hate to be negative about the attempt to develop creative garden solutions. However, just because something seems like it *ought* to work doesn't mean that it will in reality. There's no sense wasting time and materials on tasks that you can accomplish even better with a little planning and forethought.

crops, so it makes sense that they developed and selected varieties that needed less water than their modern counterparts. Native Seeds/SEARCH, a Tucson, Arizona–based seed company that collects and preserves edible varieties from native Arizonan, Texan, and Mexican people, offers varieties of vegetables that were used for their drought tolerance or their quick-cropping abilities.

## FERTILIZING FOR GOOD GROWTH

Despite what you've been told, fertilizer is *not* plant food. Plants make their own food through the process of photosynthesis. Perhaps a more apt name would be "plant vitamin supplement." Sure, it doesn't roll off the tongue quite as well, and it might not sell as much fertilizer, but it more accurately describes the true role of fertilizer in our gardens.

In theory, plants can get everything they need for healthy, vigorous growth from their surroundings, much like we can theoretically get all the nutrition we need by eating a diverse, well-balanced diet. However, plants have no choice in where they grow and can't just pick up and move if the nutrients they need are lacking. As plants grow in a site, particularly a site of limited volume like a container or raised bed, they use up the minerals that are in the soil where they're growing, and this is where fertilizer comes in. Fertilizer replenishes essential plant nutrients, enabling the edible plants that we grow to be productive and provide us with a harvest. It is absolutely essential to fertilize regularly, especially when you grow in containers.

to collect water from your downspouts helps to keep rainwater from running off your property and carrying pollutants into storm sewers.

**Recycle water used for washing vegetables or for cooking.** When you're giving just-picked veggies a prewash before taking them indoors, swish them around in a watering can or spray them with your hose over a garden area so the still-growing plants can use the water. Keep a pan in your kitchen sink to collect the water from the final wash, too. And don't waste the water left from cooking your harvest: Let it cool to room temperature and take it out to the garden. Even starchy pasta water can be used to water plants if allowed to cool first.

**Select drought-tolerant varieties.** Our farming and gardening forebears didn't have the luxuries we have today for watering their

## Choosing and Using Fertilizer

I recommend using a combination of granular and liquid fertilizers to keep your plants in top shape through the growing season.

**Granular (dry) fertilizers for before planting.** In containers, layer in a granular organic fertilizer before planting in spring. Notice I said *layer*, not *mix*. Interspersing fertilizer through the entire container is a waste, as the plant cannot use the fertilizer at the bottom since its roots don't reach that far down. Fill the container about halfway, add a light layer of fertilizer, then fill another quarter of the container with potting soil. Add another light layer of fertilizer and gently mix it in, then finish filling. This keeps the fertilizer well within the zone that the plant can use, and the granular fertilizer breaks down relatively slowly, furnishing the nutrient load over a longer period.

In a raised-bed garden, scatter the dry fertilizer over the soil surface based on the label directions, and rake it into the top few inches of soil before planting.

**Liquids for regular fertilizing.** When your plants begin blooming, it's time to start applying a liquid fertilizer regularly to help give them the extra nutrients they need to continue growing, flowering, and fruiting.

I do not recommend fertilizing every time you water, no matter what the package of fertilizer you purchased says. After all, the manufacturers want you to use as much of their product as possible so you'll have to buy more! Once every 7 to 10 days during the growing season should be sufficient for very demanding crops, like tomatoes and corn. Less-needy crops, like herbs and salad

## DON'T DISCARD IT

If I mix up liquid fertilizer for crops that need a highly fertile soil and have some left over, I like to top off the watering can several more times with fresh, clean water and use it to fertilize less-needy plants, like my salad greens or herbs. This gives them a small measure of nutrients and helps keep the fertilizer from merely being rinsed away and wasted.

greens, may not require any supplemental fertilizer at all.

## Build Fertility Naturally

Supplemental fertilizer is important for productive, healthy edible plants, but the most natural, organic route to keeping a fertile soil in your raised beds especially, is amending your soil liberally with compost every year. Compost is a type of organic matter made from the remains of plants, and many of the minerals and nutrients that they took from the soil when they were growing are preserved and can be passed on to the next crop. Compost also helps the soil retain more water and hold on to nutrients in supplemental fertilizers. It takes matter that would otherwise be wasted and turns it into something valuable. Composting is quite an amazing process, and it is about as easy as falling over; see "Composting 101" (on page 94) for information on making your own.

If you can't make enough plant-based compost for your needs, you can also use composted

*(continued on page 96)*

# COMPOSTING 101

Compost literally just happens. You can take any organic matter—food scraps, weeds, branches, mown grass, garden trimmings—and pile it up somewhere, and it will eventually break down and turn into compost.

## GATHER THE INGREDIENTS

If there is any secret to making compost, it is in combining the right balance of dry and wet materials.

☀ Dry ingredients are commonly called "browns," as they tend to be brown in color. Browns include dead plants, fallen leaves, hay and straw, newsprint, and wood chips.

☀ Wet materials are commonly called "greens," as they are usually fresh, green (or another color, like red apples or yellow squash, for example), and moist. Greens include food scraps, grass clippings, living plant matter (like trimmings or weeds), and manure from herbivorous (plant-eating) animals.

If you pile up only brown material, decomposition will eventually happen but will be almost imperceptibly slow. If you pile up just green material, decomposition will be fairly quick, but the material will be slimy and foul smelling. Put these two types of ingredients together, however, and they form the ideal environment for a host of microorganisms that in time consumes every cell, breaking the components down into a rich, dark brown, soil-like material.

## PUT A PILE TOGETHER

To begin composting, you will need at least two layers' worth of brown and green materials. Unfortunately, these are rarely equally abundant at the same time of year. Autumn leaves, the best and

most abundant source of browns, are obviously only around in autumn, while greens are most abundant in spring and summer, when our plants are actively growing and we're mowing our lawns.

Probably the best solution to this conundrum is to bag up autumn leaves, collecting all you can find, and storing them until you need them. Newsprint, torn into strips, makes an acceptable substitute, but you should use only matte newsprint papers: nothing printed in color on glossy paper. You can also use a combination of brown materials to create the layer. This is a good idea if you have a lot of dense material, like branches or wood chips that will not decompose quickly on their own.

Lay down a thick layer of browns to begin with, then layer on the greens. The recommended ratio is 2:1 (twice as much brown material as green by volume). This isn't always possible, however, so do your best to simply have more brown material than green. Now add a second layer of brown material, and top it up with a layer of green. If you have more materials, by all means, continue! But two layers will be enough to get you started.

## ENJOY THE RESULTS

Compost needs to be moist to decompose—water sustains the microorganisms that break down the material. Water your newly built pile, drenching it completely and thoroughly. The ideal compost pile is always kept about as wet as a just-wrung-out sponge. The water will evaporate and drain off into the ground as the pile rots, so you will need to check the moisture level regularly. If you live in a very wet climate or a very dry climate, you may want to cover your pile with a tarp to keep it from becoming too wet or to conserve precious moisture, respectively.

Congratulations! You've started composting. Even as you walk away, microorganisms are already beginning to consume the material. Insects and earthworms will soon join the party, and they'll bring their own colonies of microorganisms along. If conditions remain optimal, you'll have finished compost in 2 to 3 months. It's that easy!

(or aged) manure from livestock animals, such as horses, chickens, or cows. ("Aged" means that the waste has been allowed to sit and decompose for several weeks or months, depending on the type of manure and the quantity.) Fresh manure can be too concentrated in certain forms of nitrogen and can burn your plants if you apply it directly to your crops.

To increase the fertility of your raised beds, dig the compost or composted manure into the top 3 to 5 inches of soil in your raised beds, or mix it into your potting medium before refilling your containers. You can amend your soil by as much as 50 percent compost every year. Compost will continue breaking down as the season goes on, so it's best to stir in some soil, sand, or potting mix with it to provide bulk. You can also top-dress your entire garden area or just specific plants with a layer of compost.

Yet another way to build fertility naturally is by applying "compost tea." This is made by converting finished compost into a liquid fertilizer. "Manure tea" is the same thing, but made with manure instead of plant-based compost. While these provide a rich, immediately usable nutrient boost to the plants you apply them to, few of us are fortunate enough to have enough compost at our disposal to make teas as often as we'd like. Ready-made compost and manure tea bags are available in garden centers and online, though. These products are generally ready to use: All you have to do is steep them for 24 to 48 hours in a bucket of water and then apply the resulting liquid to your plants.

If you are lucky enough to have a surfeit of compost or manure and would like to make your own tea, it's a pretty simple process. Put a shovelful of compost or manure in a 5-gallon bucket, cover it with water, and allow it to steep for 48 hours. Strain and then use the water to irrigate and fertilize plants; leftover brewed compost can be returned to the pile. Use only finished compost (compost with no recognizable ingredients) or composted manure in your garden, whether for direct application or for making tea.

## STAKING AND PRUNING

You've probably invested a good amount of money and time acquiring containers or building raised beds. The best way to get the most out of your investment is to use some savvy horticultural techniques that allow you to grow more plants in less space.

Staking and training methods can add a third dimension to your garden, creating unique new spaces. For example, you can build a simple archway out of sturdy bamboo according to the instructions on page 118. Stick one end of the arch into each of two pots or two adjacent raised beds and train beans up it, and you've created a dramatic structure for edibles that defines your garden space.

Staking can be useful for supporting damaged plants, too. Sometimes, heavy rains or strong winds can cause a previously strong plant to flop over or lean into its neighbors. Pets and wildlife may damage roots by digging around them or knock into stems when they walk through your plantings. With a little creative staking, you can disguise the damage and keep your plants producing a harvest.

Staking and pruning make gardens look

neat and well tended, especially those with dense plantings. These methods can minimize pest and disease problems, and they make fruit easier to harvest, too. By keeping your plants neater and more compact, you allow more sunlight to reach each one, resulting in greater productivity.

If there's a disadvantage to staking and training, it's that keeping crops supported and well groomed does take a regular commitment of time. You can't let their growth get too far away from your intended direction or the situation can be difficult to correct. That doesn't sound too challenging, but in summer, when things grow like gangbusters, a tomato can put on several inches of growth in a matter of days, making it a rather overwhelming task to get that riot of branching arms back on track to being a svelte, pruned, and well-supported

plant. (You'll find much more about the types of crops that benefit from these training methods in Chapter 6.)

## Support Systems

Ask a dozen gardeners how best to stake plants, and you're likely to get a dozen different answers. Still, there are basics that apply to any approach.

**Materials.** A supply of bamboo stakes is useful to have around. Inexpensive, versatile, and long lasting, bamboo is easy to cut to any length, and you can lash the canes together to create a wide variety of support structures. I prefer the undyed type, even though the pale color stands out a bit more in the garden than the green-dyed bamboo does. Check out the Bamboo Ladder Trellis (page 116) and the Bean Archway and Arbor (page 118).

The plastic-covered metal stakes sold in garden centers are a good option, especially for tomatoes. This type is more expensive, however, and bends easily, especially when you're trying to remove them at the end of the season.

Heavy 1 × 1-inch wood stakes provide heavy-duty support, which can be used for very rampant tomatoes. If you don't see these at your favorite garden center or in the garden section of your hardware store, look for them with the fencing materials. Wood stakes and other types of stakes make an easy three-legged support; take a look at Try a Tripod! (page 122) for a support you can create in less than half an hour.

If there's a fence or wall next to your raised bed or containers, you can use that to your advantage in many different ways. It's easy to tie tomatoes right to a chain-link fence, for instance, and it's possible to install a masonry nail into the mortar of a brick wall to use for securing string to train plants. The Fence Net project on page 149 is a nice, straightforward way to manage your plants on a fence using readily available materials.

I've also designed a support that's strong and reliable for growing tomatoes. The Tomato Ring (page 143) uses a metal wreath form and bamboo stakes to keep tomatoes upright and contained.

**Securing plants to stakes.** Simply leaning the stems on a stake can work for certain plants, such as eggplants and peppers. Most, though, need to be secured to the stake with some sort of tie to get the extra support they need to stay upright and out of the way of their neighbors.

You can use a wide variety of materials to tie a plant to a stake, as long as they are reasonably soft and flexible. Many gardeners like compostable materials, like cotton or sisal twine, but I find that when I am cutting my plants down at the end of the season, I have to snip the ties anyway, which gives me a chance to remove them and dispose of them or collect them for reuse.

Garden suppliers sell many effective ties and connectors, including Velcro loop closures, little clips, and fancy twine in lovely tins imported from England. You can also find many suitable ties around the house, such as kitchen twine, bits of yarn, or strips cut from old tights and stockings. If you are using a light-colored material to tie up a plant and think it's too visible, rub some moist soil into

the material; that will dirty it just enough to blend in.

The best way to tie a plant to a stake is to first secure the connector material around the stake itself, tying it to the stake with a firm double knot so that it will not slip down. Then cross the free ends over one another to form a figure eight before bringing the ends around the plant stem and tying them together. The figure eight leaves a little play in the tie and prevents the stem of the plant from rubbing directly against the stake, which could cause damage. As you secure the free ends around the plant, leave plenty of room in the loop for the stem to expand and sway. Do not tie it tightly to the stake.

**Trellising.** Plants that have twining stems

The figure 8 tie is the safest, most secure way to support a staked plant. Double a piece of twine and tie the center of the string tightly to the stake. Bring the ends around, cross them to form an 8, wrap them around the plant's stem, and then secure them to the stake in a firm double knot.

(such as pole beans and Malabar spinach) or that climb by tendrils (such as cucumbers, melons, peas, and pumpkins) are generally trellised instead of staked. Trellising these plants turns them from spillers into thrillers, so they become a useful design element that saves space and encourages productivity. Depending on its size and construction, a trellis may be difficult to incorporate into a container, so have a plan before planting if you wish to trellis container-grown vining crops. Though the word *trellis* conjures up elaborate structures, there are several simple ways to craft a trellis for beans, cucumbers, and the like. Try the fast and inexpensive trellis shown on page 116.

I've found that copper plumbing parts can be assembled into an attractive support; see the Copper Trellis project on page 137. Or get into the spirit of upcycling with the Window Frame Trellis on page 160.

### Pruning Your Crops

We typically associate the task of pruning with trees and shrubs, but it's useful—and sometimes even necessary—for edibles, especially in containers. For example, pinching back basil plants to keep them densely branched and to prevent or delay their flowering is a type of pruning. Harvesting a lot from a perennial herb like thyme or oregano to dry it for storage is also a kind of pruning.

One pruning technique that I use frequently in my edible pots is leaf pruning. This means removing individual leaves that are blocking the sunlight for neighboring plants or to the interior of the plant that's being pruned. I do this a lot on warm-climate crops like tomatoes and peppers that are combined with other plants, but sometimes on other crops as well.

While it's true that every leaf is a little solar collector, creating food and energy for the plant, pruning off a few leaves does not harm the plant and can help minimize pests and disease (by increasing air circulation) and improve quality of the fruit (by exposing it to more sunlight). More important, it helps less-vigorous plants get additional sunshine when they're paired with rampant bully plants.

Though heavy pruning shears (sometimes called secateurs) are useful in vegetable gardens for cutting bamboo and heavy old growth, a pair of light snip-type pruners are invaluable for leaf pruning, harvesting, and deadheading. These lightweight, scissor-action cutters are a bit more convenient to keep on hand than traditional pruning shears, so don't go into your garden without them. You'll invariably need them for something on most every visit to the garden.

# DEALING WITH PESTS AND DISEASES

Let's face it: Pests and diseases are a reality of any sort of gardening. However, containers and raised beds offer several advantages when it comes to observing, identifying, and controlling these potential problems.

- The nontraditional layout of crops in containers and raised beds—particularly those planted in the thriller-filler-spiller combinations you'll learn about later in the book—can confuse insects. Many common vegetable pests have adapted to find their prey by recognizing the patterns of long, straight rows so common to traditional vegetable gardens. From the vantage point of flying insects, your nontraditional garden may not signal the presence of vegetables, so the airborne critters may pass it by.

- Looking for signs of disease and insects and their egg masses, also known as scouting, is one of the key tenets of organic gardening, and this is far easier to do in containers or raised beds, where you don't need to bend and kneel and stoop to see your plants. If you set your containers on dollies, it's a simple matter to spin them in a complete circle, allowing you to quickly look over the entire plant. I designed a simple dolly for keeping containers mobile; see the Pot Caddy project on page 151.

- Growing crops in or close to your outdoor living space makes it much easier to keep an eye on them, so you can spot the first sign of damage and choose a control strategy right away.

- Combinations of different crops make it much more difficult for insects and diseases to spread than row plantings, where pests and pathogens that are adapted to one particular crop can quickly leap from one plant to the next.

- Diseases—especially those caused by fungi, which are the most common—tend to infect plants that are not growing in ideal conditions. You can easily move container plants to keep them in optimal light conditions, and raised beds offer the improved drainage that can help prevent soilborne problems.

- For many pests, keeping them from reaching your plants in the first place is the most direct way to prevent damage. Covering crops with floating row cover (shown below) during periods when the pests are known to be feeding or laying eggs—a task that's much simpler in container and raised-bed

# SLUG BUSTERS

Slugs are usually not an issue in containers, although they may be in raised beds. But few people know that slug eggs begin hatching long before the gardening season begins—usually in mid- to late winter. If slugs are a problem in your garden, you should begin your management techniques months before you're thinking about slug damage. Put out saucers or tuna cans full of beer or soda to attract those slimy mollusks, and empty the traps in the morning. Set out thin sheets of wood (such as cedar shingles) in the garden at night; in the morning, scrape off the slugs clinging to them. Starting these simple, nontoxic practices early in the season can help thwart bigger issues later.

gardens, which are designed for easy access—forces the pests to go elsewhere.

## Get Smart

The first thing that comes to mind when we talk about pest control is spraying. However, nothing in your edible pots or spots is worth spraying with any chemical, even if the label on the bottle says "organic." This is a bit of a bold statement, I realize, but I truly believe that at the scale of the home gardener, there is never any reason to apply pesticides. Sometimes, this may mean the loss of a plant, and that is undeniably heartbreaking. But I would rather rely on my farmers' market to fill in a gap in produce than to spray any kind of pesticide in my own garden.

As important as our homegrown food is to us, gardening is ultimately a hobby. We will not suffer an economic hardship if we have fewer cucumbers in our garden because the flowers were damaged by cucumber beetles. It hurts, and it's disappointing, but at the end of the day, we aren't farmers who make our living from the soil. We may grow food to save money, but nonetheless, we have no economic reason to apply poison in our backyards.

Many alternatives to spraying pesticides—such as tolerance, knowledge, and creativity—can help you maintain a safe, productive, organic garden. They involve a different approach than the traditional "see damage/ apply pesticide" model does, but they can be equally—or possibly more—effective and result in a healthier place to garden.

**Tolerance.** Tolerance is a vital part of being a gardener and a good steward of the environment. For the home gardener, tolerance simply means acknowledging that pests are natural, expected, and not necessarily catastrophic. While our tendency to concentrate a bunch of delicious plants together for our own convenience and benefit is a bit unnatural and can lead to heavier infestations than in nature, this doesn't change the fact that plants can generally withstand the presence of a pest population.

Tolerance does not mean sitting back and doing nothing, surrendering your garden to marauding slugs or Japanese beetles or cabbage loopers. It means understanding that these are natural occurrences and that with knowledge—the next tool we'll discuss—there are simple, nontoxic ways to manage them.

**Knowledge.** Knowledge of the pests and diseases common in your area, their habits, and their life cycles is a powerful organic gardening practice and vital garden management tool. When you understand how the pests and diseases common to your region operate, you can begin to use that knowledge to thwart them.

Powdery mildew, for example, is a common fungal disease that grows on the foliage of many garden plants, but it's most common on cucumbers and zucchini. It manifests itself as a silvery-gray growth on the leaf surface. A light infestation does not severely harm the plant's ability to photosynthesize, so you can tolerate it; more important, though, you can minimize or even prevent it when you understand what conditions it requires to take hold. Powdery mildew grows on foliage that is alternately wet and dry; if the leaves are too wet or too dry, the disease can't get started. Thus, careful watering of plants prone to powdery mildew, which means directing the water directly into the soil without wetting the leaves, can help. It's also a good idea to water these plants in the morning only, so that they have all day to dry and don't stay wet for long periods. You can mulch the plants to minimize the need to water, or you can install drip irrigation, which will prevent the foliage from being wetted regularly. You can also try siting your powdery mildew–prone plants in your sunniest, breeziest locations, which speeds drying of wet foliage.

Also important is the ability to identify common insects and recognize their damage. This way, you can target your control efforts to the exact pest and its current life stage.

It's equally important to learn what benign and beneficial insects look like, so you won't mistake them for pests and harm them. If you

# UNDERSTANDING GROWING DEGREE DAYS

Growing degree days are a system that meteorologists use to quantify the gradual warming trend through the spring, and gardeners can use these observations to their advantage in pest-control efforts. Beginning on January 1 of each year, each day's maximum and minimum temperatures are added together and divided by 2 to find the day's average temperature. From this a constant, based on the area's winter low, is subtracted. Any remainder is the number of growing degree days that that day's warmth has contributed to the year. There are apps for smartphones and tablets that tell you the growing degree days for your area; you can also find it on the National Weather Service Web page for your area.

Horticulturists and entomologists have correlated the growing degree day phenomenon to the emergence of flowers on woody ornamentals, the best time to take cuttings for propagation, and—most important to organic gardeners—the emergence, flight periods, and egg-laying times of insects. Using growing degree days, we can predict almost exactly when we need to start looking for and protecting against pests like cucumber beetles and squash vine borers. For example, squash vine borer scouting must begin at about 950 growing degree days.

You can find this information by doing an Internet search for the pest name followed by "growing degree days." It is best to get this information from your state's land grant university or Cooperative Extension, as the growing degree day figure for each pest will be determined by the winter temperature constant used to calculate growing degree days in your region. By monitoring the growing degree days that have accumulated in your area and researching the emergence of your most common pests, you can focus your energies when and where in the garden they are most needed and minimize the duration that you need to keep floating row cover over certain plants.

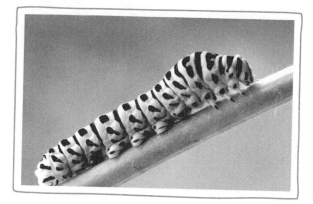

see striped caterpillars munching on dill, carrot, or parsley leaves, your first instinct might be to destroy them. If you know that they are the larvae of swallowtail butterflies, though, you'll tolerate their presence in favor of seeing the beautiful adults emerge in the garden, and you'll simply sow more of the crop for a later harvest. Without knowledge of the insects you're likely to encounter, you stand to miss out on some of the biggest rewards of having a garden. For this reason, every gardener needs a couple of good pest identification books; see the Resources on page 286 for some suggestions.

**Creativity.** Gardeners are pretty ingenious folks and, armed with the knowledge about the pests present in the garden, can come up with unique, natural ways to thwart them. Sometimes, the best solution is the simplest. For example, my first year in my current garden, something started devouring my basil. At first, I tried tolerance. I watched the plants, inspecting them carefully for the tiniest caterpillar or beetle, but found nothing. Then one evening, as I sat outside, beetles began flocking to our porch. I looked at my basil plants

and there were the culprits: small, shiny, copper-colored beetles, iridescent under our porch light, all gorging themselves on my tender, fragrant basil leaves, leaving only the midrib behind.

I collected the pests and researched them. They turned out to be Asiatic garden beetles, horrible creatures that are active only at night and that love to feed on herbs in the mint family. For the following 2 weeks or so (until the beetles' appetite abated), I brought my pots of basil indoors at night. I realize this isn't practical for everyone in all circumstances, but it is a simple solution to a pest problem.

## Creative and Nontoxic Pest Control

There are lots of ways to deal with pest infestations big or small. Some require outside-the-box thinking, and others demand taking swift action. Choose the method or combination of methods that's right for your garden situation.

**Choose resistant varieties.** One of the best ways to avoid having to deal with an infestation or infection on your crops is to plant varieties that won't be troubled by the problem in the first place. Choosing insect- and disease-resistant varieties requires a bit more research than simply heading up to your local garden center and plucking some seed packets off the shelf. For the widest selection and most information, spend a few weeks in winter doing research on the various resistant varieties offered in your favorite seed catalogs.

**Rotate your crops.** Many pests and diseases are specific to a type of vegetable or to a family of vegetables (the carrot family, the tomato family, etc.). You can thwart those that spend the winter in the soil simply by planting their host plants in a new place the following season. For example, plants in the cabbage family are susceptible to club root, a fungal disease that disfigures the roots and eventually kills the plant because it interferes with water uptake. The fungal spores overwinter in the soil, so if you plant a cabbage relative in that same spot the next year, you encourage the disease to stay. If, however, you plant lettuce or cucumbers there the following year, the club root will begin to wane, because it will have no host to feed on.

**Encourage beneficial insects.** One of the reasons pests have become so virulent in vegetable gardens is because a regular, inground vegetable garden all planted in rows isn't remotely like anything found in nature. As such, it does not encourage the balance of insect predator and prey that is found in natural ecosystems like forests and prairies.

Predatory insects—those that eat other insects as their main food source—are also known as beneficial insects. These types of insects can provide serious pest control in your garden. Common beneficial insects include ladybugs, lacewings, syrphid flies, praying mantises, aphid lions, predatory wasps, and minute pirate bugs. Some of these are indiscriminate feeders, eating anything that crawls or flies; others have specific diets, as in the case of ladybugs, which eat aphids.

It is important to understand that beneficial insects might be predatory only at certain stages of their lives. For example, syrphid flies (also known as hoverflies) are the most predatory in their larval stage, when they devour aphids. However, to get the larvae, you need to entice the adults to stop in your garden, and the adults rely on nectar for their primary food source. By growing nectar-rich flowers alongside your edibles (or even *as* edibles, in the case of fennel, dill, and borage), and by creating mixed-up communities of plants, you encourage a diversity of insects to take up permanent residence, leaving their eggs and their voracious younger generation. Dense, intermingled plantings are also more appealing to birds, which can provide significant natural pest control as well.

**Release beneficial insects.** There is a growing industry in selecting, rearing, and selling

beneficial insects for release in home gardens. Everything from parasitic nematodes to control grubs to predatory mites to the time-honored ladybugs and praying mantis egg cases are available to be shipped to your door for release in your garden. You generally can't rely on these as preventive measures: After all, if none of these insects' favorite foods are available in your garden, they'll have to go find it elsewhere. However, they are worth experimenting with as long as you buy them from a reputable source that provides all the information you need to know (whether or not that beneficial will work in your area, and how many you'll need) and can ship them so they'll arrive alive, healthy, and ready to do their stuff in your garden.

**Hand-pick pest insects.** I am a big fan of this method, but I will be the first to admit that it is not for the squeamish. Many pest insects are easy to spot and handle, and you can simply pick these off and smash them. Japanese beetles, Asiatic garden beetles, potato beetles, cabbage loopers, tomato hornworms, and stink bugs can all be controlled this way

Hand-picking is easiest and most effective early in the morning, when insects move more slowly and are less likely to fly away. (The exception is the Asiatic garden beetle, which is nocturnal.) You can either squash them or drop them into a bucket of water with a film of dish soap on top, which will keep them from flying out. Some gardeners even use vacuum cleaners to suck insects out of flowers and off leaves!

Hand-picking may seem futile, especially in the case of Japanese beetles, which can appear in daunting numbers all at once. How-ever, every individual you pick means a little less damage now and reduces future generations. Practiced regularly, it can be quite effective—even more so if you can get your neighbors to do it, too.

Hand-picking is especially well suited to pest control in edible spots and pots, as the height boost given by containers and raised beds makes it much easier to inspect plants from above and below and to spot any pest insects or egg masses.

**Apply physical barriers.** You can physically block access to your plants through the use of a floating row cover, a specially made light fabric that you lay over your crops to physically prevent insects from accessing the leaves and stems. These fabrics are designed to allow light and air to reach the plant, so the plant can continue healthy, vigorous, pest-free growth. Row covers come in pieces that are large enough to drape over a whole plant. To completely prevent pest access, however, you'll need to secure the fabric to the soil around the base of the plant. Specially designed "staples" are available for this, or you can use rocks or even soil to seal off the gap.

While a floating row cover isn't exactly attractive and may cause problems for pollination with certain crops, such as cucumbers and squash, you usually need to use it for only a short time, depending on the life cycles of the insects you're trying to exclude. Using the growing degree days system (see the sidebar on page 103) helps you minimize the amount of time that you need to maintain the row cover on your crops.

Another type of physical barrier is kaolin clay sprays. Kaolin clay is the same type of clay used in making ceramic dishes. A special grade of it is available in bags for garden use. When you mix it with water and apply it to your plants, it not only prevents insects from making a meal of your plants, it also prevents many fungal diseases from becoming established. Some gardeners claim that it makes plants more productive, too, as the pale coating minimizes heat and drought stress.

Kaolin clay is nontoxic and very effective; however, it has a few significant drawbacks. First, it turns your plants an ashen beige color, severely diminishing the aesthetic qualities of your garden. It becomes even more problematic for edible spots and pots, given that the clay will drip and cling to the containers and raised-bed sides. Depending on the material, this can cause permanent staining. It also means that you'll have to wash all of your harvest thoroughly. Second, you need to reapply it fairly frequently, as new growth emerges and as rain washes it off.

Though kaolin clay is a good, effective product, I would recommend it for those using the methods in this book only in extreme infestations. A row cover takes less effort to use, and it's equally effective if well timed. Plus, you can easily remove it if you are expecting guests and would like to show off your beautiful, healthy, organic garden.

**Try water sprays.** A simple spray of water is an effective way to control soft-bodied pests that tend to congregate on leaves, shoots, or fruits, such as aphids and mealybugs. To avoid damaging plants with a very strong stream, I use a gentler stream and rub the insects off at the same time. Water sprays work only on soft-bodied insects, so they're not a widely appli-

cable control solution, but they do have a place in your nontoxic pest control toolbox.

**Set out sticky traps.** Sticky traps are small, stiff cards—usually bright yellow—that are coated with a sticky glue. Placed on a little stake or hung from a strong plant, they can be very effective at catching small flying insects. Check sticky traps frequently to see what you've caught. They won't trap heavy pests, such as Asiatic garden beetles and Japanese beetles, but they're good for controlling whiteflies, flea beetles, leafhoppers, and a host of other pests that are too small or too fast moving to catch otherwise.

Sticky traps are inexpensive and last until they are so covered with insects that no vacant

sticky surface remains. They do have a few disadvantages, though: They're nonselective, so they catch good insects as well as bad, and they readily catch your hair if you're working too close to them. If you decide to try sticky traps, don't expect to find them at your local garden center; you'll probably have to order them from a supplier of organic-gardening products or greenhouse supplies.

**Keep it clean.** Cleanliness is a key part of pest-control strategies at commercial greenhouses, and it applies to home gardens, too. When you work with a plant that you know has a pest infestation, wash your hands and your tools before moving on to the next plant to avoid carrying the pests and their eggs to your other crops.

Sanitation is especially important at the end of the year, whether or not your plants showed signs of pest problems. Remove the withered foliage of anything that cannot survive winter; otherwise, it will provide shelter to pests and a cue that their favorite food source will probably be back again in roughly that same spot next year. Garden waste like this can typically be composted, though if it hosted a fungal disease or a severe infestation, it is

better to put the material in the trash than in the compost bin.

In spring, when you are preparing for a new season of gardening, pull out any root masses that are left in the soil and compost them. In both containers and raised beds, you are likely to encounter grubs in the soil as you dig, dump out old soil, or plant; destroy them or put them in your bird feeder.

When it comes to nontoxic pest-control strategies, every little action does have an impact. It may be a minor impact, but as long as it contributes to lowering the pest population in the long run, it is worth doing.

## Keep Critters Out

Insects aren't the only pests that can attack your crops: You'll also need to watch out for larger plant eaters, such as deer, rabbits, squirrels, voles, and raccoons. You can manage them with the tolerance, knowledge, and creativity guidelines I recommend earlier for insects. Chicken wire, hardware cloth, and wire mesh are all excellent ways to physically exclude these pests from your plants. Deer netting is also effective, and it is more flexible and less expensive than its wire counterparts.

## Minimize Diseases

Fungi cause the majority of plant diseases, including powdery mildew, blight, anthracnose, and fusarium and verticillium wilt, to name just a few. Generally speaking, you can't cure a plant that is diseased; you can only prevent the problem. The best defense against diseases is to give your plants the best possible growing conditions: placing them in full sun, keeping the leaves as dry as possible, and siting your garden where there is good air circulation. Gardening in pots and raised beds gives you extra help in this effort, as the potting mixes used for container plants are not as able to host disease as garden soils, and the additional elevation of a raised bed or container reduces the chance of disease spores splashing up on the leaves.

manage to get the seeds in and growing while the weather is still warm, so don't wait too long to sow seed in these areas.

If you are using a cover crop on your raised bed as described in "Cover Crops" on page 68, be sure to sow it with sufficient time to germinate. Each crop has different temperature requirements for germination and different lengths of time it must grow to have the desired effect. Plan carefully, as timing is crucial to success.

# WINDING DOWN IN FALL

Shorter days and cooler temperatures trigger a decrease in growth and production by mid- to late August. Though there are still many weeks of harvest ahead for most crops, physiological changes are taking place to usher in death or dormancy. There are several ways to prolong the season, however. You can turn to the floating row cover, the same stuff you used to protect against insects, and use it to shield tender plants on nights when temperatures dip into the 40s. You can even enlist old bedsheets or towels for the task; use some bamboo stakes or a tomato cage to create a framework to hold up the cover. (This method also works well early in the season when you have the odd cold night that threatens tender plants—temperatures much below 53°F can cause tomato plants to stall their growth and flowering.)

Late August, September, and even October (in warmer climates) are fine times to revisit some of the crops you may have grown in spring, such as radishes, peas, spinach, and salad greens. Cold-climate gardeners will have much better success with fall crops if they

## Cleanup and Winterizing

Though a hard frost will blacken and wither everything but the most cold-tolerant crops, you don't need to wait that long to pull unproductive, stressed-looking plants out of your garden. While it is ideal to remove plants from the garden entirely, this isn't always possible and often results in a huge waste of soil, as so much clings to the still-living roots. You can remove the upper portions in fall and wait until spring to remove the root masses; they'll be easier to pull out after they've died and started to decompose. Add the results of your garden cleanup to your compost pile.

Anything that is still green and alive can stay in place for the winter. Some crops will survive and grow again in spring, if the winter isn't too severe, and these can provide a welcome treat early in the season, before anything else is growing. In my USDA Zone 6 garden, for example, scallions, Swiss chard, chervil, and parsley all overwinter well.

Move any pots that are not weatherproof to a dry, frost-free area. You don't need to empty them first. You can reuse the potting soil next year if you amend it with compost and fertilizer as outlined in "Recycled Potting Soil" on page 33. Protect perennial crops with a winter mulch.

## Thinking Ahead

"Next year, I'll..." is the gardener's mantra. And now that the season is over, it's time to reflect on the successes and missteps of the past year and plan how you'll improve next year. Spend the winter poring over seed catalogs and sketching out new plans for next year's garden. Review photos to refresh your memory and get a new perspective on the garden. Plan a crop rotation scheme, and think about how you'll amend your soil to enjoy the same vigorous, bountiful garden in the coming season. And as the snow or rain comes down and the gray days linger, take heart: The next gardening season is right around the corner.

# Six Ways for Vegetable Gardeners to Make Winter Go More Quickly

Winter is a welcome period of rest for most gardeners. No matter how enjoyable and productive your garden was in summer, there's something satisfying about winding up and storing the hose and knowing that you won't be dragging it around for many more months. With the busyness of the holidays facing us, most of us look forward to November and December and curling up on the couch with a good book. But once January rolls around, many start feeling the itch to get gardening again. Here are six ways you can make the most of winter and help the cold, gray days pass more quickly.

1. **Care for potted herbs that you've brought in from the garden for winter.** This can include many beautiful and useful plants, like lemon verbena, scented geraniums, and specialty bay laurels. Not-quite-hardy plants that tolerate some cold temperatures, like bay laurel and rosemary, can even be grown in unheated sunrooms if they are protected from extreme cold.

2. **Research.** Between garden magazines and the constant flood of information on the Internet, there's never any shortage of new ideas, new discoveries, new products, and new solutions for gardeners. Winter is the perfect time to read up on what has changed in the last year and gain the up-to-date knowledge you need to make the upcoming season the best yet.

3. **Shop.** Seed catalogs begin appearing in the mailbox just as soon as the holidays end—sooner even, it seems anymore. I never tire of poring over them and thinking about what I will grow in the coming year, where I will plant it, and what I will combine it with.

4. **Plan.** You can sketch out your planting plans for your containers or raised beds—if you don't feel confident in your drawing skills, you can cut photos of crops from your old seed catalogs and tape them to a plan of your garden to experiment with different combinations long before the first seed sprouts. You can also come up with a seed sowing and planting schedule for your favorite crops. Even though many of those tasks will depend on the weather at the time, you can still schedule it in for larger blocks of time, like "early April" or "midspring." I have learned that organizing your ideas in winter definitely leads to a much more productive and efficient spring!

5. **Attend talks.** Your local public gardens, garden centers, garden clubs, and even public libraries usually host meetings with guest speakers where you can learn a lot for little or no cost. It's the perfect opportunity to spend some time with like-minded folks in your town and get excited about the coming season.

6. **Sow seeds.** Depending on your climate, seed-starting time may be as early as mid to late February (though mid to late March is typical for most of North America). Starting my tomato and pepper seeds indoors always feels like gardening to me, and I consider it the kickoff of the new season. It's a fun, easy way to get excited for spring, even if outdoor gardening is still weeks away.

## chapter four

# SPOTS & POTS PROJECTS

Whether it's the hands-on aspect of working outdoors or a natural tendency toward thriftiness, gardeners tend to be do-it-yourselfers. That's why I created these 16 projects that will make your edible spots and pots more useful, more affordable, and more fun. Nearly all of these items have ready-made counterparts, but making them yourself affords a freedom in materials, design, and size that is especially perfect for the adaptable nature of raised beds and containers. Besides, what better way is there to spend the off-season than working on accessories that will lessen your work, increase your yields, or make your garden a little more stylish and unique?

The following projects incorporate a range of skills and techniques but are all well within the ability of even the most novice handyperson. They are made from readily available materials and are built with tools that most folks already have around. If you are a confident crafter or builder, by all means, use these instructions as guidelines only and customize the project for your space. After all, I wouldn't have gotten this far if I hadn't taken that liberty with items that I saw in the first place! These ideas are absolutely yours to own, improve, and adapt.

Some of these projects require materials (such as a roll of chicken wire or landscape fabric) that can only be purchased in larger quantities than you'll need to make a single project. While you will easily find other uses for these materials around your home, you could always split the cost with a gardening pal and spend a day making the items together. Or, perhaps, strike a deal wherein one person with a sewing machine makes fabric projects for both while the other with power tools makes wood projects. The point is to have fun, create something unique, and save money so you can devote your cash to items you can't make, like new plants and tools.

## ROSTER OF PROJECTS

### BAMBOO

Bamboo Ladder Trellis 116

Bean Archway and Arbor 118

Try a Tripod! 122

### FABRIC

Fabric Grow Bag 125

Hanging Basket Sling 128

Modular Hanging Planter 130

Planting Hammock 134

### METAL

Copper Trellis 137

Mesh Tower 140

Tomato Ring 143

### WOOD

Deck Corner Shelf 147

Fence Net 149

Pot Caddy 151

Raised Beds 153

Stacked Pot Planter 158

Window-Frame Trellis 160

# BAMBOO

For many gardeners, bamboo stakes are so ubiquitous that it's easy to forget how handy and versatile they are. We just sort of accumulate them, and they're generally so long lasting that we end up with a pretty significant assortment of stakes without ever having tried to do so. But bamboo is useful in the garden far beyond serving as a single support stake: It is easily cut and joined with other pieces to create any number of garden structures, both decorative and functional.

Despite its hard surface and durable nature, bamboo is not wood. Botanically speaking, it is a type of grass, which is why it is so lightweight and flexible. This also accounts for its sustainability—it is extremely fast growing, which makes it earth friendly and inexpensive. There are many bamboo species that can be cultivated in the garden to cut and use as light-duty stakes, but for these projects, I recommend that you purchase bamboo specifically grown for stakes. Imported from warm climates, the bamboo sold in stores tends to be straighter and stronger than the cold-tolerant bamboos we grow in American gardens.

Though these projects are quick, it's best to invest in top-quality materials so your finished product will be safe and sturdy. Wherever possible, purchase "first-cut" bamboo, which is the highest quality and the most structurally sound. That said, it is always important to inspect each stalk of bamboo carefully that you intend to use for your project, as it is a natural product and can contain small faults that could cause problems later. Evaluate each piece by bending it slightly and listening for cracking or breaking. Look also for weak points or rotten areas, which may appear as a blackish crust. Finally, look at the joints, known botanically as nodes, along the stem. These should all be round and thicker than the surrounding stem. Make sure they are not compromised, and try to visualize your project to ensure they won't be in the way of any cuts or joins, as the stronger tissue makes these tasks much more difficult than when done on the internodes, or round stem sections.

One last word of advice: Though lightweight bamboo can be cut with pruners, heavy bamboo must be cut with a saw.

# BAMBOO LADDER TRELLIS

*Trellises are an important and productive way to maximize space in raised beds and containers, and there are many types of trellises available—plastic, wood, metal, and more! However, the one-size-fits-all nature of store-bought items doesn't always work in every spot and application or for every plant. It's much better to create your own trellis at a height and width suitable for the location where you'll use it. This bamboo ladder-type trellis is the perfect place to start: Not only is it easy, fast, and inexpensive to construct, it's also sturdy and long lasting. It's perfect for cucumbers and other plants that climb by means of tendrils, like peas.*

> Time: 30 minutes / Cost: $7
> Size: 12" wide × 6' high, which works well
> for a 16"-diameter pot

## MATERIALS (FOR 1 TRELLIS)
**Four ½" bamboo stakes, each 6' long**
**36 light-duty zip ties**

## TOOLS
**Hand pruners**
**Tape measure**
**Pencil**

## DIRECTIONS

1. Choose two of the sturdiest, straightest stakes for the trellis uprights. To determine where to start securing the trellis crossbars, place one upright into the pot or raised bed and mark the soil level (or potential soil level) with a pencil.

2. Using the hand pruners, cut the remaining two stakes into eight 15"-long crossbars.

3. Lay the uprights, parallel to one another, flat on the ground. Place one 15" crossbar at the soil-level mark on the right upright, angling it 45 degrees upward to the left upright and allowing the crossbar to extend beyond the uprights about 1". Use a zip tie to secure the crossbar to each upright, but do not pull the zip ties tight. Position and secure a second crossbar, crisscrossing the first crossbar to create an X; do not tighten the zip ties yet.

4. Start the second course of crossbars just above the first, lightly securing the bars in position with zip ties. Repeat for two more sets of crossbars.

5. Once all the pieces are in place, even, and at a consistent angle, pull the zip ties tightly to secure. Place one additional zip tie at the X intersection of each crossbar and tighten completely. Trim the tails on all ties.

6. If you have an additional length of bamboo, you can place a single crossbar horizontally across the top of the trellis to add more stability.

*Using the Bamboo Ladder Trellis: Ideally, place the trellis in a container or raised bed before planting your cucumber or peas, though it can be put into place after they've begun growth but before they are vining vigorously. For the best-looking display, check growth frequently and try to position it on the trellis to provide maximum coverage. You may also wish to prune away the occasional leaf so that sunlight reaches the ripening fruits.*

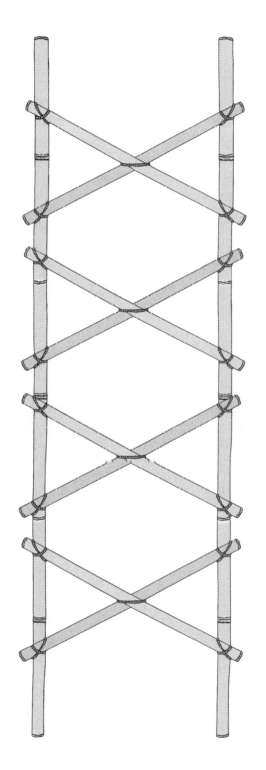

# BEAN ARCHWAY AND ARBOR

*With just three lengths of bamboo stakes, you can create a dramatic single-span archway; add a few more stakes and you can build a double-span arbor for the season for a fraction of the cost of buying a ready-made product or building something similar out of wood. These simple but useful projects not only give your edible twining crops a place to grow but also create a focal point in your garden. Both of these structures are suitable for growing lightweight twining annuals, such as Malabar spinach, pole beans, and ornamental vines like morning glory or moonflower.*

*The key to making the archway and arbor sturdy and serviceable is using large, 1"-diameter bamboo poles. Though these are not as widely available as the flimsier garden-stake size, they are worth seeking out through a specialty or professional horticultural supplier, like A.M. Leonard or Gempler's. And a word of advice: Build the projects on-site; they will be unwieldy and cumbersome to move once built.*

## Bean Archway

Time: 30 minutes / Cost: $15
Size: 5½' wide × 6½' high

### MATERIALS (FOR 1 ARCHWAY)

**Two 1"-diameter bamboo poles, each 8' long***

**One ½"-diameter bamboo garden stake, 6' long**

**6 heavy-duty zip ties**

*\*Using 8'-long bamboo poles allows for a 15"–20" sink into raised beds or containers to anchor the project and an arbor height of 6½'. If you'd like a deeper anchor or a higher arbor, you may wish to use 10'-long bamboo poles. If you need to cut 1"-diameter bamboo, it must be done with a sharp hacksaw (ideally) or a pruning saw.*

### DIRECTIONS

1. Decide where you'll place the archway. It can be sited at the corner of two adjacent raised beds or in two large, heavy-based containers. The 6'-long bamboo stake creates the span of the archway for a total width of about 5½', once the horizontal piece is attached. If you need a longer span, either find longer slim stakes or use light-duty zip ties to add a section of thin bamboo. Do not go wider than 6½' for the span or it may sag.

2. Lay the 8' poles on the ground about 5½' apart. Place the thin bamboo stake perpendicular to the poles about 2" from the top to create the span and secure lightly at each end with two zip ties crisscrossed into an X. Do not tighten all the way.

3. Make sure the span is straight and even, then pull the zip ties tightly to secure. Add an additional zip tie immediately below each

junction to prevent slipping, and tighten down completely. Trim the tails on all ties.

4. With a helper, place the end of each bamboo pole into a corner of a raised bed or into a soil-filled container. (Note: If the bed or container is newly filled with soil, water the soil thoroughly first so that there is minimal settling once you install the archway.)

*Using the Bean Archway: Once it is installed, plant seeds or starter plants of a vining crop in the soil around the base of each upright. Sometimes, plants need a little help reaching the upright post to begin twining, and once again, bamboo comes to the rescue: Simply cut a short piece of light bamboo and position it as a "bridge" to direct growth toward the arch.*

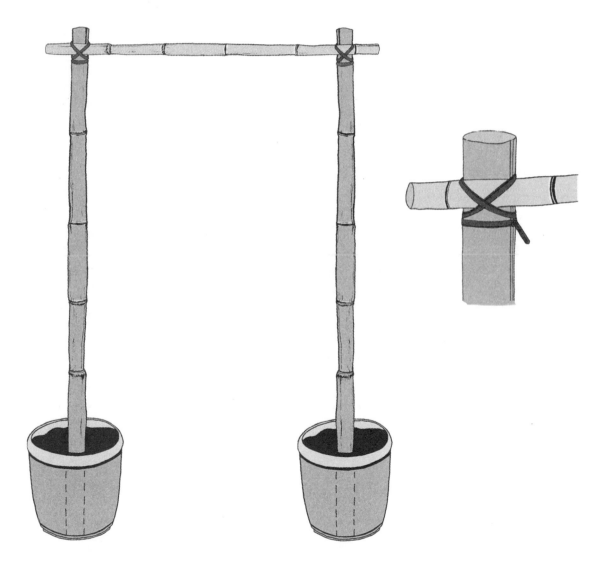

# Bean Arbor

*As with the Bean Archway, you should work on the site where you'll install the arbor. A small stepladder will come in handy when positioning and securing the zip ties.*

Time: 1 hour / Cost: $38
Size: 5½' wide × 6½' high × 5½' deep

## MATERIALS (FOR 1 ARBOR)

Four 1"-diameter bamboo poles,
  each 8' long

Seven ½"-diameter bamboo garden stakes,
  each 6' long

24 heavy-duty zip ties

12 light-duty zip ties

## DIRECTIONS

1. Begin by assembling two archways as described on pages 118–119. Position and install the archways in containers or raised beds about 5½' apart, or use helpers to hold the archways upright while you construct the overhead portion of the arbor.

2. Install one 6' bamboo stake perpendicular to the span of the archway by placing one end of the stake in the inside corner of one archway below the previously secured cross bar and overhanging it by 3"; secure lightly with a pair of crisscrossed heavy-duty zip ties over the ties you installed in Step 1, but do not pull the zip ties tight. Place the other end of the stake on the opposite archway in the same manner. Repeat for the second stake, again working in the inside corner below the cross bar you installed in Step 1. Once these two perpendicular pieces are even and level, pull the zip ties tightly to secure. Install a third heavy-duty zip tie on the inside of these pieces to keep them snug against the corner junctions.

3. Install the remaining three 6' stakes across these bars, with one placed at the midpoint and the other two equally spaced between this middle stake and the horizontal pieces of the archway. Secure the stakes on each end with a pair of light-duty zip ties, crisscrossed in an X. Do not tighten the zip ties completely until all pieces are in place and even and level. Pull the zip ties tightly to secure. Trim the tails on all ties.

*Using the Bean Arbor: If the arbor is not yet in place, insert the poles in four containers or in the corners of four adjacent raised beds. Plant with an annual vining crop (see suggestions on page 118) or a perennial that dies back to the ground every year, like hops vine. This arbor can be left outdoors year-round if desired, though it will last a few seasons longer if you bring it in. You can simply cut the zip ties for storage and retie the structure the following season.*

# TRY A TRIPOD!

*Whether you call it a tripod, a pyramid, or a tepee, this easy-to-make garden accessory is a true must-have. Though simple in its components and construction, this three-legged structure is surprisingly versatile. It can be used to train almost any crop that needs support, whether the plant climbs on its own (like beans, Malabar spinach, and cucumbers) or requires the gardener to tie up its long, rambling stems (like tomatoes and potatoes). A tripod saves space, maximizes sunlight, and makes pests easier to spot since they're at eye level. It adds a welcome geometry to informal gardens, providing structure and height and dramatically shaping the space. Tripods are also handy to use as season extenders if you wrap them in landscape fabric to keep frost off plants or wrap them with heavy plastic to create a mini-greenhouse.*

*You can use a variety of materials to make a tripod, depending on the look you'd like, your budget, and what materials you have on hand. You can also make these in any height you'd like, from a diminutive 2'-tall structure for spring peas to an 8'-tall giant for pole beans. When determining the height you want, add an extra 6" to 8" to secure the trellis in the soil (or add more length if you're using the trellis in a container, where it is generally best to sink the stake all the way to the bottom).*

Time: About 15 minutes / Cost: $6
Size: Variable

## MATERIALS (FOR 1 TRELLIS)
**22-gauge green paddle wire (aka floral wire)**

**3 sturdy stakes of equal length**

**Sheet moss (optional)**

## TOOLS
**Hand pruners**

## DIRECTIONS

1. Bend about 1" of wire to a 90-degree angle and place this flat against the first stake, holding it securely with your thumb. Wrap the wire twice around this first stake, going over the 1" piece as you come around it to secure. Pull tightly and begin to bring the wire around the second stake, about 1½" from the top, starting around the back (what will be the inside of the tripod) and coming around the front of it. As you work, keep the stakes at a slight angle (say, 30 degrees) from one another. Do not hold them parallel.

2. Pull the wire tight and bring it around the third stake, 1½" from the top, coming around the back and over the far side. As you bring it around to the front, hold the third stake at about a 30-degree angle to the first one, pull the wire tight, and go around all three stakes with the wire three times.

3. Bring the wire over the center where all three stakes meet and through the junction on the inside. Repeat this three times,

# CLAIM YOUR STAKES

For this project, you'll need three sturdy stakes of equal length (they don't need to be precisely equal, but they must be very close). You can use your choice of new or reused materials, such as:

- ☼ Bamboo stakes
- ☼ Wood stakes
- ☼ Heavy branches at least 1" in diameter
- ☼ Plastic-coated metal garden stakes
- ☼ Metal stakes or light-duty rods

You should avoid very heavy metal rods, like rebar, for this project because they can't be securely fastened into a tripod with floral wire. Rebar, however, does have many wonderful uses in the garden, especially as individual stakes—so save your rebar for other projects.

each time alternating which two stakes you thread the wire through.

4. Use the wire-cutting notch on your pruners to cut the wire; leave an 8" to 10" tail. Finish by wrapping the tail around all three stakes and tuck the end between previous wraps.

5. If you wish to dress up the tripod, tuck several sprigs of sheet moss around the wraps and secure it as you wrap the last few inches of wire. This makes the wire nearly disappear visually and is a nice accent for tripods that will be seen up close.

*Using the Try a Tripod!: This project can be used in one large (14" or larger) container or in raised beds. I like to plant seeds around the base of each stake and let them scamper upward, but it works well with young plants, too. If you'd like, try a different variety or a different crop at each stake!*

# FABRIC

Pass the days until the growing season starts by whipping up a couple of these fun garden projects on your sewing machine. You don't need any experience or sewing skills to make these items—after all, they're going to be filled with soil and placed outdoors! Whether you have a cutting-edge sewing machine or Grandma's vintage model, these projects require just a few seams—most of them simple straight lines. I have provided a recommendation for a particular type of canvas, fabric, or landscape fabric (also known as weed barrier) for each project, based on the durability and strength needed. Of course, if you're interested in upcycling, you may already have materials that you can put to good use; they may perform a bit differently than the fabrics used here, but you can still enjoy the benefits of DIY garden projects.

As you get started, I'd like to pass along a few tips for success with these projects:

☩ Always use a heavy-duty needle (size 16 or a denim needle) in the machine when sewing canvas.

☩ Use only 100 percent polyester thread. Cotton thread will disintegrate shockingly fast outdoors.

☩ Backstitch securely at the beginning and end of all seams.

☩ All of these fabrics will be much easier to cut and far more accurately done if you use a rotary cutter setup (including a rotary cutter, self-healing rotary mat, and see-through rotary ruler). This system, favored by quilters for more than 2 decades, makes it fast and easy to cut very long, straight lines and minimizes the need to mark and measure on the pieces of fabric. Investing in the rotary cutting equipment may cost about $75, so you may wish to ask a quilting friend if you can borrow the equipment. Of course, pieces can be marked and cut conventionally with a ruler and scissors as well, but the rotary system is much faster, more accurate, and less frustrating.

☩ Drainage holes are not necessary for fabric items, as water seeps out readily. However, if you choose impermeable materials like oilcloth or woven plastic, install several grommets for drainage. You'll find grommet installation directions on the package; grommets are available in hardware, fabric, and craft stores.

# FABRIC GROW BAG

*For a lot of container at little cost, you can't beat these fabric grow bags! They are really inexpensive and fast to create out of landscape fabric from the garden center. You must use a nonstretchy fabric, not plastic landscape sheeting—to test its suitability, pull a piece taut and poke it with your finger. The material should not stretch or turn lighter in color where you apply pressure. Further, the material must not be impregnated with any type of herbicide. Read the label carefully to be certain.*

*Not only is landscape fabric cost effective, it is surprisingly handsome and long lasting in the garden, too. Another benefit: Since it is nonwoven, you needn't worry about fraying. I recommend using a double layer of weed barrier fabric for a sturdy container.*

*Fabric grow bags will probably last only one season in most climates. However, you can prolong their life by placing them on a surface that allows airflow to the bottom, such as decking or a pallet, and facing the bags toward the sun so they dry quickly, ensuring that the fabric is less prone to rotting.*

Time: About 1 hour / Cost: $4
Size: 14" high × 14" diameter

## MATERIALS (FOR 1 BAG)
1⅜ yards 4'-wide landscape fabric
100% polyester thread
Length of string

## TOOLS
Ruler
Permanent marker or pen
Small spring clip or clothespin
Tailor's chalk or fabric marking pen
Scissors
Sewing machine
Straight pins

## DIRECTIONS

1. For the grow bag bottom, fold the landscape fabric in half lengthwise, then trim the length to exactly 49". Fold down 10" from the top, then fold in 8" on one vertical side.

2. Cut a 12" length of thread. Securely knot one end of the thread and measure 7½" from the knot, marking the spot clearly with a permanent marker or pen.

3. Place the knot at the outer corner of the fold and clamp securely with a spring clip. Align the thread with the side edge of the fold.

4. Press down firmly on the clip and stretch the thread taut. Place the point of the tailor's chalk at the 7½" mark and draw an arc, compass style, on the fabric from folded edge to folded edge.

5. Holding all four layers securely together, cut along the arc line with scissors to create the bag bottom.

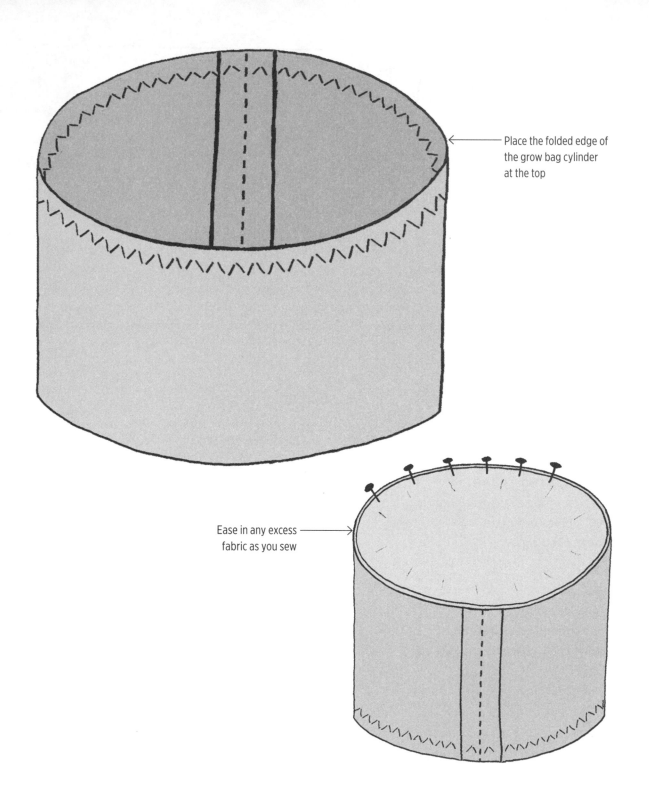

Place the folded edge of the grow bag cylinder at the top

Ease in any excess fabric as you sew

6. For the grow bag sides, unfold the fabric and cut off the portion where the circle was cut. Now cut a 30″ wide strip off the remaining length. Fold this strip in half; the folded edge will the upper edge of the grow bag.

7. To add strength to the bag and keep the side piece evenly folded while you complete the bag, sew along the folded edge, 1″ from the fold, with a zigzag stitch.

8. Fold the bag in half so the side edges meet and the wrong side of the bag is facing outward. Sew the side seam 1″ from the edge, using a straight sewing stitch to create a cylinder.

9. Place the opened cylinder upright on a flat surface with the wrong side of the bag facing outward and the top, or folded edge, facing down. Lay the right side of the bag bottom on top of the cylinder, centering the bag bottom and aligning the cylinder edges with the circumference of the bag bottom. The bag bottom should dip slightly inside the cylinder to allow you to pin the two pieces together. Note: The fabrics should have some "give" so you can gather or stretch the bag bottom to be evenly distrib-

uted around the cylinder. If there's excess fabric, push it toward the existing seam on the cylinder to lessen puckering. Use straight pins to hold the pieces together for sewing.

10. Sew the bag bottom and cylinder together 1″ from the edge, easing in any excess fabric as you sew. If you are unable to ease in all of the excess fabric, push the excess toward the seam where it's less likely to be noticed.

11. Turn the grow bag right side out, pushing out the thick areas along the seam lines to expand the bag.

*Using the Fabric Grow Bag. Before filling the bag with soil, place it where you plan to keep it all season; it is not easy to move. When filling, add soil carefully and completely, deliberately placing the soil evenly around the walls and filling in the center. If you do not fill the entire volume of the bag, it will be slouchy and misshapen instead of well formed and supportive. Any plant, or combination of plants, can be grown in grow bags, and the bags can be planted like regular containers. Depending on your site, however, they may dry out more quickly than ceramic containers, so schedule time each day to check on their water needs.*

# CUSTOMIZE THE SIZE

You can make Fabric Grow Bags any size you'd like, though it's best to keep them under 18 inches in diameter for stability. To make a custom-size grow bag, first decide what diameter you'd like it to be. Divide this number in half and add ½″ to determine how large to cut the circle, and adjust the sides accordingly using the following formula:

**Length of side = circumference of circle (3.14 × total diameter of circle);
add 2″ for seam allowance (1″ on each side).**

# HANGING BASKET SLING

Hanging baskets and containers are the perfect way to claim a bit more growing space than the ground allows and to bring your garden up into a vertical plane. However, you don't need to invest in expensive hanging metal baskets with coir liners, nor do you need to settle for ugly one-piece molded plastic baskets designed for summer annuals! This simple, sleek Hanging Basket Sling is easily made out of fabric or heavy webbing and will last for years. Best of all, it can be used with almost any size (12" or less) terra-cotta pot, so you can transform your existing stash of pots into hanging planters. You can change out the pot if a heavy harvest leaves the crop looking a little stubbly. The sling is also perfect for potted crops that need repeated sowings for a constant supply, like cilantro and arugula. I use cotton ticking for my slings, but most heavy canvas or twill fabric should work, as long as the fabric doesn't stretch. Old denim jeans, for example, would be a good choice. Vary the length of the planter to fit your preferred basket and the height of the hook or bracket you'll be using. Your planter should hang at a length that is convenient for harvesting, but where it is safely out of the path of people and pets. The steel ring used in the project can be purchased in any hardware store in the chain section.

The amount of fabric listed below will leave you with quite a bit left over. You can use the remnant to make more Hanging Basket Slings (you'll have enough fabric to make 10 additional slings) or to create a small Fabric Grow Bag or several Planting Hammocks.

Time: 90 minutes / Cost: $6.50
Size: Varies based on the desired hanging location; mine has a drop of 25" from the ring for a total length of 26½"

## MATERIALS (FOR 1 SLING)

Bracket or hook for hanging

1½ yards 55"-wide canvas fabric*

One 1½"-diameter × ³⁄₁₆"-thick welded steel ring

100% polyester thread

## TOOLS

Rotary cutter, mat, and ruler (or ruler and scissors)

Iron and ironing board

Sewing machine

Pencil

*Determine the length of the sling (Step 1) before purchasing the fabric. This will dictate how many yards you need to buy.

## DIRECTIONS:

1. To determine the length for the sling, install the bracket or hook at the desired location. Measure the distance from the bracket to the desired height of the bottom of the

sling. Double this measurement, then subtract 1½" to account for the hanging ring; this is the length you'll cut the fabric hanging straps.

2. Using rotary cutting equipment or scissors, cut two 2"-wide strips at the length calculated in Step 1.

3. To create the hanging straps, fold each strap in half lengthwise with the wrong sides together. Press firmly with the iron to crease the fold line. To enclose the raw edges of the fabric to avoid fraying, fold each long edge in toward the center fold line, pressing each new crease firmly. Fold the strap in half again to create a thick ½"-wide strap; press firmly. Using a zigzag stitch, sew along the open edge of the strap, keeping the stitching close to the edge.

4. Fold each strap in half widthwise to find the center point, and mark it with a pencil.

5. Place the straps on a flat surface and cross them to make an X, matching the center points. Sew the straps together at the center points by stitching a small rectangular shape and then backstitching at the beginning, corners, and end of the rectangle. Thread the hanging ring onto two straps, sliding it to the sewn rectangle.

6. Cut two 3"-diameter circles for the base of the sling. (A drinking glass makes an excellent template. Trace around and cut carefully with scissors.)

7. To find the center of one base piece, fold it in quarters and mark the center point with a pencil. Place the base wrong side up on a flat surface.

8. Place one strap end about ½" from the center point, making sure the strap is not twisted; pin the end in place. Take the opposite end of that strap, position it across from its partner, and repeat this process. Repeat for the second strap, leaving a neat, open square in the exact center of the base; this prevents overlapping and keeps the lengths as even as possible. Make sure the straps are not twisted, then sew the strap ends securely to the base. Place the remaining base, right side out, on top of the sewn ends. Sewing as close to the edge as possible, zigzag-stitch around the perimeter of the bases, sewing over the straps when you come to them and keeping them flat.

*Using the Hanging Basket Sling: Position the ring at the top intersection of the straps and hang from a secure bracket. Fill a 10" terra-cotta pot with soil, plant as desired (I recommend parsley, cilantro, or other leafy herbs), and slip it between the straps, centering the pot bottom over the circle base of the sling.*

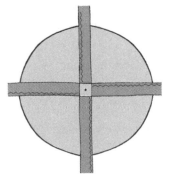

# MODULAR HANGING PLANTER

*The Internet abounds with photos of hanging shoe organizers used as wall planters. Despite their cuteness, I've found that these products are ill suited to the garden: The pockets are far too small to grow anything larger than an herb or a single lettuce plant, and the material is thin and weak, tearing and staining badly well before the season is over. The idea of growing several small plants in pockets is still an appealing one, though, so I designed a project that does work and yields good results.*

*This hanging planter is a touch more complex than the previous sewing machine projects, but it's not outside the reach of someone reasonably confident in his or her cutting and sewing skills. It has gusseted pockets, which add a minor extra step, but they make planting and watering easier. The overall size of the planter, along with the dimensions and arrangement of the pockets, can be wholly customized to suit your space and needs, and I'm happy to pass along this vital bit of wisdom: If you change this design, don't make any of the pockets longer than 16" or deeper than 10". Beyond those sizes, the volume and weight of the soil (especially when recently watered) cause severe bulging and can fray or rip the fabric.*

Time: 3 hours / Cost: $15
Size: 36" wide × 40" long

**MATERIALS (FOR 1 PLANTER)**

**2 yards 60"-wide undyed heavy canvas, such as 14-ounce weight canvas\***

**Heavy-duty 100% polyester thread**

**Grommet kit with five ½" brass grommets**

**TOOLS**

**Rotary cutter, mat, and ruler (or ruler and scissors)**

**Pencil**

**Iron and ironing board**

**Size 16 needle**

**Sewing machine**

*\*Purchase additional canvas if you prefer to match stripes or patterns.*

## DIRECTIONS

1. For the background: Using the rotary cutting equipment or scissors, cut a piece of canvas 40" × 44"; this size allows for a 2" hem on all sides. On the wrong side of the fabric, use the ruler and pencil to mark a line 4" in from the edge on all sides. Fold each cut edge in toward the line to make a 2"-wide hem, and press flat. Using a size 16 needle and a zigzag stitch, sew close to the cut edge to secure the hem in place.

2. To create the pockets, cut three 10"-wide strips of canvas perpendicular to the selvage edges of the remaining piece of fabric. Lay each strip flat and measure and cut the following lengths:

   ⚜ Three 14" pieces
   (finished pocket size is 8" × 8")

   ⚜ Three 16" pieces
   (finished pocket size is 8" × 10")

   ⚜ Two 18" pieces
   (finished pocket size is 8" × 12")

3. Place the pocket piece on a flat surface. On the wrong side of each pocket, mark a line 2" from the top and bottom edges (the longest edges on each pocket); these will be the hem guidelines. On the 10" sides of each pocket, mark a line 1" from the edge for the hem and a second line 3" from the edge for the gusset (the gusset is the extra fabric that gives the pockets greater capacity and makes them easier to plant).

4. To prepare the pockets, place each pocket wrong side up on an ironing board. On the top edge, fold in the cut edge to meet the marked hem guideline and press the fold firmly. Using a zigzag stitch, sew the top hem in place, then press firmly. In the same manner, fold in the side and bottom edges to meet the marked hem guidelines and press the fold firmly; do not stitch these hems in place.

5. To create the gusset, fold each 10" side along the 3" gusset line and press the fold firmly, keeping the original hem turned under. Then fold each gusset back on itself once, accordion style. Press firmly, but do not sew.

6. Lay the background canvas flat on a work surface, and arrange the pockets in three rows, keeping the top 3" to 5" free for the grommets. For my planter, I placed the pockets in this order:

   ⚜ Top row pockets: 8" × 8", 8" × 10", and 8" × 8"

   ⚜ Middle row pockets: 8" × 10", 8" × 8", and 8" × 10"

   ⚜ Bottom row pockets: 8" × 12" and 8" × 12"

7. When you're satisfied with the position of each pocket, mark the location of the upper two corners of each pocket, being sure that the gusset is folded accordion style as it will be when it is attached to the background canvas. Set aside all but the centermost pocket: Pin the centermost pocket at the top two corners and at the bottom edge (or as needed).

8. To sew the pocket to the background canvas, beginning at the top right corner of the pocket and keeping the upper gusset folds free, backstitch securely and use a straight stitch to sew down the side edge about ¼" away from the fold. When you are ½" from the bottom right corner, keep the needle down but lift the presser foot. Flatten the gusset folds and continue sewing through all layers until you reach the corner. Keep the needle down, raise the presser foot, rotate the canvas 90 degrees, then lower the presser foot over all layers. Using a straight stitch, sew along the bottom edge about ¼" away from the fold, flattening and sewing over the gusset folds. Stop at the corner and keep the needle down. Raise the presser foot and rotate the piece 90 degrees.

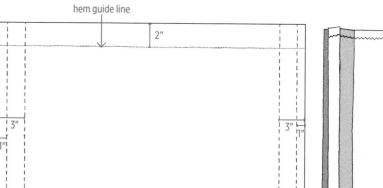

hem guide line

2"

3"

1"

3"
1"

2"

hem line

gusset line

Marking the hem and gusset lines

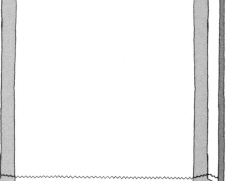

Folding the gusset

SPOTS & POTS PROJECTS

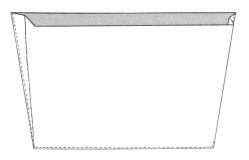

Sewing the pocket to the canvas

Using a straight stitch, sew up the side edge ½", sewing through all layers about ¼" from the folds. Keep the needle down but lift the presser foot, pull the upper gusset out of the way, and continue to sew along the side edge about ¼" from the fold. When you reach the top of the pocket, backstitch securely, then cut the thread. Repeat for all the pockets.

9. When all the pockets are attached, mark the grommet locations on the background canvas. Measure 1½" in from each side and 1" down from the top to determine the location of the first two grommets, then mark three more locations evenly spaced across the top of the piece between the corner grommets. Follow the package directions to install the grommets through all layers of background canvas.

*Using the Modular Hanging Planter:* This project is best hung under an eave or overhang out of the rain. Heavy rains will wash soil out of the upper pockets and into the lower ones, so it is better to rely exclusively on hand-watering to maintain it. Site this in full sun only, so the fabric dries quickly and all plants get plenty of sunshine.

*Use the grommet spacing on the planter as a guide to install sturdy nails or hooks into the wall, sinking them securely into a stud or other strong support (I used a window sash, for example). Hang the planter on these hooks or nails and heap soil into the pockets, packing it down gently to fill each pocket completely. This planter creates excellent spots for growing small, leafy crops. I recommend that you plant each pocket with a different plant. Fill some with plants that will grow and provide a harvest all summer long, like nasturtiums, salad burnet, and basil, and some with crops that need to be sown throughout the season, like lettuce, arugula, and spinach. This creates an interesting tapestry effect, and the season-long crops keep the planter looking full and vibrant while new crops of greens come in. Plan the layout of crops before you plant, however, and place smaller, shorter crops at the top and taller crops at the bottom, so one level doesn't shade out the one below it.*

# PLANTING HAMMOCK

*Create an instant edible spot with this easy planting pocket. If you're a beginning sewer, this is a great first project! Based loosely on the design of a hammock, this project has minimal sewing but maximum versatility in the garden. It can be hung by S hooks on a chain-link fence or under a low eave or from screws on the side of a wooden raised bed or stockade fence. Deck rails, walls, and windowsills can all be transformed into edible spots with this quick project. Its sturdiness comes from its simple doubled construction. Whether you make one or a dozen, you'll find that hammocks are a fast and easy way to make use of every bit of outdoor space. Their size makes them well suited to growing herbs, salad greens, or small crops like kohlrabi, radishes, and Swiss chard.*

Time: 30 minutes / Cost: $1-$3, depending on the fabric (landscape fabric is cheapest)
Size: 5" high × 10" long

## MATERIALS (FOR 1 HAMMOCK)

20" square of landscape fabric or undyed heavy canvas

100% polyester thread in a matching color

Grommet kit with two ½" brass grommets

## TOOLS

Sewing machine

Straight pins

## DIRECTIONS

1. Sew around all the edges of the fabric square with a zigzag stitch to keep the edges from fraying.

2. Place the square on a flat surface and bring each of the four corners to the center to make a smaller square; pin in place. Sew along the X created by these folds with a wide zigzag stitch, catching all edges as you sew.

3. Place the square on a flat surface with one straight edge at the top and the X edges facing down. Fold the bottom edge up to meet the top edge, creating a rectangle. Pin, then sew across each short end with a straight stitch, about ¼" from the edges, backstitching at each end to secure the thread. Turn the hammock right side out.

4. Install grommets at each upper corner, about 1" diagonally from the corner, following the manufacturer's instructions.

*Using the Planting Hammock: Hang the hammock from the grommet holes using either screws (if installing on a wall, wood fence, or windowsill) or hooks (if on a chain-link fence or an eave). Heap a lightweight potting mix into the pocket and plant either seeds or seedlings of small crops like those suggested above. It is important to keep the hammock well watered, as the relatively small volume of soil can dry out quickly. When watering, use one hand to apply the water and the other to lift and level the hammock so that the water doesn't simply run off. Replant as needed throughout the season.*

# METAL

No welder required! These metal projects use inexpensive, easy-to-work-with metal wire products or lightweight plumbing pipe, not heavy-duty stuff that requires a whole lot of special tools and know-how. All of the materials can be readily found at a hardware or craft store. These projects are lightweight but strong and, more important, very long lasting in the garden. Your investment in time and money will give you projects that will perform for several growing seasons. And in winter, these items can be tidily stowed up in the garage rafters or in an out-of-the-way corner.

There are a few important tips for working with metal in these projects:

⚜ You may wish to wear gloves. A light, flexible leather glove not only provides protection against sharp edges and pointed ends, it also makes the metal easier to handle and work. If you find that leather is too slippery (particularly in the Copper Trellis project), try a knit cotton glove with rubber grip dots.

⚜ Wear old clothes. Metal is frequently oiled for shipping and may be dirty from being stored.

⚜ If you lack hand strength, use needle-nose pliers to fit the components together and make the bends.

⚜ Use true wire cutters. Though most hand pruners are equipped with a wire-cutting notch, you'll want to use proper wire cutters here. The wire for these projects is too heavy to cut neatly with the notch built in most hand pruners.

All three of the following projects are made from noncorrosive materials, so rust will not be an issue. The Copper Trellis will lose its shiny, coppery look with time and will instead sport that lovely bluish green patina.

# COPPER TRELLIS

*The common copper pipes that are used in plumbing installations are far too pretty to be relegated only to walls and basement—bring them out into the garden! Copper plumbing components are relatively inexpensive, convenient to work with, and easy to find at any hardware store—and they happen to hold extensive creative construction possibilities for garden trellises and ornaments. Here I've given instructions for an appealing, versatile, two-way garden trellis, perfect for raised beds that have been outfitted with tube straps to hold the legs securely to the edge. This simple, straightforward design is really just a jumping-off point for the concept and process. If you feel inspired to take this project to the next level or to create your own custom design, go for it! With so many different types of tubes, elbows, tees, and couplings, a determined gardener can craft almost anything from this beautiful, resilient material.*

*You will need to buy one special piece of equipment for this project: a tube cutter. They are quick and easy to use, and you do not need an expensive, professional model; just be sure to select one that was designed for copper and metal pipes.*

Time: 2-3 hours / Cost: About $55 ($65 with a tube cutter) / Size: About 3' wide × 5½' high

## MATERIALS (FOR 1 TRELLIS)

Three ½" copper plumbing pipes, each 10' long

Two ½" copper 90-degree elbows (unthreaded)

Twelve ½" copper tee connectors (unthreaded)

One ½" copper tube cap

Heavy-duty adhesive for metal

Sturdy garden twine or monofilament

## TOOLS

Tape measure

Permanent marker

Cotton swabs

Tube cutter

## DIRECTIONS

1. Using the tape measure and a permanent marker, measure and mark the three 10'-long pipes to create the following pieces:

   ⚜From the first pipe: one 50¼", one 11½", three 10¼", and three 1"

   ⚜From the second and third pipes: a total of seven 1' and seven 1½'

   ⚜Seven 1½'-long pieces

2. Using the tube cutter, cut on each mark: First, place the tube cutter wheel at the mark and spin the cutter around once to score the pipe at the mark. Leaving the

cutter in place, turn down the cutter's screw to keep the cutter in place (but do not turn the screw too tight or you will crimp the pipe). Spin the cutter around the pipe once and then tighten the screw and spin the cutter again—each time you tighten the screw and spin, you cut the pipe a bit deeper. Continue in this manner until the section is cut free; repeat on all marked measurements on all three pipes. Set aside the remaining pipe for another project.

3. Assemble the trellis as shown. For each connection, apply a generous bead of adhesive and use a cotton swab to cover the entire inside of the female connection (the tee or elbow for most of the connections). Let the adhesive set on all pieces before proceeding, following the manufacturer's directions. Work in the following order:

⚓Attach tees to each end of five 1½' pieces.

⚓Attach the 1' pieces to the lower arm of each tee on three of these 1½' pieces.

⚓Attach one tee and one elbow to each end of the remaining two 1½' pieces.

⚓Attach the 50¼" piece to one of the 1½' pieces with the elbow.

⚓Insert the three 1" pieces as shown.

⚓Attach the two 10¼" legs and the 11½" leg.

⚓Assemble the entire trellis, working from the top down, then install the end cap at the top of the middle upright. Let the adhesive set completely before moving the trellis.

*Using the Copper Trellis: This trellis is designed to be used with one side as a frame for taut monofilament or garden twine for tomatoes or pole beans and with cucumber or melon vines climbing the ladderlike rungs of the other side. Since the trellis is relatively crop specific, plan your plantings first and*

*then decide where it should be placed. To install, simply push the legs into the soil as far as they will go. Use your hands or foot to firm the soil around the legs and steady the trellis.*

*The open section is yours to customize as you wish. You can tie in several single strands of twine or monofilament and give each plant its own path to grow up, or you can create a network or grid of twine. It simply depends on how you'd like to fill the space. You can, of course, adapt the directions for the ladder side to entirely redesign the open side, and create your own scheme of tubing to fill the space. I designed the trellis this way to keep costs down and versatility high, but you know what works best for your space and the crops you like to grow.*

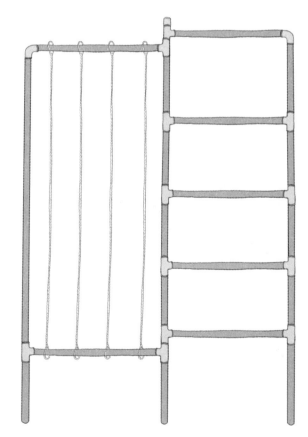

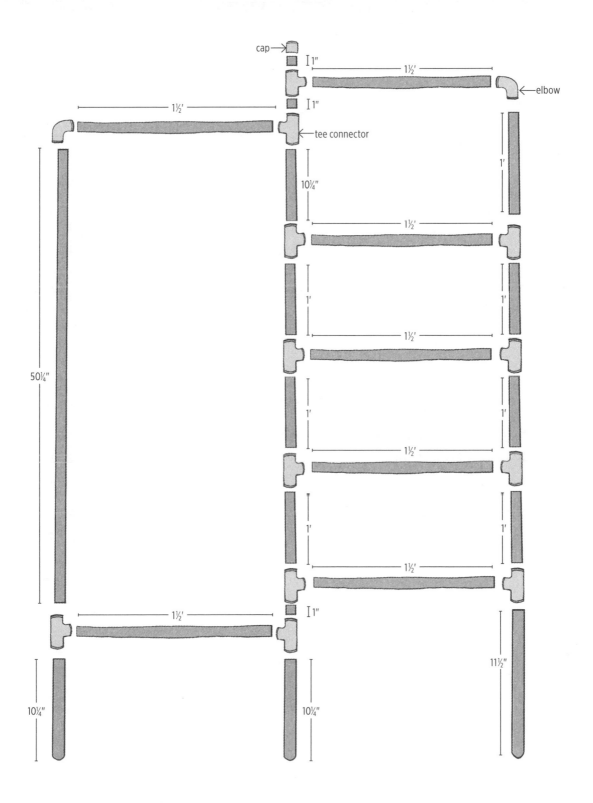

cap →

1"

1½'

← elbow

1"

1½'

tee connector

1'

10¼"

1½'

1'

1'

1½'

1'

1'

1½'

1'

1'

50¼"

1½'

1"

1½'

11½"

10¼"

10¼"

10¼"

# MESH TOWER

Gardeners often use cylindrical towers to grow potatoes, since the towers lend themselves so well to the "hilling" method that encourages maximum production for most potato varieties. But don't think these grow towers are suitable only for potatoes! They're an easy-to-construct, quick-and-dirty container suitable for most any crop or combination of edibles. Summer squash is a particularly good choice for a grow tower because the towers accommodate large plants, and their off-the-ground design makes it easy to scout for the most nefarious summer squash pests—squash bugs and squash vine borers.

I use landscape fabric to line my Mesh Towers; it keeps the soil contained and blocks light from reaching the developing potatoes (which causes them to turn green). I've found that landscape fabric has several advantages over the straw or hay that you may see in other grow tower projects: First, it is more permanent, of course, than straw or hay and can be reused for a few seasons; second, it creates a sleek, good-looking grow tower; and third, straw and hay are messy, are only sold in large bales, and aren't always easy to find.

When shopping for landscape fabric, be sure to choose a nonstretchy fabric instead of plastic landscape sheeting, which will stretch and rip easily if pulled (see the fabric project tips on page 124). And don't be deterred by the teeny bit of hand-sewing required in this project; the landscape fabric is a cinch to sew, and its long-lasting nature makes it more than worth the 15 minutes required to secure the fabric to the wire frame.

Time: About 1 hour / Cost: About $10 for each
Size: 2' high × 2' diameter

## MATERIALS (MAKES 7 TOWERS)

One 50' roll of 2'-high 2" × 4" welded wire mesh

One 50' roll of 2'-wide landscape fabric or weed-block fabric (make sure it is not treated with herbicides)

100% polyester thread

## TOOLS

Tape measure

Two bricks or large stones

Snub-nosed pliers with wire cutter

Scissors

Large sewing needle

**DIRECTIONS (FOR EACH TOWER):**

1. Unroll the wire mesh and measure out a 77″ length, placing bricks on the first edge to keep it from rolling. Using wire cutters, snip the horizontal wires at the point where they meet the next vertical wire. This leaves little "tab extensions" to secure the tower closed. Using bricks or stones for weight, keep the wire mesh flat.

2. Unroll the landscape fabric, then measure and cut one 81″ length with scissors (this leaves a 4″ overlap inside the tower to provide coverage and allow for slight soil bulging). Fold the fabric in half lengthwise.

3. Lay the fabric on top of the wire mesh, aligning the bottom edge of the wire mesh with the bottom edges of the landscape fabric.

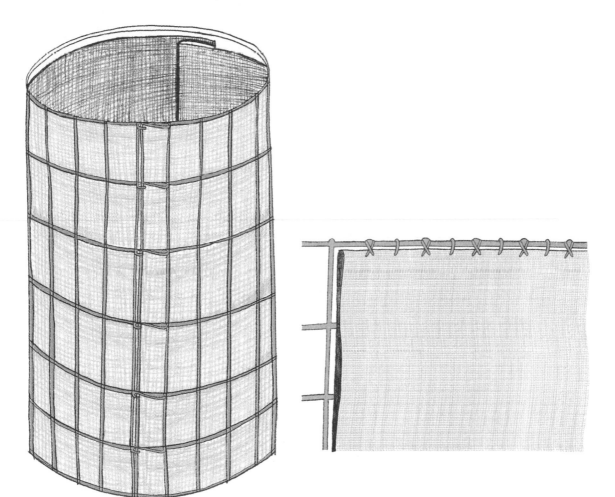

4. Thread the needle with a 30"-long doubled length of thread, and tie a large knot at the bottom. Secure the folded top edge of the landscape fabric to the wire mesh first, making an X out of thread at each wire so that the fabric is secured to all points of each wire intersection. This prevents the fabric from slipping downward. As you near the end of the thread, sew around the last X stitch several times to secure it; cut the thread, leaving a long tail.

5. Continue to sew along the top edge, along each side, and along the bottom to attach the fabric to the wire mesh. The side and bottom edges do not require as secure a connection as the top edge, and the bottom edge can be secured every two wires instead of every wire.

6. Stand the lined wire mesh upright and form it into a cylinder. Bend the "tab extensions" around the adjoining wire mesh edge to secure the cylinder shape, using pliers if necessary.

*Using the Mesh Tower: Place the cylinder in a sunny spot and fill it with at least 8" of a topsoil-and-composted-manure mixture. For potatoes, space seed potatoes evenly over the surface of the soil and then top with an additional 2" to 3" of soil. Water well. The potato plants will begin growing in 7 to 10 days. Once the aboveground growth has reached 10", begin mounding soil around the stem, up to the top 2 or 3 sets of leaves to encourage increased tuber production. Continue mounding until you reach the top of the lined grow tower. Harvest the potatoes 1 week after growth has withered.*

*For other crops, plant and harvest as directed in Chapter 6.*

# TOMATO RING

*If you are growing a tomato as part of a thriller-filler-spiller combination, the sucker-pruning, single-stake method described on page 256 yields the best growing results since it keeps the tomato narrow so there's room for neighbors. However, if you are growing tomatoes as a solo act, this easy, inexpensive grow ring is an excellent way to keep your plants strong, upright, and attractive. Similar to the rings used to keep peonies from flopping over in the flower garden, this DIY version is tailor-made for tomatoes. It is unobtrusive, supportive, requires little effort from the gardener to help keep a plant tamed, and can be made to the exact diameter of a pot for a neat, trim fit.*

Time: 30 minutes / Cost: $8
Size: 16" diameter, height varies with the height of the container and tomato

## MATERIALS (FOR 1 RING)

**Five ½"-diameter bamboo stakes, each 6' long**

**Flat, double-rail wire wreath form to match container width, or 14", 16", or 18" in diameter**

**8 light-duty zip ties**

## TOOLS

**Tape measure**

**Pencil**

**Hand pruners**

**Coping saw (can be purchased for less than $10 at any hardware store)**

## DIRECTIONS

1. Measure the depth of your container and use a pencil to mark this height on four of the bamboo stakes. Measure 24" above this point and mark a second line. Be sure there isn't a node within 1" of the top of the stake;

if there's a node at that spot, you'll need to make adjustments or use another stake. Using hand pruners, cut the stakes at the second line. All four stakes should be identical in length once cut because these will be used for the grow ring legs. (Note: If one end of the bamboo stake is thinner than the other end, cut off the thinnest portion and reserve it for a different use.) Set the legs aside.

2. From the fifth stake, cut two cross pieces to the exact diameter measurement of the wreath form, measuring from outermost wire to outermost wire.

3. Place one grid-work piece under the wreath form at the 12 o'clock and 6 o'clock positions. (If using a box-type wreath form, work on the flat side and place the grid-work piece under the topmost wire.) Lightly secure each end of the bamboo to the wreath form with two crisscrossed zip ties, but do not pull the zip ties tight.

4. Place the remaining grid-work piece on top of the wreath form to form a grid of four quadrants (for a box-type form, place the grid-work piece on top of the uppermost wire). Crisscross two zip ties where the bamboo crosses the wreath form and lightly secure them.

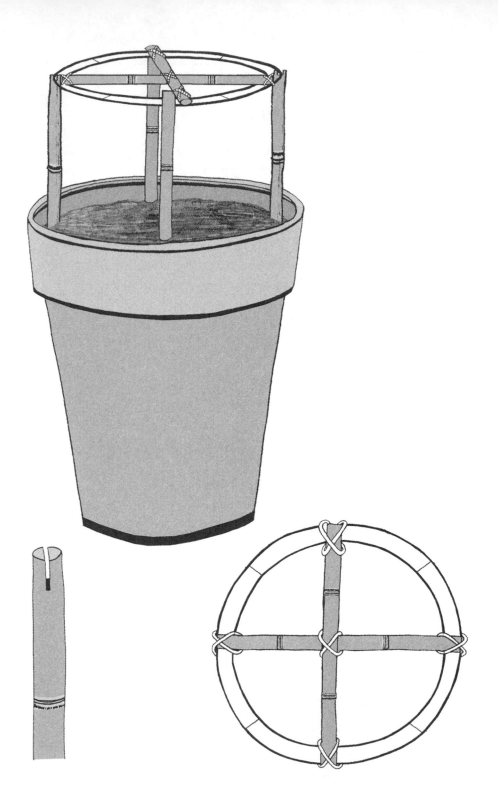

SPOTS & POTS PROJECTS

5. Once the grid-work pieces are evenly spaced, pull the zip ties tightly to secure.

6. To prepare the legs of the grow ring, measure and mark ½" from one end of each leg stake. Use the coping saw to cut a narrow notch into the top end of the stake, barely large enough to accommodate the wire of the wreath form. Cut down to the ½" mark but no farther. It may take only a few strokes of the saw to create the right-size notch; try making one or two strokes at a slight angle to enlarge the notch a bit without making the tip of the stake too thin or cutting too deeply. As you work, check for fit frequently, placing the outermost wire (whether it's a flat form or a box-type form) into the notch. It should fit securely, without much play or looseness. Repeat for the remaining three stakes, trying to make each notch the same depth and width.

*Using the Tomato Ring: Once a tomato plant has reached 12" to 18" high and is planted in a container or raised bed, drive the grow ring legs into the soil at the 12, 3, 6, and 9 o'clock points. Carefully fit the wreath form into the notches, aligning the bamboo grid with the legs if possible. As the tomato plant grows, gently place any errant branches into one of the sections of the grid. Growth will continue up through the grid, and the wire form and bamboo grid will support the stem and branches.*

*You may find that this grow ring is useful for supporting other plants that often need staking, particularly eggplant and bell peppers. In these cases, you may not want the "legs" of the grow ring quite so tall, so simply reduce the measurement between the soil surface and where you cut to account for these shorter plants. Since these crops tend to be a bit smaller over all, you may even be able to use the built-in grid to grow four different varieties in one large pot, training each one through a quadrant of the grid. In this case, you would want to have the grow ring in place when the plants were still quite small, as once they begin branching, it will become more difficult to separate them.*

# CHOOSING A WREATH FORM

The Tomato Ring offers the best support when the diameter of the wreath form matches the diameter of the container you'll use. The grow ring also adapts well to raised beds, in which case you should opt for a 16" or 18" wreath form for each tomato plant.

Wire wreath forms, sometimes called wreath rings, are available at craft stores and floral suppliers. You'll want to look for the flat, "double-rail" form. The "box-type" form, which looks a bit like a rounded Bundt pan, has four concentric rings and is the most common form available. If you can only find the box-type form, you will use it upside down—with the rounded, raised section of wires facing the ground. Flat, double-rail wreath forms may be ordered from mainewreathco.com if you cannot find them locally at a floral or craft supplier.

# WOOD

You don't need an arsenal of woodworking techniques and knowledge to build simple, useful, beautiful items for your garden. The following projects utilize readily available materials (framing lumber and plywood) and common power tools (a drill and circular saw), so they are well within the reach of most reasonably handy homeowners. There are some important woodworking basics that you should know before you begin, however:

- When working with screws, always drill a pilot hole first. A pilot hole is a starter hole that not only helps you to install the screw straight and at the exact right spot but also prevents the wood from splitting. Mark the site of the pilot hole with a pencil, and use a drill bit a size or two smaller than the diameter of the screw. Clamp the two pieces of wood together, or have a helper hold them while you join them.

- Use hardware rated for outdoor use—many nails and screws that are designed for indoor construction will rust outdoors. A good place to shop for appropriate materials is at the deck-building section of your lumberyard, where everything may be a bit more expensive but is rated for outdoor use, conserving your investment of time and money.

- These projects are not about fine carpentry, but it still pays to use some finishing techniques for the most professional result. A bit of sanding may be required, depending on the grade of lumber you purchase. Look carefully over all materials to be sure you are purchasing the best—not all lumber is of equal quality, and it is up to you to select pieces that are free of defects.

- Always measure twice before cutting.

- As any woodworker will tell you, safety is key. Always wear eye and ear protection when sawing or drilling (earplugs and safety goggles can be purchased very inexpensively). Take your time as you work and stay focused to avoid error and injury.

# DECK CORNER SHELF

*If your deck is the most-used part of your home in nice weather, consider making this simple corner shelf to hold more containers—especially herbs for summer meals since they'll be right outside the kitchen door! The shelf fits neatly over the flat railings of any 90-degree corner on your deck, making the perfect perch for a collection of basil, scented geraniums, or edibles in smaller pots.*

*This project does require the use of a power saw to cut the boards. If you don't have the tools or aren't comfortable using them, you may be able to cajole a friend, neighbor, or local carpenter into making the cuts for you. Since one half-sheet of plywood makes exactly four of these nifty shelves, you could always repay your helper with a shelf for his or her own deck!*

Time: 2 hours / Cost: $30 / Size: 2' wide

## MATERIALS (FOR 1 SHELF)

One 2' x 4' sheet ¾" plywood, MDF, or hardboard*

Two 2" x 4" × ½"-thick boards, one 22" long and one 21½" long

One 2" L-shaped metal corner brace with hardware

Eight 1" #6 wood screws

¾"-wide decorative wooden trim, 34" long (optional)

1" finish nails (optional)

Exterior paint or stain (optional)

Four 2½" #6 deck screws (optional)

## TOOLS

Tape measure

Pencil

Power saw

Safety goggles and ear protection

2 bar clamps

Power screwdriver or drill with screwdriver bit

*This plywood sheet will make four shelves total, so multiply other materials as necessary to make the number of shelves you desire.*

## DIRECTIONS

1. On the plywood sheet, measure and mark the 2′ center line. Cut along the line to create two 2′ squares. (Note: Wear safety goggles and ear protection for all cuts.) On one square, mark a diagonal line from corner to corner. Cut along this line to make two equal triangles. You will use one triangle for this project; set aside the remaining triangle and 2′ square.

2. To make the shelf support, abut the two 2″ × 4″ boards with their 4″ ends together at a right angle, then secure with the metal corner brace.

3. Place the shelf on top of the support, and use bar clamps to align the edges and hold it securely. You may wish to test-fit the shelf over your deck railing, making adjustments as necessary. Working from the shelf side

from the ends and spacing the screws evenly along the edges. Remove the bar clamps.

4. If desired, attach the trim to the front edge of the shelf, using finish nails.

5. Paint or stain the shelf, as desired.

6. To hold the shelf in place, use deck screws to attach the support boards to the fence railing, placing two screws on each board, if desired.

*Using the Deck Corner Shelf: Fit the shelf over any 90-degree corner of your deck and create a display with potted plants. This is the perfect place to show off a collection of scented geraniums, herbal topiaries, or tender edibles like bay laurel and small citrus plants. Any pot much larger than 10″ will look out of scale on this shelf, so reserve the shelf for small pots with scented foliage that invite discovery and sampling.*

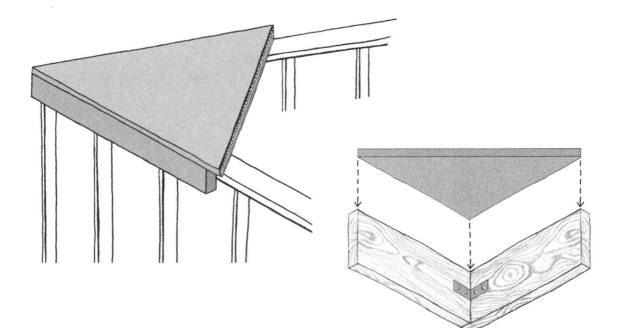

# FENCE NET

*If your edible spot or pot is located near a wood fence, here's a super-simple way to turn it in an asset: Use it to train vining and climbing plants! But don't risk the plants twining over to your neighbors' yard and giving them all your harvest: This net trellis can be attached directly to the fence to keep everything tidily on your side. By using a simple but sturdy wood frame as the basis for the netting, the entire piece can be detached and moved each growing season, allowing you to properly rotate your crops to different parts of your bed. It adds an attractive and useful vertical component to your garden, reminiscent of a lush green wall. The gridlike structure of deer netting not only provides support for naturally climbing plants, it also provides the perfect place to tie the stems of tomatoes, eggplants, or peppers. Just slip a length of twine through the squares and around the stem!*

Time: 30 minutes / Cost: $20
Size: 3' high × 4' long

## MATERIALS (FOR 1 FENCE NET)

**Two 1" × 2" untreated pine or redwood stakes, each 3' long**

**5'-long section polypropylene deer netting, cut to 3' high**

**2 pieces twine**

**Six 2" #6 wood screws**

## TOOLS

**Tape measure**

**Pencil**

**Staple gun and staples**

**Drill with ⁹⁄₆₄" bit and screwdriver bit (Note: This is the recommended bit size for #6 wood screws; if using a different size wood screw, adjust the bit size accordingly.)**

## DIRECTIONS

1. Make three marks on the widest side of each stake: one mark 3" from the top; one mark 3" from the bottom; and one mark in the center, 18" from either end. Fit the drill with the ⁹⁄₆₄" bit and drill holes at each of these sites on both stakes.

2. Measure 6" in from each end along the 5' length of deer netting and mark this point on each edge by loosely tying the twine at the top.

3. Lay the netting on a flat surface and place one stake along the 3' side. Use a staple gun to secure the entire 3'-length of the netting to one flat side of the stake. Wrap the netting around the stake, keeping it tight to the stake (have someone assist you by keeping tension on the other end of the deer netting while you work). When you reach the 6" mark indicated by the twine, stop wrapping but keep tension on the netting. Use the staple gun to secure the netting to one of the wide sides of the stake, stapling through all layers of netting and as many netting

intersections as possible. Staple again on the opposite side of the stake, if desired, or if the netting is a bit loose. Repeat for the second stake and the opposite side of the netting.

4.  Position the constructed fence net against the fence to determine the desired height and location. (Suggestion: Place the fence net about 4" to 6" above the edge of an adjacent raised bed; that's a good height to encourage vigorous vining early in the season and offers great coverage for the net and fence.) Mark the position of the upper two corners with a pencil. Predrill pilot holes in both the stakes and the fence, then screw the fence net to the fence at each of the predrilled holes.

*Using the Fence Net: You may need to do a little finessing to get the plants to grow on the fence, depending on what you've chosen to grow and how high you install the net. If necessary, use short lengths of bamboo or sticks to direct stems toward the fence net until a plant's growth is long enough to vine through the netting on its own or to be tied on to the netting, as in the case of tomatoes. If the deer netting rips and needs repair during or after the season, it can be easily mended or rewoven with a needle and polyester thread.*

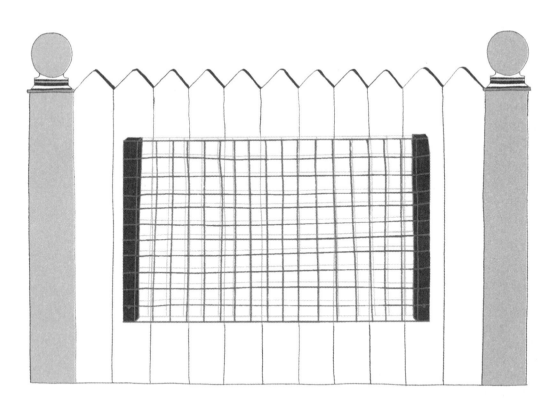

# POT CADDY

*This simple wheeled dolly to move your heaviest containers around the garden or into winter storage is a convenient, hardworking addition to your collection of edible pots. Made from attractive, rot-resistant cedar, this handsome, well-crafted dolly will be as useful for your indoor plants all winter as it will be for your outdoor ones during the growing season.*

Time: 1 hour / Cost: $20-$30, depending on
the quality of the cedar
Size: 18" square × 5" high

**MATERIALS (FOR 1 CADDY)**

One 2" × 6" cedar board, 8' long

Four 2" swivel-plate casters (with brakes, if desired)

3" #8 or #9 decking screws (minimum of 18 screws)

1" wood screws (approximately 16 screws, if the casters do not come with hardware)

**TOOLS**

Pencil

Drill with star bit head (decking screws have a star head)

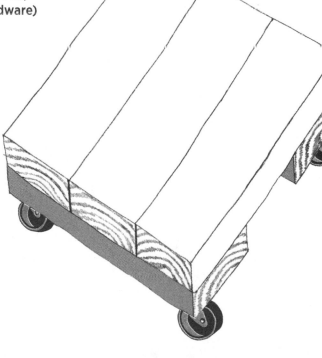

## DIRECTIONS

1. Cut the board (or have it cut at a hardware store) into five 18"-long pieces (there will be one 6" piece left over). On the underside of two pieces, position the caster plates almost to the corners and trace around the plates with a pencil, marking the position of the screw holes. (To determine the underside of a board, look at the ends—if a tree's grow rings are visible, the arcs should point down like a rainbow.)

2. To hide the screw heads and create a neat appearance, the entire caddy will be built from the underside as follows: Lay out the three unmarked pieces horizontally on a work surface to create the upper deck; the underside of the boards should be facing up.

Place the two marked pieces at the side edges, aligning the outer edges of the pieces.

3. Fasten the marked pieces to the upper deck by installing three 3" decking screws in each board, spaced about 2" apart in a zigzag (staggered) pattern; be sure to avoid placing any of the decking screws near the caster plate markings.

4. Install the casters at the previously marked areas, using four 1" wood screws or included hardware for each caster.

*Using the Pot Caddy: By choosing naturally rot-resistant cedar for this project, you can leave it in place under your pot all summer long. It also makes an excellent choice for large, tender plants that you'd like to move indoors for winter.*

# RAISED BEDS

Building your own raised beds lets you determine their materials and dimensions; it also allows you to recycle appropriate materials from other projects, as Chris and Katie did for their raised beds (page 46). Because the basic design and procedure for making raised beds is so simple, there are multiple ways that you can construct them. All have their merits and are about equally as easy to accomplish, so this project is mostly about choosing which corner-joining technique you'll use.

The following instructions describe how to build a basic 2' × 4' raised bed. The 4' sides do not require any sort of cross bracing, and these dimensions allow you to make efficient use of a 12' board (an easy-to-find length). You can, of course, make raised beds to almost any dimension you'd like, though those with sides over 6' long will benefit from a bar installed in the center to prevent bowing. Organic Gardening magazine has excellent instructions for making larger beds, if you're looking for more guidance; see www.organicgardening.com/learn-and-grow/how-to-build-a-raised-bed.

**MATERIALS (FOR 1 BED 2' WIDE × 4' LONG × 10" DEEP)**

One 2" × 10" untreated board, 12' long

**MATERIALS FOR CORNERS (CHOOSE 1 METHOD)**

**For the Corner Posts Method:**

One 2" × 2" untreated furring strip (usually sold in 8' lengths)

3½" #10 corrosion-resistant wood screws (approximately 24 screws)

Bar clamp

**For the L-Shaped Corner Braces Method:**

Eight 4" corrosion-resistant steel L-shaped corner braces

1¼" #6 corrosion-resistant wood screws (approximately 32 screws)

**For the Framing Angle Method:**

Four 7" heavy-duty L-angles for framing

1¼" #9 corrosion-resistant wood screws (approximately 24 screws; quantity depends on model of framing angle)

**TOOLS**

Drill with screwdriver bit

Bar clamp (Corner Posts Method)

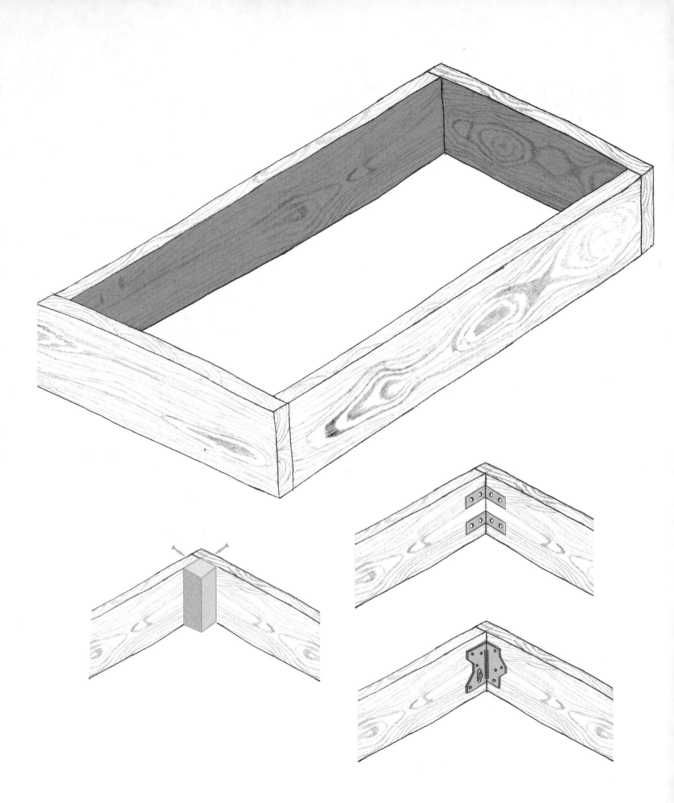

## DIRECTIONS FOR ALL METHODS

1. Cut the board into four pieces: two at 2' long and two at 4' long.

2. Prepare the raised-bed site. Measure out a 2' × 4' flat area and mark the perimeter with a dusting of flour or sawdust; if the area has vegetation growing, cover it with sheets of newspaper or cardboard and water thoroughly.

3. Lay out the boards on the perimeter of the bed. Join the boards to create a raised bed using one of the following methods.

**To use the Corner Posts Method:** Cut the 2" × 2" furring strip into four 10" lengths. Use three of the wood screws to attach one length of furring strip to each edge of the 2'-long boards, placing one screw near the top, one at the center, and one near the bottom. Match the corner of one of the 4'-long boards to the furring strip, abutting the corners of that piece and the 2'-long piece. Use a bar clamp to secure the pieces together, then join them with three wood screws; be sure to slightly offset the placement of the screws. Repeat for the three remaining corners.

If you wish to make your beds deeper than 10", simply plan to add another course of 2" × 10" boards. For the corner posts, just cut furring strips or 2" × 4" boards to match the bed depth.

**To use the L-Shaped Corner Braces Method:** Use two corner braces for each inside corner of the raised bed. Mark the placement of the braces, placing one about 1" from the top and one 1" from the bottom on each raised bed piece. Attach the raised-bed sides using wood screws. Join together each corner completely before moving on to the next corner.

**To use the Framing Angle Method:** First, a little background: Framing angles are found in the deck-building section of lumberyards. These heavy-duty metal pieces are used to join 90-degree angles on outdoor decks because they are strong, weather resistant, inexpensive, and easy to install. The only caveat is that they should be used with corrosion-resistant fasteners, which cost a bit more than typical wood screws. Framing angles work well on 10" or shallower beds, since this size bed requires only one framing angle per corner.

Center and install a framing angle on each inside corner, using wood screws and alternating which side of the brace you work on to keep the corners together snugly and to prevent slipping. Join together each corner completely before moving on to the next corner.

*Using Raised Beds: For terrific ideas for planting crops in raised beds, see page 65.*

# Raised Bed Extras

Before filling the bed with soil, you may wish to make one or more of these convenient adaptations for added protection or versatility:

☼ **Pest control:** Line the wooden raised bed with wire mesh to protect crops from digging and burrowing animals. The animal may attempt to dig in from the side but will be unable to actually access the roots of your crops. Cut a 3' × 5' piece of hardware cloth or chicken wire. Bend up the edges about 6" and maneuver the mesh into the raised-bed box, making adjustments to the bends as necessary. Press the mesh to the bottom of the box and use a staple gun to attach it.

☼ **Fancy finishes:** Install a cap on the upper edges of the raised bed. Attach a length of untreated 1" × 6" board at a right angle to any or all of the edges of your raised beds with 2½" #6 wood screws. This provides a shelf for tools or harvested crops and can give your beds a more finished look. If you're confident in your woodworking skills, make handsome mitered corners.

☼ **Versatile hardware:** Install several tube straps (semicircular metal brackets used to secure plumbing pipes to walls) along the inside edges of your bed, using galvanized wood screws. These can hold stakes for training plants or, if positioned directly across from one another in a series of several tube straps, they can be fitted with heavy wires or flexible plastic piping to make arcing hoops for supporting row covers, heavy mil plastic, or frost blanket to exclude pests or extend the season. Tube straps can also be used to anchor lengths of string from bean poles or other trellises. Add tube straps when they're needed; it is not imperative to have these in place before filling the bed with soil.

☼ **Irrigation hookup:** By building your own hose outlet with readily available plumbing parts, you can easily give each of your raised beds its own drip irrigation system or soaker hose. Simply hook each up to your main hose and leave it to run as necessary. Use ¾"-diameter components and assemble them as shown, covering all threads with Teflon tape (a nonsticky plastic film available in the plumbing section that prevents leaks on threaded pipes). The swivel adapter makes it possible for you to connect your main hose without twisting it—you twist the swivel end of the adapter instead of the hose to attach it. Attach the irrigation hookup to the upper corner of the raised bed closest to your water source, using two ¾" tube straps placed at the bend of each elbow and screwed into the side of the raised bed.

☼ **Mailbox tool storage:** Purchase an inexpensive horizontal wall-mount mailbox and affix it to one side of your raised bed, using heavy-duty screws for maximum strength. Store tools and supplies to keep things handy.

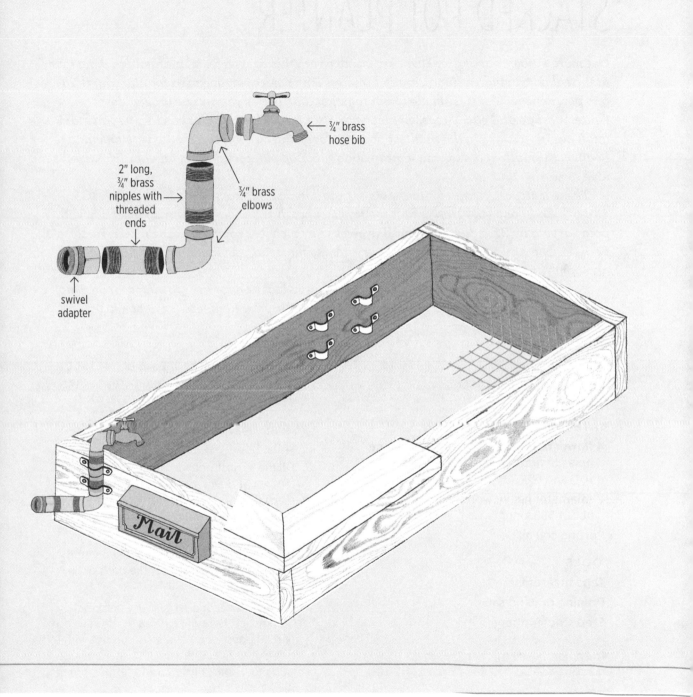

¾" brass
hose bib

2" long,
¾" brass
nipples with
threaded
ends

¾" brass
elbows

swivel
adapter

*Mail*

# STACKED POT PLANTER

*Get more edibles out of a small, narrow space with this easy vertical planter. Stacking four identical pots in increasingly small diameters lends more surface area for planting than one pot alone would! It is simple to put together and, better yet, can be broken down for winter storage and easily reassembled year after year. This design aims to give you maximum planting space in the smallest possible footprint, but you can create versions that begin with smaller pots to create interesting tabletop planters or gifts for your friends who love to garden and cook.*

*These instructions call for four pots in graduated sizes, starting at 18" (18", 14", 10", and 6"). An 8" pot will also work for the topmost pot. If you wish, you can do a version with pots varying by 2" in diameter, but this gives you much less room for planting. Terra-cotta pots work best, but the planter will work with any material provided the pots are identical and come in a wide range of sizes.*

*You'll need to construct the planter in its desired location for the growing season. Due to the weight of the pots and soil, the planter cannot be moved unless it's deconstructed.*

Time: 30 minutes / Cost: $50
Size: Variable

## MATERIALS (FOR 1 PLANTER)

4 flower pots with 1"-diameter drainage holes in graduated sizes, such as 18", 14", 10", and 6"

1"-diameter heavy wooden broom handle, about 55" long*

Potting soil mix

## TOOLS

Tape measure

Pruning or hand saw

Step stool (optional)

*\*The broom handle must fit through the flower pot drainage holes.*

## DIRECTIONS:

1. Measure the height of each pot and add the numbers together to determine the length of broom handle necessary for the project. Cut the broom handle to this length, leaving its rounded or finished end intact.

2. Fill the largest pot with the potting soil, tamping it down as you work. When you reach the top of the planter, water it well, let it drain, and water again. Add more soil to fill to within 1½" of the container rim.

3. Drive the broom handle into the center of the pot, fitting its end into the pot's drainage hole.

4. Thread the second-largest pot onto the broomstick, letting it rest on the soil surface of the largest pot. Fill the second pot with soil, water it, let it drain, and water again. Add more soil if necessary to form a firm, full base.

# STACKED POT PLANTER RECIPE

This project is perfect for planting with the thriller-filler-spiller method described in Chapter 5; just use smaller-scale plants. Try mixing and matching these crops throughout all of the tiers of the planter for a wild, jubilant "birthday cake" effect that is sure to get all of your friends and neighbors talking. As a bonus, all of these crops are delicious in salads (or dressings), so they will be as useful as they are beautiful. Choose from these thrillers: spinach, arugula, lettuce, or Greek basil; and fillers: cilantro, saltwort, chamomile, or chervil; and spillers: nasturtium, Johnny-jump-up, or thyme.

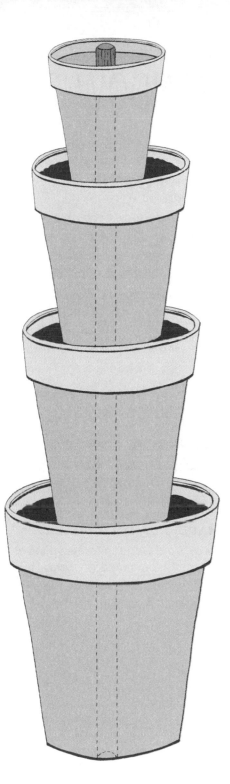

5. Repeat for the third and fourth pots, filling with soil and watering well. If desired, use the step stool to fill the pots as the planter gets higher.

*Using the Stacked Pot Planter: The planter is best suited for growing salad greens, herbs, and edible flowers, either grown from seeds or transplanted as young plants. The narrow planting bands will make it difficult for fruit-bearing crops to grow and produce well. Have an extra pot handy when planting to hold the excess soil you remove to install the plants. Be aware that because clay is so porous, the pot tower may take a bit more watering than you would expect. Water each tower pot carefully to avoid washing out soil onto the pot below. Use a watering wand with a breaker or rose and a very gentle stream. As the soil stabilizes over the growing season, this will become less of an issue.*

# WINDOW-FRAME TRELLIS

*Do you brake for garage sales and thrift stores? If so, keep an eye out for old wooden window frames for this quirky yet functional trellis and garden accent. All it takes is two or three same-size window frames that have lost their glass plus a few hinges and a power screwdriver.*

*Two windows become a versatile trellis that can be installed either vertically or horizontally in a raised bed, perfect for keeping cucumbers and other vines off the ground. A two-window trellis can even be used horizontally in early spring, covered in plastic or frost fabric, to create a small shelter in the garden. Three windows make a dramatic focal point in a raised bed and can form a support or a backdrop for an exuberant mix of edibles. The three-window version could even find a home among an array of containers, winding its way around pots of vining plants to keep them off the ground so the plants are easier to harvest and appreciate. In either case, the trellis will fold away neatly for storage over winter so you can stash it in the garage or basement.*

Time: 1½ hours / Cost: Varies based on the windows you purchase; expect to spend about $10 for hardware and other tools to complete the project / Size: Variable

## MATERIALS (FOR 1 TRELLIS)

2 or 3 old wooden frame windows with muntin bars (and with glass removed)

3"–3½" inexpensive door hinges or broad utility hinges with hardware*

## TOOLS

Wire brush

Pencil

Power screwdriver

*\*Two windows need two hinges; three windows will need four hinges. For shutters (see opposite page), substitute an equal quantity of 1"–1½" narrow utility hinges.*

## DIRECTIONS

1. Working on a tarp or concrete surface, scrape the window frames vigorously with a wire brush to remove any excess paint or varnish flakes. You do not need to strip them to bare wood, but there should not be any loose, flaking chips that could fall onto the soil and contaminate your bed. Do not compost the paint chips and shavings. Because of the risk that chips may contain lead paint, follow your county's regulations for proper disposal.

2. Determine the placement of the hinges. This will depend on the size of your windows, but they should be positioned approximately 3" from each end. Hold the hinge plate to the side of the window and trace its outline.

3. Using the power screwdriver, place the hinge plate on the first window and install screws in the holes on that side of the hinge. Repeat for the second hinge.

4. Align the second window next to the first window and mark the placement of the

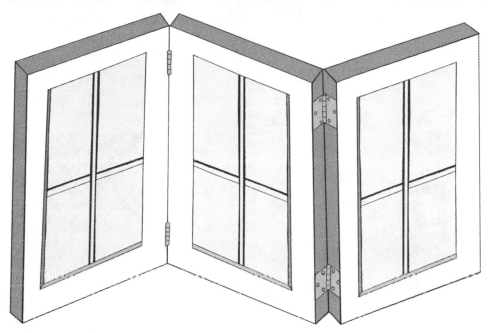

hinge plate. Install screws in the upper and lower hinges.

5. If you are including a third window, you can position the hinge on the second window facing out or in to create a zigzag or a triptych effect (zigzag shown above).

*Using the Window Frame Trellis: Place the finished project in a raised bed, nestling the window frame into the soil and firming the soil around the frame with your hands or foot. Some additional settling will occur naturally. Depending on the spacing of the window muntins, your plants may need help growing through the piece to your satisfaction. Pull stems through the bars to encourage them to wind around and, if necessary, use monofilament (like fishing line) to help the plant reach the height or position you'd like.*

# TAILOR YOUR TRELLIS

This simple stand-up trellis can inspire the crafter, designer, and recycler in you! Wooden shutters upcycled from a remodeling project indoors or out are perfect for this project. Many architectural salvage yards offer shutters, too, allowing you to mix and match shutter styles for an eclectic trellis. This project is so versatile that you can attach as many shutters as you'd like to create a multihinged trellis, and you can even feature shorter shutters on each end to give the trellis a step-up design. For best results, choose shutters with real slats so vines can pass through the slats as they grow.

When shopping for windows, be sure they have crossbars, known as muntins, for the best support for climbing plants and the most interesting presence in the garden. If they do not, you can make crossbars by hot-gluing heavy twigs, small branches, or even bamboo stakes into the channel routed out of the frame.

## chapter five

# THRILLER, FILLER, &
# SPILLER COMBINATIONS

If gardening for you is more about the nitty-gritty than the pretty-pretty, you're not alone. Most gardeners, and certainly vegetable gardeners, don't spend a lot of time thinking about garden design: They simply plant what they like in the spot best suited to the plant's needs. The words garden design seem to imply that people need esoteric knowledge about a passel of theories on color, form, and composition to do it right. Hogwash! Garden design is based on a few simple principles that even veggie gardeners can readily apply to their containers and raised beds to improve both looks and yields. The trick lies in using this nifty little rhyme as a scheme for putting together plant combinations: thriller, spiller, and filler.

This idea has been popular since 1997, when writer and designer Steve Silk introduced the concept in *Fine Gardening* magazine. He outlined a method of creating jaw-dropping container combinations by choosing plants for three distinct growth habits: a thriller, the dramatic, center-of-attention plant; a filler, a spreading plant that plays off the thriller and helps create the overall shape; and a spiller, a plant to peek over the edge of the pot and extend the visual effect of the planting downward. The results of this type of plant composition are so dramatic and satisfying, it's hard to believe that they can be simple to attain. Ornamental gardeners embraced this guideline and have been practicing it ever since, but for some reason, vegetable gardeners have not yet made it their own. To understand how the thriller-filler-spiller method applies to edibles, let's look deeper at each role.

# THE SIMPLE SECRET TO PERFECT PLANT PAIRINGS

**The thriller-filler-spiller concept** is an excellent way to combine vegetable plants and is especially well suited to gardening in both containers and raised beds. It offers aesthetic, practical, and productivity benefits, such as:

## NO GUESSWORK!

The thriller-filler-spiller formula shows you how, why, and where to place vegetable plants—easy enough for everyone.

## FOR ANY SIZE GARDEN!

These plant combinations work in any size pot or raised bed.

## BE CREATIVE!

Dozens and dozens and dozens of vegetables, herbs, and edible flowers work in these combos.

## HEALTHY GROWING CONDITIONS!

The mixed heights of the plants allow light to reach all plants in the combination, meaning less disease and more air circulation and fewer pests, too—you'll be able to spot potential issues faster.

## BIRD, BUTTERFLY, AND BENEFICIALS MAGNET

The diversity of the plants' habits attract nature to your garden for seeds and pest control.

## BEAUTY BEYOND COMPARE

The variety of heights, textures, and colors mean magazine-worthy combinations right in your backyard.

# THRILLERS

The thriller element is the main event. It is the anchor of each combination, the centerpiece and focal point, the movie star, the drama queen, the main attraction. It is almost always the largest plant, but size alone does not necessarily make a plant a thriller. This centerpiece plant contributes other qualities as well—bold or interesting foliage, brightly colored fruit, or a striking overall form. These plants tend to be upright, tall, and expressive.

The thriller element is one that can typically stand on its own, needing neither spiller nor filler to make a statement. Its dramatic presence is enough to easily carry an entire container. Or it could be used along with a spiller, which can act as a groundcover to help conserve water and can set off the thriller through its contrasting color in foliage or flowers. Think about a few burgundy okra plants surrounded by some gold-leaved sweet potato vines as an example—no filler required for that fabulous combination!

## Try a Thriller

*Good edible thriller plants include:*

TOMATOES

BEANS OR MALABAR SPINACH
GROWING ON A TRIPOD

ARTICHOKES

ROSEMARY GROWING AS A TOPIARY

OKRA

Typically, there will be only one thriller per container, though the thriller may consist of multiple individual plants, as would be the case for beans and okra.

The thriller is the best place to start when putting together a combination. As it is the largest element, the thriller you choose for each planting will determine how much space is required in the raised bed or what size container is needed to accommodate the plants. It also dictates the filler and spiller that will best pair with it, whether based on color, habit, or size.

# FILLERS

Though "filler" sounds like a dull, workaday role for a plant to play, its presence can make the difference between a merely interesting container and a dynamic one. The filler is the supporting cast to the thriller's star player, giving the main attraction something to play against and helping to minimize any of its flaws. It makes the thriller look even better by adding substance to a combination and tieing together all the elements. It is a bit of an unsung hero and easy to write off, but a well-chosen filler makes the difference between a combination that sings and one that merely hums.

What makes a good filler plant, then? It's one that offers interesting foliage or fruit and has a spreading habit so that it grows in multiple directions, broadening its impact across the whole combination. Because it must grow wide and with an open habit, the filler tends to be a quite productive member of each group. It should provide as much foliage and branching as possible.

In addition, most herbs tend to be fillers, not only because they aren't quite as showy as vegetables but also because their leafy good looks and spreading habit make them perfect for the role.

Most combinations look best if you use more than a single filler—either multiple plants of the same type or perhaps two or three different kinds of plants. For example, you could put together a combination in which a large bell pepper was the thriller and a few small hot pepper varieties and some cilantro plants functioned as fillers. Filler is the most abstract of the three roles, so it's a bit difficult to generalize as you can for thriller and spiller. On the other hand, it isn't exactly a catch-all category, as good filler plants provide much-needed form, volume, and color to a combination.

By definition, filler plants aren't used on

## Find a Filler

*Good edible fillers are:*

BEETS

CARROTS

EGGPLANT

PEPPERS

PEAS

their own. That's because a filler automatically becomes a thriller when there are no other plants in the container or bed.

## SPILLER

The spiller in a combination is like the perfect accessory—the right shoes or scarf that turns a good-looking outfit into something that gets not just noticed but remembered. To be a spiller, the plant must break over the edge of the container to some degree, where it does the important jobs of softening any hard lines in your raised bed or container, extending the visual impact of the combination toward the ground plane, and making the view of the garden more about plants than about the vessel they're in. Even stunningly beautiful containers and raised beds benefit from the use of spillers to accentuate their best features and mitigate their hard, unyielding nature. Of all three elements, spillers are the hardest to find as edibles, although some crops are obviously vinelike and perfectly suited to spiller roles.

Because many spillers consume lots of space, it can be difficult to pair them with other plants. And considering the rather limited selection of edible spillers to choose from, you may question just how many cucumber or sweet potato vines you really want to grow in the first place. As an alternative, think creatively: Look for a crop that has a particular variety bred for a prostrate or weeping habit and make that your spiller.

### Spot a Spiller

*Good plants for the spiller role include:*

BEANS

CUCUMBERS

MELONS AND PUMPKINS (both better suited to raised beds than containers)

SWEET POTATOES

THYME

*Specific crop varieties with a spiller habit are:*

TRAILING TOMATOES, LIKE 'TUMBLING TOM'

PROSTRATE ROSEMARY

TRAILING OR VINING NASTURTIUM (you'll find this info on the seed packet)

Because most spillers tend to be large plants that require a lot of water to produce a crop, you may not be able to accommodate more than one per pot. To get the most impact from your spiller plants, separate the individual vines when they are young to encourage them to grow in different directions so you achieve better coverage.

Choose spillers based on the amount of

space you have to give them and for their color and leaf form. Try to select spillers that accentuate the surrounding plants and also look good against the container or raised bed, because spillers have the most visual interaction with the colors and textures of pots and bed materials. And of course, make your decisions based on crops you like to eat—if you don't much care for sweet potatoes, there's little sense in planting a bunch of them solely because they are such an excellent spiller plant!

Spillers can readily be used by themselves and are especially effective in hanging baskets.

The roles of thriller, filler, and spiller have clear characteristics that work together to create amazing designs. However, the roles are not set in stone for each plant: Each plant changes and functions differently if used on its own. Other factors can change a plant's role as well, especially that of scale: the size of your container or raised bed relative to the size of your plants. Small pots allow smaller plants to become thrillers. For example, in a 12-inch pot, a purple basil, which would be more of a filler in a large pot, functions as a thriller; parsley could be planted around to act as a filler; and nasturtium placed at intervals could be a spiller. The largest plant in a planting becomes the thriller by default.

The way a plant has been or will be treated can also make a difference. For example, if shiso (also known as perilla; see the plant encyclopedia in Chapter 6) is pinched back, it will branch out and form an excellent filler. But if it is allowed to grow upward, it may take on a thriller role. Similarly, plant variety can affect its function. Rosemary is a good example: You can choose from strongly upright varieties; rounded,

well-branched types; and prostrate or trailing types. Each one of these can fill a different role, but the upright type cannot become a spiller, nor can the prostrate type become a thriller. The plant encyclopedia, starting on page 217, notes where multiple varieties of a plant may influence its role.

# LAYOUT CONSIDERATIONS

When planting a thriller-filler-spiller combination, the natural inclination is to plant one in front of the other so that the tall plant is in the back, the medium-height plant is in the middle, and the low grower is in front. In most cases, that makes sense. But you'll find that you can vary their placement to devise a more effective combination—for both aesthetic and habit purposes.

## Raised Beds

The thriller-filler-spiller formula was invented as a way to create ornamental container combinations, and it is easiest to understand the principle within the limits of a pot. But thriller-filler-spiller recipes translate to raised beds just as well, because raised beds are ultimately very large containers. Designing raised beds with this method can be approached in two ways: arranged as one entire large-scale combination, or subdivided into convenient, appropriately sized sections with different thrillers, spillers, and fillers for each part. For example, in a 4 × 8-foot raised bed, you could place three tomato plants in the center and intersperse those with bold zucchini plants, well-branched basil, a few patches of carrots, and some dill plants randomly sown throughout. Then you gussy up the edge of the bed with lemon balm and nasturtiums planted to tumble along and over the rim.

On the other hand, you could choose three different thrillers—say, a tomato plant, a big tepee of beans, and an artichoke plant—and surround each one with fillers and spillers selected to work with the specific characteristics of each different thriller.

The following plans for raised beds designed with the thriller-filler-spiller method are presented as individual combinations for a roughly 2 × 2-foot space. These can be repeated as many times as space will allow across your raised beds, or you can mix them within a raised bed, as described above. Either way, you can be assured of an attractive planting that maximizes the available light and space for the best possible results.

## Containers

Sure, it's much easier to plan thriller filler spiller combinations within containers, but you still have important decisions to make. One is how you will place the plants within the container. The thriller doesn't necessarily have to be smack in the middle—it can be set off to any edge, the other plants nestled around it. The primary factors in determining the overall composition are the habit of the thriller plant (for example, summer squash doesn't make a good central plant; it's much better off to the side of a container), the other plants you're combining with the thriller, and the direction from which the finished arrangement will be viewed. Containers seen from all directions

# A Note About Salad Greens

Arugula, spinach, and lettuce are popular crops that are a bit difficult to characterize within the thriller-filler-spiller theme, for several reasons. One, they are typically ephemeral, ceding to more heat-loving plants once the weather warms. Two, they are low growing and clump forming—far from thrillers, possibly working as fillers, or even verging into spiller territory if they are planted near the edge of a container and allowed to droop over the side.

They are also difficult to pair with other plants because of the way they are best harvested—simply cut down with scissors. If other plants are mixed in, you must snip the greens carefully to avoid snipping the neighbors, which needlessly complicates harvesting. The best way to design with salad greens is to give them their own pot, let them be productive in their season, and then turn the space over to a more summery combination. If you want to experiment with combining greens (sometimes, the shade provided by neighboring plants can prolong their harvest), plan to use them as fairly dense, nonspreading fillers, and expect to devote extra care to harvesting them than you would in a dedicated planting.

generally look best when the thriller is centered and the supporting cast is arrayed evenly around it so that the composition is the same all the way around. Containers nestled against a wall or in a grouping of other containers will be viewed only from one side. They don't need to look their best from every direction.

Container size is another determining factor in putting together your combinations. A very large container (more than 24 inches) can successfully host a fabulous combination of a large zucchini plant, a clump of dill and/or fennel, and perhaps a single sweet potato vine, but attempting to use such large, demanding plants in a smaller container would be a watering nightmare and would limit the productivity of all three. On the other hand, a smaller container could host a thriller-filler-spiller combination of more compact plants, like an eggplant, a kohlrabi, and marjoram. The container recipes that follow are organized by medium and large containers. These are suggestions that demonstrate how to combine plants beautifully and successfully. I hope that you will be inspired to adapt these ideas in new ways for your own crops, containers, and personal tastes!

# COMPANION PLANTING

The thriller-filler-spiller formula is an example of companion planting—placing plants in close proximity to gain some kind of benefit. In this method, we rely on the complementary physical characteristics of different plants to help maximize sunlight and air circulation, to encourage beneficial insects and discourage bad ones (or at least make them easier to spot

and manage), and to look better than more random combinations of plants. Another example of companion planting that capitalizes on plants' physical attributes is the Native American "three sisters" method, which is a sort of thriller-filler-spiller method itself: Corn is the thriller; squash is the filler, planted around the base and shading the roots of the corn; and pole beans are the spiller, growing up the cornstalk and along the ground. The benefits of these types of companion plantings are obvious and readily identifiable, as we can see how the plants' natural sizes and habits work well together.

Not all companion planting is equal, however. A lot of information online and in old books asserts that pairing certain plants together can result in increased production, better flavors, and protection from pests or diseases. These sources also claim that some plants are natural "enemies" and, if planted together, both will suffer. While these old adages are quirky and interesting, it is important to note that despite controlled studies, no scientific evidence backs up most of this folklore. In fact, science has disproven some oft-repeated companion planting advice, such as that marigolds deter nematodes. (A very few varieties of marigold are capable of controlling a very few varieties of nematodes, but simply planting any marigold in an effort to deter nematodes is unlikely to have an effect.)

In contrast, there are scientifically proven situations in which plants cannot be grown in combination due to the form of chemical competition known as allelopathy. Allelopathic plants exude a chemical from their roots to deter the growth of neighboring plants. The best-known example of an allelopathic plant is the black walnut tree, which secretes juglone, a chemical that interferes with many plants' respiratory abilities. The black walnuts on their property are what caused Chris and Katie (page 46) to begin raised-bed gardening at their home. There are very few proven allelopathic interactions between edible plants, and any that do exist primarily affect nonedible species and so are not likely to be a problem in your garden.

Beliefs about "friendly" garden companions are largely anecdotal, deriving from a desire to personify plants so we can better understand them. These beliefs imply that merely planting two specific types of vegetables together is the silver bullet that will solve your pest problems or negate the need to fertilize. This simply isn't true. If, for example, cabbage moths were as deterred by the presence of mint nearby as the old adages claim, we wouldn't have nearly as many cabbageworms or moths—yet most gardeners have no shortage of either in season! While there is little harm in following most of the advice if it appeals to you, I do not recommend avoiding or constantly repeating certain plant combinations solely out of superstition.

## MAINTAINING YOUR COMBINATIONS

Anytime you plant edibles in close proximity to one another, you increase maintenance requirements to some degree. Thriller-filler-spiller combinations will usually require more water and fertilizer than would each of the three plants grown in single plantings, because

# SUMMER BRAISED VEGETABLES

Inspired by a recipe that my husband's grandmother made frequently, we affectionately call this dish Miriam's Zucchini. It's a simple, healthy, and delicious combination that makes a great side dish for a barbeque or as a summer lunch when eaten with bread. It's also a good way to use small amounts of many vegetables.

½ red bell pepper (or whole cherry pepper), cut as finely as possible
2–5 cloves garlic, finely chopped
2 tablespoons olive oil
4–6 cups mixed summer vegetables (zucchini, thinly sliced; okra, cut in half if large; green beans, halved if large; eggplant, cut into bite-size pieces; bell peppers, cut into strips; and corn, stripped from the ear)
Several fresh tomatoes, chopped into ½-inch pieces, or 8 ounces canned tomatoes or canned tomato sauce
3 tablespoons water
Juice from ½ lemon

In a large pot, saute the pepper and garlic in the olive oil until softened and very fragrant. Add the mixed vegetables and stir to coat (if using corn, add in the last 3 to 5 minutes of cooking). Add the tomatoes and stir. Add the water and lemon juice. Cook over medium-low heat, with the lid slightly ajar, for 20 to 30 minutes, until the vegetables are very tender but not falling apart. If necessary, cook without the lid to reduce the sauce to a stewlike consistency. Enjoy hot, warm, or at room temperature.

the soil volume is shared by the roots of three (or more) plants, all competing for moisture and nutrients. However, you will be rewarded with three different crops to harvest out of a small amount of space.

Though the three different plant habits are perfectly complementary in their heights and spread, maintaining optimum growing conditions for all of them may require a bit of help from you now and then. You may need to perform some strategic leaf pruning, trellising, or staking (see page 256) to keep plants in proportion with one another and to curtail especially enthusiastic growers that might outpace their companions. This maintenance will depend on your weather, the soil, and even the variety of plant you've chosen; it can be as simple as physically moving a branch in the direction you'd like it to grow or removing a leaf here and there when it is blocking a neighboring plant.

Finally, some plants grown in combination will mature faster than their neighbors and thus get harvested or bolt or otherwise start to look poor in comparison. The best way to maintain an attractive, productive combination is to sow new seed, or perhaps transplant something from another bed or container. Keep a supply of seeds handy to fill in gaps. You can also pop ornamentals or houseplants in empty spots to keep up the full, lush, appearance.

## USING YOUR HARVEST

By planting in combination, you get a lot of beauty and variety from a small space, but you don't get the kinds of enormous yields that require all-day canning and freezing marathons. For some, that may be a good thing, but for oth-

ers, harvesting vegetables just a few at a time can present some challenges for meal planning.

When I plan my garden, I always plant multiples. These thriller-filler-spiller recipes are guidelines and suggestions, and I encourage you to mix and match elements so you'll have plenty of your favorite crops spread over several containers. For example, I use collard greens and kale in at least a dozen different containers so my husband and I can enjoy about two harvests a week during the peak season.

Even when you have just a few okra, zucchini, peppers, beans, or eggplant ready for harvest, you still have lots of opportunities to use them. I use small harvests in the following ways:

**Refrigerate:** Store a small harvest in the fridge until the plants produce more. Most fresh-picked vegetables will keep for at least 5 days or so. Look to the grocery store aisles for the best way to store different crops, such as keeping vegetables misted or in a plastic bag.

**Small plates:** Use them in recipes (see page 171) that require small amounts. A few of my favorites include:

- Thai curries. Purchase a can of curry paste and a can of coconut milk at your local Asian grocery, along with your favorite meat or tofu, and cook according to package directions. Add vegetables in any amounts.

- Stir-fries or fried rice. These classic refrigerator-cleanout meals can be garden cleanout meals, too.

- Pasta. Let's face it, is there anything that isn't delicious with pasta?

**Single-serve sides:** When there's just a teeny harvest, serve each person a different vegetable or offer a lazy Susan of veggies Chinese restaurant–style.

# CONTAINER RECIPES
## *for Large Pots*

Though large pots and the considerable volume of soil they require constitute a significant investment, they are an important component of your edible pots collection. It takes at least this much space to successfully grow the large crops that are the reason so many of us garden in the first place, like tomatoes and summer squash. Large pots are also the only way to have enough space left over to create these combinations and still get a sizeable harvest out of all of the crops. Plus, big containers make a welcome presence in the garden, keeping your arrangements from feeling too scattered and bitsy. Any type of container that is at least 16 inches in diameter qualifies as a large pot; 18-inch diameter is ideal for most of the following recipes. Try to amass a selection of shapes and depth to keep your garden interesting and unique.

# CUCUMBER LOVERS ONLY

It's easy to grow cucumbers in a container if you give them a fertile environment and plenty of water. Start this combination in spring by sowing salad burnet in a horseshoe shape around the edge. Its delicious cucumber-watermelon foliage will tide you over until temperatures are warm enough to plant cucumber seed. In the meantime, sow a few seeds of purple shiso, a delicious and unusual herb that looks beautiful with its companions and, when shredded, makes a tasty addition (and gives a rosy tinge) to cucumber salads and pickles. Finally, when it is warm enough, build and place a Bamboo Ladder Trellis (page 116), then sow the cucumber seed.

### THRILLER
*Cucumber on a trellis*

Be sure to select a vining type like 'Garden Oasis'.

### FILLER
*Purple shiso*

Use shiso in pickles, in home-brewed iced tea, shredded on hot cooked rice, or even in flower arrangements.

### SPILLER
*Salad burnet*

The delicate leaves of this plant are a welcome contrast to the coarse cucumber foliage.

# LOW RIDER

Most thriller plants get tall. Not so with summer squash, which stays low and wide. Its large, attractive foliage makes this plant a definite thriller, however, and it's a nice way to add interest to low, wide containers and contrast with taller neighbors. Pair it with trailing rosemary (if only for summer) on the sides and leave a patch open in the front for cilantro seeds, which you can sow at intervals through the season and harvest frequently and easily while the herb is still tender and mild. The heavy watering that summer squash needs may improve the flavor of rosemary by making the pungently piney herb taste slightly milder.

 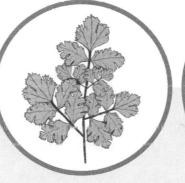

### THRILLER
*Summer squash*

'Ronde de Nice' is a productive, compact choice.

### FILLER
*Cilantro*

Sow a few fresh seeds every 2 weeks or so.

### SPILLER
*Trailing rosemary*

This plant readily tolerates the excess water needed by the summer squash as long as the soil is well drained.

# POTLUCK

You're in luck when you grow a small cascading tomato like the popular 'Tumbling Tom'—this variety gives you the chance to treat tomatoes as spillers instead of thrillers! Mix them with colorful Swiss chard or beets and a few tall okra plants (choose a purple variety for extra drama) for a vividly colored grouping. If you grow beets, you'll need to carefully harvest them and resow through the season; a single spring planting of Swiss chard should last as long as the okra and tomatoes in most climates.

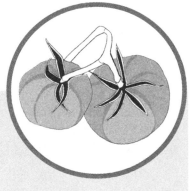

### THRILLER
### Okra

Okra is a beautiful plant and the pods can be useful in craft projects if they become too large to eat.

### FILLER
### Swiss chard or beets

Choose seeds for mixed-color or single-color plants, depending on how rowdy you'd like this combination.

### SPILLER
### 'Tumbling Tom' tomato

It may take planning to find this tomato variety. Call your favorite garden centers in winter and ask if they'll be carrying it.

# THE SOPHISTICATE

The artichoke is a commanding plant, with its silvery white, highly dissected foliage and large, vaselike growth habit. Honor its dramatic tendencies—while keeping things on the light side—by combining it with pretty bronze fennel and a few variegated thyme plants. This combination will need less water than most. Gardeners in cold climates may not get any fruit on their artichokes; however, the plant is so beautiful and such fun to grow that it more than merits inclusion in your garden.

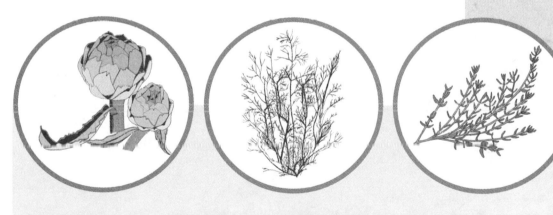

### THRILLER
### Artichoke

To increase the chance of harvest, get plants in the ground as soon as possible in cold climates, even if it means protecting them through cool nights.

### FILLER
### Bronze fennel

This plant is best started from seed; it can be transplanted from elsewhere in the garden if you already have it.

### SPILLER
### Silver variegated thyme

This thyme may not "spill" until it is mature—especially if you cut from it frequently.

# SOUTHERN SPRAWLER

Let the long, languid vines of sweet potatoes cover your patio in this combination of Southern-cuisine favorites. Large, glaucous leaves of collard greens preside above, and wispy scallions sprinkled here and there provide a finer texture. In autumn, when the sweet potatoes are ready for harvest, pull out the remaining collards and scallions and, if your climate allows, sow new seed for a fall/winter crop.

### THRILLER
*Collard greens*

Kale or broccoli can be substituted, if desired.

### FILLER
*Scallions*

Depending on your use of the crop, allow it to grow to maturity or harvest and sow new seed regularly.

### SPILLER
*Sweet potato*

Be sure to select a variety appropriate for your climate; buying locally is recommended.

# SUMMER DELIGHTS

Take advantage of summertime by growing these warm-climate favorites together. A lush tomato placed to the rear of the pot can be staked and leaf pruned (page 100) as needed to allow basil and marjoram—two delicious, hot-weather herbs—to provide grace notes below. Purple basil looks best with the green tomato and silvery marjoram foliage, but if you prefer the taste of green basil, by all means, swap it for the purple.

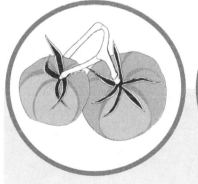 

**THRILLER**
*Tomato on stake*

Cherry tomatoes are the highest yielding and easiest to manage in combinations.

**FILLER**
*Purple basil*

After basil reaches 6 to 8 inches tall, pinch the center to encourage branching and a bushier habit.

**SPILLER**
*Marjoram*

Marjoram acquires its spiller habit during and after flowering.

# SUMMERY SIDES

Fresh beans, sweet peppers, and plenty of parsley to top it all off—that's what summer, and this container, is all about. In early spring, sow parsley seed in a ring around the center of the pot, which will get the herb established and growing well. Once the weather warms so that nights are consistently above 55°F, plant a bell pepper in the center and a ring of easy-care bush beans around the edge between the parsley plants. The low leaves of the bean plants will give the illusion of a spiller plant. Didn't get your parsley started early enough? No worries—just swap the position of the parsley and the beans, then the faster-growing beans won't shade the parsley.

### THRILLER
### *Bell pepper*

Most any color bell pepper can be eaten green, so choose a red or orange pepper and harvest them while green, if desired.

### FILLER
### *Parsley*

Sowing seed, rather than buying plants, guarantees the longest parsley harvest.

### SPILLER
### *Bush beans*

Bush beans become more spillerlike as they grow.

# TEMPTING TRIPOD

Using a garden tripod (see page 122) adds a unique accent that a plant alone simply cannot duplicate—it's almost like adding a piece of sculpture! Choose beans or Malabar spinach to cover the bamboo stakes, then fill spaces between them with trailing nasturtiums and Tuscan kale. For the lowest-maintenance combination, use Malabar spinach, which branches little, thus leaving plenty of light and air for growing the Tuscan kale.

| THRILLER | FILLER | SPILLER |
|---|---|---|
| *Malabar spinach* | *Tuscan kale* | *Trailing nasturtiums* |
| Malabar spinach is the more colorful and dramatic choice for this combo, but beans work just as effectively. Use a bamboo trellis to carry the vines skyward. | Plant kale between the stakes so that it doesn't get smothered by the vine. | A few seeds on either side of the kale is sufficient to create a dramatic spill. |

# VAMPIRE REPELLENT

Garlic is fun and easy to grow, and its strongly upright stems make a powerful statement in the garden. The only trick is that it is sown in fall and harvested in summer, making combining it with other crops difficult. This combination solves that by mixing it with spring crops that will be nothing but ghosts by the time the garlic stalks wither and harvest time comes. Since garlic needs to be outdoors all winter, use only weatherproof containers for this recipe. If you wish, you could even re-use it for the following year's garlic crop a few weeks after the harvest.

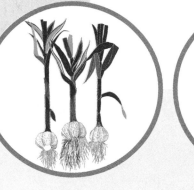 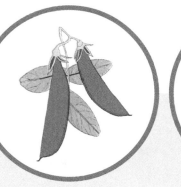 

### THRILLER
*Garlic*

You can plant 6-10 individual cloves, depending on your pot size. Stagger them throughout the pot.

### FILLER
*Peas*

Peas will be finished just a few weeks before garlic is ready. While they grow, they can climb on to the sturdy garlic stalks for support.

### SPILLER
*Spinach*

Spinach likes the same conditions as peas, so it too will be cleared out before the garlic harvest comes.

# NUTRITION STATION

If you're looking for a nutrient-packed combination that's as beautiful as it is tasty, this one's got you covered! Super-healthy broccoli presides over a ring of carrots and vitamin-C-packed parsley for the makings of a super healthy salad or side dish. The trick is to take advantage of the more colorful, vitamin-filled varieties offered in your favorite seed catalog and not just settle for the conventional supermarket colors. That way, you're getting more beauty and more nutrients for your time and money.

### THRILLER
*Broccoli*

Look for very dark green or purple-tinged varieties, like 'Bay Meadows.'

### FILLER
*Carrots*

For the most nutritious and prettiest carrots, you can't go wrong with 'Purple Haze' or 'Atomic Red.'

### SPILLER
*Parsley*

All varieties of parsley are rich in vitamins and excellent raw or in salad dressings.

# CONTAINER RECIPES
## *for Medium Pots*

Medium pots—those 12 inches to 16 inches in diameter—are about as small as you can go in a conventional pot and still enjoy beautiful, productive plants. The following combinations use smaller-scale crops, though they still involve three different types to ensure you get the most out of your space. This means that you are guaranteed a varied and diverse selection of plants in your edible spots and pots, rather than the same types of plants, repeated in the same ways, throughout your garden. Because there is a range of pot sizes that qualify as "medium," use your judgment in interpreting these recipes for the sizes you have. For example, if you are planting a 12-inch pot, sow fewer of the filler or spiller plants than if you are planting a 14- or 16-inch pot.

# BEAN SCENE

This combination can eventually be turned over to a fall or winter crop—it will be productive in spring and much of summer, leaving the container open for peas, radishes, or arugula in autumn. Scallions and cilantro can both be sown as soon as nights have warmed into the 40s; once it gets a bit warmer and drier, in late spring, go ahead and sow a few bush bean seeds. Depending on your weather and your family's consumption, subsequent sowings of cilantro and scallions may be needed to keep this container looking abundant and beautiful.

### THRILLER
#### Scallions

You could try a large chive plant or plant a few onion sets instead.

### FILLER
#### Bush beans

Varieties with yellow beans are the easiest to harvest, as they stand in contrast to the foliage.

### SPILLER
#### Cilantro

If you don't care for cilantro, try chervil or parsley as a substitute.

THRILLER
+FILLER
+SPILLER

# BOLD STATEMENT

This combo makes a big impact in a small pot. Start with a garlic chive plant in spring, then sow lovage or parsley, according to your preference (note that lovage becomes much larger than parsley, especially if you don't harvest regularly). When the weather gets warm enough, add a nice healthy eggplant seedling—choose your favorite variety or a small-fruited, colorful type like 'Rosa Bianca'. In most climates, garlic chives and eggplant will bloom together for an especially pretty effect.

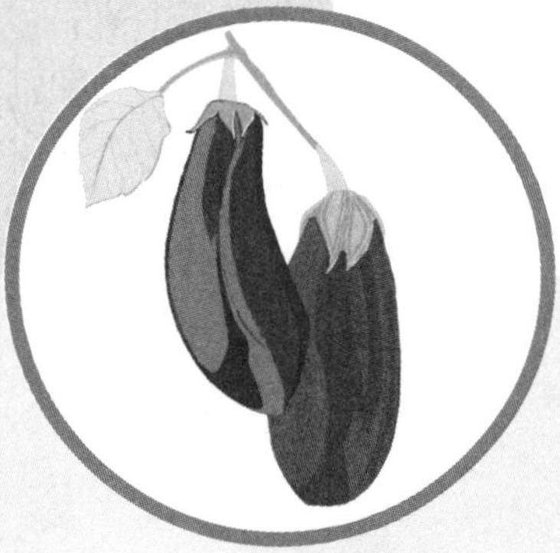

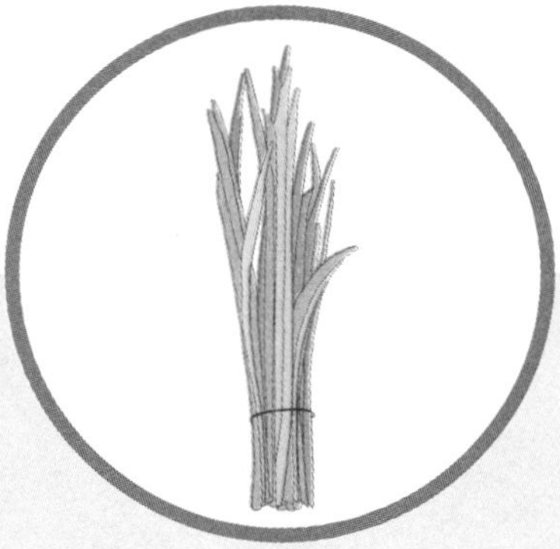

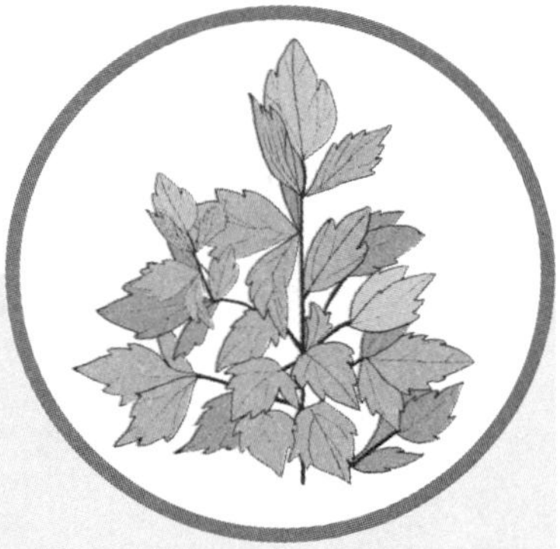

### THRILLER

*Eggplant*

Site eggplant off to the side so you don't catch its thorns while working in this container.

### FILLER

*Garlic chives*

Garlic chives are a perennial; transplant them at the end of the season if your pot is not weatherproof.

### SPILLER

*Parsley or lovage*

Harvest lovage frequently to keep it in scale with the container. It can be frozen for use in stock if you can't use it all fresh.

# LEAFY GLADE

Basil and chives are two of the most useful and popular garden herbs, but they're not much on color. Remedy this by grouping them with crayonlike 'Bright Lights' Swiss chard. For the basil, opt for a bold lettuce-leaf type like 'Napoletano', which not only provides a better contrast with the fine foliage of the chives but gives you much more from each harvest, too. Though chives become large, a young plant will work well for this combination for the entire season (it can be planted out in the garden in fall or left to take up more of the container if the container is weatherproof). Place three to five Swiss chard seeds at the front edge of the container, where the plants' foliage will dip over the edge for a spiller effect.

### THRILLER
*Basil*

A big, bold basil is necessary for this combination. Try starting from seed indoors 4 weeks before frost.

### FILLER
*Chives*

Substitute scallions or garlic chives if you prefer.

### SPILLER
*Swiss chard*

It is best to harvest frequently to keep this combination in scale, so try adding small chard leaves to salads each week.

# LUNAR LANDING

If there's an edible plant that looks like it's from outer space, it is kohlrabi. Take advantage of its unique growth habit by planting three to five of them across most of the surface of the pot. Place a single 'Tumbling Tom' tomato at the front of the pot, then tuck some salad burnet in around the edges. Since kohlrabi is quick to grow, plan to sow a second (and possibly even a third) crop in between the plants of the current crop.

### THRILLER
## Kohlrabi

Sliced kohlrabi makes a crunchy addition to your salads.

### SPILLER
## 'Tumbling Tom' tomato

Choose any color from the 'Tumbling Tom' series.

### FILLER
## Salad burnet

The young foliage of salad burnet is the tastiest and mildest; prune frequently to encourage new growth.

# PEPPER PARTY

Hot pepper plants are generally smaller and easier to group together than bell peppers, so take advantage of their growth habits and fruit colors and shapes by pairing them closely together. This pot features two of my favorite peppers—yellow hot lemon (also seen as lemon drop) and red Thai hot. Not only do the colors contrast, but so too do the habits: Lemon peppers hang seductively from the plant, while Thai peppers point straight up. Round out the composition with some marjoram, the perfect herb to accompany roasted or marinated peppers.

### THRILLER
*Hot lemon pepper*

Though this pepper is beautiful and tasty, any pepper with pendulous fruit will do.

### FILLER
*Thai hot pepper*

These are easy to find and quite ornamental. They're also very hot, so don't let their tiny size fool you.

### SPILLER
*Marjoram*

Marjoram adds a delicious Mediterranean summer flavor to any vegetable dish and is especially nice with peppers.

# PROVENCE PROVENANCE

Close your eyes and focus on this container—you can, just for a moment, pretend you're on a patio overlooking the sea in the south of France! After all, nothing epitomizes Provence like lavender, which anchors this container. Pair it with a narrow, fine-textured French tarragon plant and several nasturtium seeds for the makings of tasty salads and vinaigrettes all summer long. English lavender, the hardiest lavender, is the only type suitable for eating; harvest the entire flower stem once two or three flowers on it have opened, then dry the blossoms and store for later use.

## THRILLER
### French tarragon

Imperative for authentic French vinaigrettes, French tarragon can also be used to infuse vinegar for winter use.

## FILLER
### Lavender

Lavender's edible harvest is fairly short. When its flowers are gone, the leaves can be used for sachets.

## SPILLER
### Nasturtium

Choose any color flowers you like or choose a mix of colors; either is fine—as long as it is a vining type.

# SPRING GREENS

Get a gorgeous, productive container early in the season with this cool-weather combo. As soon as nighttime temperatures are in the 40s, sow broccoli in the center, and sow arugula seed from the 10 o'clock to 2 o'clock position as well as from the 4 o'clock to the 8 o'clock position. Between 2 and 4 o'clock and between 8 and 10 o'clock, plant a golden variegated thyme. In midsummer, when these plants have given up the ghost, use the pot for late-season crops like watermelon radish or for another sowing of broccoli and arugula.

### THRILLER
*Broccoli*

Experiment with broccoli raab or sprouting broccoli, if you'd prefer.

### FILLER
*Arugula*

If your arugula bolts, sprinkle the flowers on a salad before removing the plants from the pot.

### SPILLER
*Golden thyme*

Equally as useful in the kitchen as plain green thyme, golden thyme is much more ornamental in the garden.

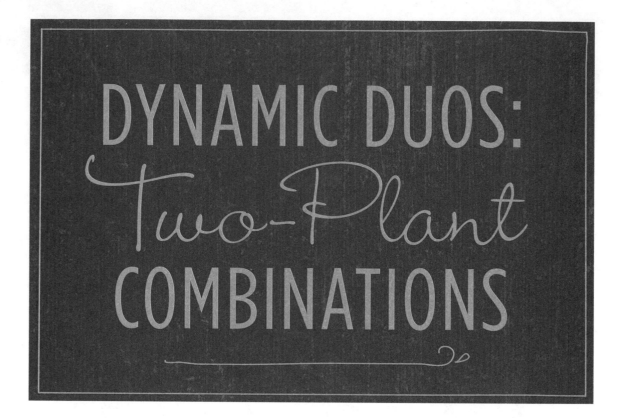

# DYNAMIC DUOS: *Two-Plant* COMBINATIONS

Sometimes, three is a crowd—especially if you have a small container or bed space to plant. Fortunately, it only takes two to tango! You can have a powerfully pretty plant combination with just two elements if you choose carefully.

**Thriller plus filler combinations** bring together the strong presence of a thriller plant with the spreading, supporting role of the filler. In these recipes, some fillers can become thrillers, and their more diminutive mate becomes the filler. It's all about context.

**Thriller plus spiller combinations** let large plants truly shine. These combinations are particularly good at highlighting plants with strongly upright habits because the spiller element droops gracefully around the base of the thriller.

# BASIL BLOWOUT

If you love basil, go overboard and plant two types together. You'll get twice the fragrance and twice the harvest of this summertime luxury. Choose radically different-looking varieties like 'Pesto Perpetuo' and 'Purple Ruffles' and most visitors wouldn't guess they are the same herb. Not only do these offer incredible color contrast, they also have very different growth habits and so complement each other in that way as well.

### THRILLER
#### 'Pesto Perpetuo' basil
This variegated basil is sterile so it never flowers; you can only purchase plants, not seeds, of this variety.

### FILLER
#### 'Purple Ruffles' basil
This pretty variety is easier to find in seeds than as plants. Sow directly in a container or start it indoors.

# THE BITTER END

Sweeten up these two edibles, mutually appreciated for their pleasant bitterness, by planting them together. Eggplant is actually a marvelously diverse crop, with a range of fruit sizes, shapes, and colors. By growing it solo with a decorative fringe of parsley all around, you can truly appreciate the merits of its big, showy flowers, bold foliage, and otherworldly fruits.

### THRILLER
## Eggplant

Go off the deep end with an interesting variety like 'Calliope' or 'Kermit'. These small-fruited varieties are prolific producers, resulting in larger harvests and more ornamental appeal.

### FILLER
## Parsley

In early spring, sow the seed directly in place, or start the seed in a different pot and then transplant the seedlings.

# BOLLYWOOD BOWL

Drawing from the flashy colors and dynamic dance moves of a Bollywood movie, this unusual pairing incorporates both color contrast and foliage contrast. Best of all, these two plants don't mind the heat, so they'll stay super showy from the beginning of the growing season until the end. Once frost has claimed the okra plants, the chard will stick around until the weather gets bitter cold.

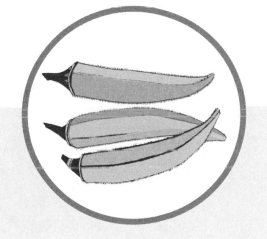

### THRILLER
*Okra*

For maximum impact, choose a red variety. The fruits contrast nicely with the pale yellow flowers.

### FILLER
*'Bright Lights' Swiss chard*

This popular variety is a must for true Bollywood style.

# CHEERFUL COMPANIONS

Looking for something unexpected? Try this pairing of collard greens and calendula. Both love the sun, and the blue green of the collard foliage benefits from the bright orange of calendula's sunny blooms. The flowers also attract a host of beneficial pollinating insects that normally wouldn't visit a container of foliage plant like collards, thus bringing even more color to your garden.

**THRILLER**
*Collard greens*

Three collard plants fit perfectly in a 14- to 16-inch pot.

**FILLER**
*Calendula*

Sow seeds between the collards and around the edges.

# DINNER BELL

When Mexican food is on the menu, you'll be glad you have this easy combination at hand! Use a large bell pepper to anchor the center of the container, then sow cilantro seeds around the edge, about 3 inches apart. After a few weeks, sow fresh cilantro seed in between the existing plants to keep a consistent supply and to maintain the appealing juxtaposition of cilantro's delicate leaves and the blocky fruits of the stately bell pepper plant.

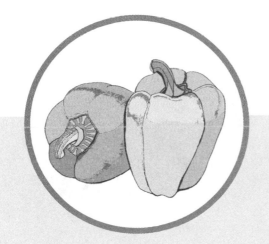

### THRILLER
*Bell pepper*

Try a small-fruited type for best productivity, like 'Lipstick' or 'Lunchbox Orange'.

### FILLER
*Cilantro*

If your cilantro bolts, don't fret. Let the seed develop and use it for next year's crop or to transform into the spice coriander.

# GREEN LANTERNS

That's the best way to describe the unique look of tomatillo fruits: large, round, green tomatoes encased in a papery coat. This easy-to-grow, incredibly productive tomato relative is essential in authentic Mexican salsas. It has a strongly lateral habit, like a low-growing tree, so it's a pretty companion for a hot pepper with upright-facing fruit, like Thai peppers or bird peppers. Choosing a hot pepper variety where the fruit points upward rather than hangs down makes a more interesting contrast to the unique habit of the tomatillo.

### THRILLER
*Tomatillo*

Try any tomatillo that will crop within your season, but a purple variety is especially nice.

### FILLER
*Hot pepper*

Pick any that works for your family's spice tolerance.

# IN A PICKLE

Whether enjoyed pickled or fresh in a salad, dill and cucumber are a natural pairing. Make combining these two in the kitchen easy by combining them in the garden: Let the cucumber plant sprawl over the edge of the container, and plant a patch of dill to one side of the pot. Depending on your weather and how much of the herb you use, you may want to sow more dill seed in early and midsummer.

**THRILLER**
*Dill*

Dill is always best grown from seed sown directly in place.

**FILLER**
*Cucumber 'Endeavor' or 'Diamant'*

Small pickling types are more versatile and productive than large-fruited varieties.

# ROMAN HOLIDAY

Every day is a celebration with these two summer favorites! Plant a small-fruited purple tomato in the center of the pot (I used 'Indigo Rose') and then underplant it with large-leaved basil. Not only do the enormous leaves of the basil act as mulch, shading the roots of the tomato plant, their vivid green color brightens up the dark stems, leaves, and fruits of the tomato. They complement one another just as beautifully on the table, too.

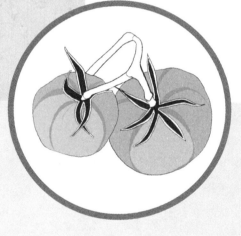

### THRILLER
*Purple or black tomato*

Choose a small-fruited tomato variety, like 'Indigo Rose'.

### FILLER
*Italian basil*

Plant 'Napoletano', a large-leaved variety.

# BOX OF CRAYONS

For rich, saturated colors, it's hard to beat nasturtium. Pair this beautiful and tasty edible flower with some equally colorful bush beans for an especially vivid combination. To keep a constant supply of beans, you may want to sow a few new seeds every 2 to 3 weeks, or you can just turn the container over to a fall crop of radishes or salad greens.

### THRILLER
*Bush beans*

Try the 'Tricolor Bush' blend from Renee's Garden Seeds in containers.

### SPILLER
*Nasturtium*

Mixed color blends are nice, especially the classic 'Jewel Mix'.

# SOW EASY

Self-sowing herbs are the lazy gardener's best friend—plant a few seeds once and these enthusiastic plants will pop up year after year. Because they are edible, they're always a welcome presence. But if seedlings should appear where they're not wanted, don't fret—they are very easy to remove. Both borage and chervil are delicious additions to salads and make them prettier and more fun when sprinkled over the top of garden-fresh lettuce.

### THRILLER
*Borage*

Borage is a large plant, so give it space. By harvesting the flowers frequently, you can limit the amount of seed it produces.

### SPILLER
*Chervil*

When the small white flowers of chervil appear, the herb itself is no longer harvestable, so it's best to let it go to seed and let beneficial insects enjoy its nectar-rich flowers.

# SWEET SOMETHINGS

Got a sweet tooth? Satisfy your craving in a uniquely horticultural way with these two popular dessert herbs. Both can be used in ice cream, cakes, and granitas (an easy-to-make frozen ice refreshment; look online for recipes), or simply layer their freshly picked foliage with some sugar in a jar for a few days to perfume the sugar with their fragrance. This flavored sugar makes a nice gift, or use it to sweeten tea or in baking.

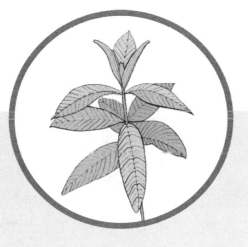

### THRILLER
*Lemon verbena*

Nothing compares to the fragrance of lemon verbena. Try growing it indoors over winter as a houseplant.

### SPILLER
*Mint*

Notoriously rampant, you can curtail the mint by removing some when you dig out the lemon verbena in autumn.

# CHIVE TALK

Potatoes and chives are a classic combination in the kitchen, and they make good companions in the garden as well. Chives readily adapt to the same cultural requirements as potatoes, and they are not overly competitive with the deep-growing potato plants. Use a very large container for this pairing; once the spuds are ready to eat, dig out the chives and transplant them elsewhere. You can try drying the tops of the chives or preserving them in the freezer if you'd like, and you can still plant out the root masses to grow again next year.

### THRILLER
*Potato*

Be sure to choose a potato variety appropriate for your region; see page 244.

### SPILLER
*Chives*

Start chives from seed, buy plants, or divide an existing chive patch.

# RHAPSODY IN WHITE

White brings a crisp and unexpected note to the vegetable garden, especially when it is the color of the fruit. Combine a white-fruited pepper with a variegated thyme to bring out one another's unique qualities and create a subtle yet quirky sophistication. If you don't like hot peppers, choose a white bell like 'Bianca'; if you do enjoy hot peppers, however, try the white habanero, also known as the Peruvian white hot pepper.

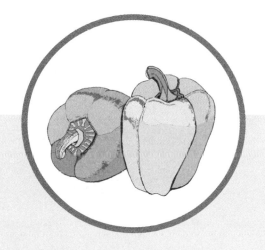

### THRILLER
*White pepper*

You can substitute a white eggplant for the white pepper, if you prefer!

### SPILLER
*Variegated thyme*

This very pretty thyme is especially nice in a brightly colored container.

# SAGE ADVICE

Lovers of variegated foliage could hardly do better than tricolor sage with its wild patterns and range of colors. Let this quirky, colorful plant show off its potential by giving it star billing in this combination: Simply underplant it with some purple-leaved sweet potatoes. Though these were developed mostly for their ornamental appeal, they do produce some fruit, and juxtaposing these two superdramatic varieties might just make you forget you've created something that was meant to be harvested!

### THRILLER
*Tricolor sage*

Carefully dig out or transplant the sage when it comes time to harvest the sweet potatoes in autumn.

### SPILLER
*Purple sweet potato vine*

The variety 'Blackie' is the one you'll want.

# SEASONAL SALAD

This combination is a great way to make use of short spans of cool weather in spring and fall. Both greens can be enjoyed at any time of the season: picked as tender baby vegetables or allowed to grow into full-size harvests if time and weather permit. Plus, these two crops are excellent when paired in a salad! Just sow five beet seeds in the center of the pot, being careful to sow deeply enough and to cover firmly or the bulbous roots won't form, then sow several arugula seeds around the edge. Harvest everything at once if it gets hot or if you need the container for another combination.

### THRILLER
*Beets 'Gourmet Golden'*

Choose a quick-cropping variety that is suitable for harvest at the baby stage.

### SPILLER
*Arugula*

If you love arugula's peppery flavor, use wild arugula. If you prefer it milder, use regular arugula, which is also known as salad rocket.

# SWEET AND GOLDEN

You may have seen stevia as a packaged sweetener in the stores, but did you know it is also an easy-to-grow and easy-to-use herb? It also makes a swell thriller plant to add to your collection. Since it isn't highly ornamental, though, its best paired with something flashy, like golden oregano. Stevia is very cold-sensitive, so plan to let it go or bring it indoors when frost threatens. The golden oregano is hardy, so you might want to grow this combination in a weather-proof pot or transplant it to a bed at the end of the season.

## THRILLER
### Stevia

Stevia is becoming increasingly easy to find among the herb selections at garden centers everywhere. Look for its neatly toothed little leaves if you can't identify it by sight.

## SPILLER
### Golden oregano

This hardy, easy-to-grow perennial herb is a more ornamental choice than the common culinary oreganos, but it is still useful in the kitchen.

# TEA TIME

When the garden gives you abundant herbs, make tea! Or more properly, a tisane: Just pour boiling water over a handful of herbs and create your own refreshing and tasty brew. It's the perfect way to use trimmings from the garden, especially of herbs that aren't at optimum flavor when dried, like lemon balm. This simple but charming combination of two popular tea herbs is easy to maintain and will keep you flush with homegrown beverages from spring through frost.

### THRILLER
#### Lemon balm

A vigorous perennial, lemon balm is very easy to grow from seed. Or ask a friend—anyone who has it in their garden will have plenty to share.

### SPILLER
#### Chamomile

Use Roman or German chamomile as you prefer. Both are pretty and well suited to brewing into tea.

# SILVER SOPHISTICATION

Artichokes are among the most beautiful, impressive edibles you can grow, but their giant, hulking habits can make them tricky to pair with a companion. This pretty combination resolves that by adding in the edible flowers of Johnny-jump-up, which does best in spring when the artichoke is small. By the time fall rolls around and the Johnnies get their second wind, the lower leaves on the artichoke will have died away, making room for the purple flowers once again.

### THRILLER
*Artichoke or cardoon*

Baby artichokes are a sought-after treat, so there's no need to wait for the artichoke to reach full size.

### SPILLER
*Johnny-jump-up*

Use the flowers in salads or on desserts, or candy them with egg whites and sugar; just look for a tutorial online.

# TO BOLDLY GROW

Few edibles are as big and bold in the garden as summer squash. With its huge foliage and wide, dramatic growth habit, it can be a difficult plant to combine with others. Instead of competing with its brash nature, though, why not complement it with the delicate foliage of salad burnet? This delicious, easy-to-grow (and much underappreciated) herb is far smaller than summer squash but manages to hold its own, thanks to its unique zigzag foliage. Just tuck it along the edge of the summer squash.

### THRILLER
*Summer squash*

Any variety will do, but small-fruited varieties, like 'Astia' or 'Bush Baby', are best for containers.

### SPILLER
*Salad burnet*

Salad burnet is delicious in salads, but it can also be used in refreshing beverages or even in an offbeat pestolike sauce.

# Solo PERFORMERS

Combining plants together in a pot or raised bed has multiple benefits: The combo looks great, it allows you to get more from a smaller space, the plants can support one another physically, and the duo or trio attracts beneficial insects. However, some plants are frankly better on their own. They are large and may cast too much shade on their neighbors, or they are especially greedy about fertilizer and water. Sometimes, we just want the increased productivity that can come from giving one of these plants more than enough space for its performance. Here are six excellent solo performers—divas, if you will—that are perfect candidates for planting alone in a container (or allocating plenty of space in a raised bed).

# BEANS ON A TRIPOD

While pole beans can be combined with certain other plants that simply peek out from between the vines, if you are aiming to maximize the notoriously high productivity of beans, go ahead and fill an entire pot with them. This allows you to plant more seed, first of all, and it eliminates the need to leaf prune and tend to the plants to allow light and air to companions. A 6' to 8' bean tripod, with its stark shape and dense, leafy covering, has ample presence in the garden on its own.

# HEIRLOOM TOMATOES

The larger fruited the tomato, the more space it will need to produce a good crop. This is especially true with heirloom tomatoes, which tend to have huge fruits and a high resource demand. Growing these plants with too much competition can severely limit yields that may already be relatively scant given the size of the plant. A well-cared-for heirloom tomato can be beautiful enough to stand on its own anyway, especially once it bears those irresistibly convoluted, colorful fruits.

# JERUSALEM ARTICHOKE

Another hardy perennial, Jerusalem artichoke is highly productive—maybe too much so. It is notorious for its ability to take over an area, bearing far more edible tubers than the average person can eat. Grow it on its own in a large container, in a dedicated raised bed, or on a grow tower (page 140), however, and you can enjoy its tasty, nutritious roots and its chocolate-scented sunflower blooms as well. If you grow it in a container, you can harvest all of the roots in autumn and store a few of them in a cool, dark place to restart your patch in spring, meaning you don't need a weatherproof pot. Jerusalem artichoke reaches well over 8 feet tall, so give it plenty of room and grow it only where it won't shade its neighbors.

# RHUBARB

This hardy perennial edible has foliage big and bold enough to merit it a place in an ornamental garden, but it really must be grown on its own in a container or widely spaced in a raised bed. It is by nature a large plant and will be productive only if allowed to reach a significant size; further, its dense, fibrous root system doesn't appreciate competition. If you choose to grow rhubarb in a container, make it a very large, and weatherproof container, as rhubarb requires a cold winter's rest to emerge in spring. It will need division in 5 to 7 years, at which point you can start afresh with a portion of the original or expand your rhubarb patch to new containers or parts of the garden. Either way, the enormous leaves lend a welcome tropical touch to cold-climate gardens.

# SWEET POTATO

With its vigorous, cascading habit, sweet potato vine is the best possible spiller plant. However, if you want to produce an abundance of sweet potatoes and maximize the lush, attractive growth, let it fill an entire container on its own. You'll get dozens of sweet potatoes, and you won't need to fret about destroying a companion crop when harvesttime comes and you need to rip the whole thing apart. Growing sweet potatoes on their own doesn't ignore their excellence as a spiller, either—place a container of them with containers of two of the other solo suggestions here, like a bean tripod and a rhubarb, and you have a super-low-maintenance, high-drama thriller-filler-spiller combination right there.

# POTATO

Even though I've included potatoes in a few of the combinations on the previous pages, there's no way to get around the fact that for the best potatoes, this crop should be grown alone. Gardeners who are serious about their potato harvest are advised to give this big, space-hungry plant all the room it wants for the very best harvest. Not only does this give the potatoes ample room to develop, it also helps eliminate potential watering problems. Potatoes can be very prone to rot, even in well-drained soils, and there's nothing more heart-breaking than digging out a healthy looking plant only to find mushy, blackened blobs below the soil. Gardeners in areas with frequent rainfall are especially advised to grow potatoes on their own, as that way there is no need to try to meet the needs of two different crops sharing the same limited space.

chapter six

# PLANT ENCYCLOPEDIA

Every home garden has its space limitations, so you have to make some compromises between everything you'd like to grow and what is worth growing given your garden's constraints. To help you decide what to try in your spots and pots, this encyclopedia goes into detail on the merits of many popular edibles and how to grow them. Watering is a particularly important issue when you use thriller-filler-spiller combinations (or anytime you grow crops close together), because you'll want to combine plants with similar needs. That's why each encyclopedia entry includes a general description of a crop's water requirements, too.

In regard to planting, growing, and harvesting times, I've stuck to seasons and temperature ranges over specific months as much as possible. Even these, I realize, are imperfect: The vernal equinox, which technically indicates the beginning of spring, is essentially meaningless in warm climates, where temperatures in the 80s may have already persisted for weeks! North America is a big place with a huge range of temperatures and climates, and even within a single geographic area, every growing season is different from the previous and the next. The best place for information on growing vegetables in your unique climate is your state's Cooperative Extension Service. To connect to yours, visit csrees.usda.gov/Extension/. For every crop described in the encyclopedia, I've included its botanical family. This isn't out of horticultural snobbery. Rather, it is important information to help you plan your garden from year to year, because plants that are in the same family are often subject to similar pests and diseases.

Similarly, each plant's listing includes its botanical name. In some cases, there is more than one botanical name. Again, this is done to clarify which varieties have the most culinary promise and to cut through the confusion when a common name (like "oregano") is applied to many plants, some of them not remotely suited to the vegetable garden. Further, I find that botanical names are the easiest way to find clear, reliable information and to search for photos of the plant on the Internet.

Finally, the Plot-Free Pointers section under each entry gives specific advice on growing the crops in raised beds and containers. These suggestions may be to recommend a specific variety or a tip on where to site the plant within your garden for the best growth and easiest harvest; others offer advice on using the crop in the kitchen or a trick for better production. Each tip is meant to help you get the very most out of your edible spots and pots and make growing your own food more fun and rewarding.

# Exploring Other Options

You may notice that some common vegetables aren't covered in this encyclopedia. That's because while they *can* grow in the kinds of edible spots and pots shown in this book, the harvest you get from them usually isn't worth the time or space they need.

Some common crops, such as cabbage and onions, are easy to find at low cost and high quality at the grocery store, so it's simply easier to buy them and save your space for more unusual edibles. Instead of cabbage, try collards; for onion flavor, consider scallions or chives.

Other familiar crops that are difficult or time consuming to grow have alternatives that are better for your edible spots and pots. Celery, for instance, is difficult to raise from seed and needs lots of water, but you can get the same flavor from the leaves of lovage, a good-looking and easy-to-grow perennial herb. And if you can't wait for months for leeks to mature, chives can provide a similar flavor all through the growing season.

I don't want to discourage you from growing any crop in your raised beds or containers: If you love it, try it, or at least do a little research to see what varieties are available. Plant breeders and seed companies are recognizing the need for smaller-scale versions of space-hogging plants like melons and squash, for example, so look for compact or faster-maturing varieties of the crops you want, such as 'Minnesota Midget' cantaloupe, 'Bush Sugar Baby' watermelon, 'Munchkin' pumpkin, or 'Gold Nugget' winter squash.

# ANNUAL Vegetables

Most of the edibles that you'll raise in your containers and raised beds are annual crops. That means they'll grow from seeds or starts, produce something you can harvest, and then die once they flower and make seeds or when frost hits, all within one growing season. Annual crops give you the advantage of a blank slate each spring, letting you start fresh with all the knowledge and experience you gained in the previous year. That means you get to try new varieties, new combinations, and new techniques every season!

Annual vegetables are an important component of your edible spots and pots: Because they are generally fast-growing, you can use them to get the most from your space. Annual vegetables with very fast life cycles, such as arugula or carrots (which doesn't technically complete its life cycle but would be inedible if it were allowed to), can be replaced with subsequent sowings of the same, or different, crops. Even in cold climates, longer-season annual crops, such as tomatoes or okra, can be replaced by fast-growing ones when production begins to drop due to cooler temperatures and longer nights. Try to keep a good supply of seed for your favorite annual vegetables handy so you can make the most out of every bit of space in your garden!

# Arugula

*Eruca sativa, Diplotaxis tenuifolia* (wild arugula)
**Family: Brassicaceae, the cabbage family**

If you've been hesitant to try arugula because of its association with food snobbery, you're missing out. Those foodies are on to something! Also known as rocket, roquette, rucola, or salad rocket, arugula is a delicious peppery crop that is extremely versatile in the kitchen, going from salad to pastas to sandwiches with aplomb. It has a pleasant crunch and is very easy to grow. In fact, growing arugula yourself is the best way to enjoy it, as its succulent stems and leaves are easily bruised, rendering most store-bought arugula rather unappealing.

**Habit:** Arugula forms a low-growing rosette of more or less lacy foliage.

**How to start:** Start this cool-weather crop directly in the garden in early spring, sowing the seeds about ¼ inch deep, as soon as the soil is thawed and dry enough to dig. Sow more seeds in late summer to early autumn, and in mild areas, even through mid- to late fall. Arugula plants can grow fairly close together: about 2 inches apart. Sow the seeds at about that spacing, or plant them closer together and then snip out the excess seedlings a week or two after they sprout and use the tender baby leaves in the kitchen.

**Season:** Spring until early summer, if the weather stays cool; fall and even into winter from a late-summer or autumn sowing.

**When to harvest:** Gather arugula as whole plants or clip single leaves as needed. You can harvest as soon as the leaves are large enough to handle and plants are bulky enough that something will be left to grow back for subsequent harvests. Once hot weather arrives, the leaves get tough and become unpleasantly peppery. Arugula may bolt (send up flowering stalks) as the season goes on. Though the foliage is not tasty at this point, the creamy yellow flowers, shot through with violet veins, are choice edibles that make an unexpected topping for salads.

**Water requirements:** Do not allow arugula plants to dry out, because they wilt readily and do not recover well.

**Light requirements:** Full sun is best, but arugula can tolerate some shade, especially in hot climates.

**Pests and diseases:** Flea beetles—small black beetles that are not remotely related to fleas but do superficially resemble them in some respects—adore arugula and mark its leaves with their telltale, perfectly round holes. You can still eat arugula that's been damaged by flea beetles, but it's better to prevent the damage by protecting your plants with a row cover.

**Recommended varieties:** Any variety sold as arugula will be tender and tasty. Wild arugula varieties differ in their leaf form and may be more peppery and less succulent than arugula; they are reputed to be hardier as well.

**Space-to-yield ratio:** High. Under ideal conditions, a single sowing of arugula can produce for a very long time in a relatively small (6-inch-square) space.

**Plot-free pointers:** Arugula is a good candidate for growing in any container that's not too big to move. Set the container in full sun in spring, then, as summer's heat comes on, move it to cooler, shadier locations until the plants bolt or the leaves becomes too strong for your taste.

**Garden role:** Arugula is mostly a filler, but it can have a spiller effect if you plant it near the edge of the container and let it grow rather large.

# Bean

*Phaseolus vulgaris*
**Family: Fabaceae, the bean family**

People seem to love or hate green beans—this innocent, wholesome vegetable is surprisingly polarizing. If you and your family dislike them, nothing will convince you to devote some of your space to this crop. On the other hand, if you like them, wonderful! Beans are one of the most productive and easiest-to-grow crops you can plant.

There are two main types of beans that are sold for eating whole: pole beans and bush beans. Pole beans have long, twining stems and need some kind of support, like a bean tepee. These can be highly ornamental and add a unique geometry to your containers or raised beds. Bush beans are much shorter and do not require support. They are generally less productive than pole beans but may be easier to pick as the pods are not hiding deep within the dense cover of leaves. Both bush and pole beans come in a variety of colors (green, yellow, and purple) and in flat- or round-podded varieties.

For something different, you can grow dry beans. This type has an inedible papery pod enclosing several beans that you can remove and cook immediately or dry for storage. The many different types are a fascinating study for those interested in Native American and heirloom crops. Grow dry beans as you would grow pole beans.

**Habit:** Beans are vining plants by nature and can reach surprising heights by the end of the season if you give them a large support to climb on. Bush beans have been developed to form short, stocky plants that bear little resemblance to their vining kin except in producing the same delicious, versatile harvest.

**How to start:** Sow bean seeds about 1 inch deep in your garden when nighttime temperatures are consistently 55°F or warmer. Most varieties are so quick cropping (50 to 60 days from germination) that you will enjoy an abundant harvest even in areas with a short growing season. Plus, their large seeds are easy to handle and emerge quickly, making them a great practice crop for gardeners who are nervous about direct sowing and for children.

**Season:** Summer through fall. In very hot

# TRAINING TIPS FOR POLE BEANS

Though beans have weak stems, they are genetically programmed to twine and twist around anything they can to climb upward to maximize their dose of sunlight. This is good news for the small space gardener, who can manipulate this quality to create focal points and lush, vine-covered structures.

**Explore your options.** Simply plant pole bean seeds near a stake, fence, or other upright structure: The shoots will readily find and climb the support. They can easily cover whatever you provide in a matter of weeks, so you must decide how to use these plants in your garden at the planning stage. There are lots of fun ways to make the most of these climbers.

☀ Grow them on a tripod, a tepeelike structure that you can fashion out of three stakes. (See page 122 for different ideas.) This results in a specimen pot with a dramatic pyramidal presence or a striking centerpiece for a raised bed.

☀ Let them climb up and over an arbor that you fashion out of wood or even sturdy bamboo stakes. This creates an archway that can mark the entrance of your garden or just provide some formality and unity to your array of containers or raised beds. See page 118.

☀ Make a series of archways for a tunnel-like effect, or erect horizontal pieces and create something like a temporary gazebo. Construct them over the pathways between raised beds to give a formerly flat area a dramatically different look, or site one over a seating area to provide a shady nook to relax right in your garden. There are instructions to create these structures on page 120.

**Consider a combination.** Creating a tunnel or arbor solely of one kind of pole beans may result in an awful lot of beans, so you may want to mix in other plants to maximize your harvest or the beauty of your arbor. For example, you could combine beans for fresh eating and for drying, or mix several colors of fresh beans like purple-, yellow-, and green-podded varieties. For extra edible interest, include some Chinese yard-long beans, which grow to incredible lengths (even if they don't usually reach a full 3 feet long).

To create more excitement, add ornamental vining plants, such as morning glories and moonflowers (*Ipomoea*), black-eyed Susan vine (*Thunbergia alata*), and love in a puff (*Cardiospermum halicacabum*). These add welcome color and floral interest to any garden, but use them only if there is no danger of children or other garden visitors confusing them with your edible climbers.

weather, the blossoms or young pods will drop off, but the plants will start producing again if cooler weather returns within 2 weeks or so.

**When to harvest:** Frequent harvesting tricks your bean plants into producing more flowers and pods, so the more often you pick, the bigger your harvest will be. Gather the pods when they are very young and tender, or let them grow a bit more if you like; if they get too large, however, they'll be stringy and tough.

**Water requirements:** Low (in raised beds) to moderate (in containers and in hot weather). Bean plants are certainly not the most demanding crops when it comes to water, but they'll produce less if they become stressed from too little moisture, so don't wait for them to wilt before watering.

**Light requirements:** Full sun.

**Pests and diseases:** The presence of the word bean in a number of the common names for certain insects and diseases is a clue that many problems can afflict this otherwise easy crop. Mexican bean beetles are their most notorious predator; Japanese beetles can be a problem, too. Both of these pests skeletonize the foliage, so pick them off and destroy them. Bean mosaic virus, anthracnose, and rust can also threaten your crop. To avoid them, check with your county's Cooperative Extension office to find out if any of these are a problem in your area and, if so, look specifically for disease-resistant varieties.

**Recommended varieties:** There are so many varieties to choose from, let your taste and sense of adventure be your guide! Many bean terms that are in common usage (like wax beans, filet beans, haricots verts, and

string beans) are merely regional terms denoting size, color (wax beans refers only to yellow beans), or area of origin. Consult a good seed catalog if you are looking for a specific type.

**Space-to-yield ratio:** High. Beans produce a lot over a long period.

**Plot-free pointers:** To save space in a container, mix individual bush bean plants with other crops or flowers. Or create a dramatic bean tepee in one large container; you'll harvest several pounds from the planting. Don't neglect beans' ability to create interesting spaces: Fashion arches from bamboo or piping to connect raised beds and cover them with pole beans to create a shady, edible retreat right in the garden.

**Garden role:** On a big tepee, pole beans are a thriller or solo performer; allowed to cascade, they are a spiller (though they will grab on to anything they can in an attempt to grow upright). Bush beans function easily as a filler but can go into spiller territory as well.

# Beet

*Beta vulgaris*
**Family: Chenopodiaceae, the beet family**

Though they're not everyone's cup of tea, beets have undergone a revival in the last several years, becoming the darling of chefs and health food enthusiasts. This is due largely to the rise of the farmers' market: Previously, the only beets you could find in stores were canned and pretty awful, nothing like the tasty, wholesome, fresh beets that began appearing in market stalls and eventually grocery stores. Beets are versatile, as both the root and leaves are edible, and they're packed with nutrition, too. Growing your own is fascinating and easy, and it allows you to experiment with a surprising range of colors and shapes.

**Habit:** Beets are swollen roots, forming underground with a tuft of upright colorful foliage above to indicate where they are growing. If their "shoulders" rise above ground level, the roots will become corky looking (though still perfectly edible); hill up some soil around them if this happens.

**How to start:** Sow beet seeds $1/2$ to $3/4$ inch deep directly in the garden in midspring. They can tolerate cold temperatures and grow best in cool weather, but wait until heavy frosts are about over before planting.

**Season:** Spring to summer and fall.

**When to harvest:** Pull the roots when they are small for tender "baby beets," or let them reach full size (use the days to maturity indicated on the seed packet as a guide for when to harvest). Clip beet greens at any size as needed, leaving some of the foliage on the plant so it can keep growing.

**Water requirements:** Medium to high. Beets need thorough, frequent watering to develop the most succulent, appealing roots.

**Light requirements:** Full sun is best, but the plants can tolerate some shade.

**Pests and diseases:** Beets are mostly trouble free. Leaf spot is a possibility, however, so choose a variety that has some resistance, such as 'Merlin', especially if you live in a humid climate.

**Recommended varieties:** Choose beet varieties based on days to maturity (some are ready to harvest in as few as 48 days), color (red, yellow, pink, white, or striped), and shape (round or cylindrical). 'Chioggia' is a classic Italian heirloom variety with red-and-white roots; 'Red Ace' and 'Early Wonder' are proven varieties with delicious, uniform roots and greens.

**Space-to-yield ratio:** Medium. Beets earn bonus points for producing two different edible parts on each plant.

**Plot-free pointers:** Because beets are fast growing and shade tolerant, you can plant them in crowded containers and raised beds and still produce a crop. For an autumn harvest, tuck beet seeds into small openings left by other plants in late summer.

**Garden role:** Fillers. It's best to pair them with crops that mature earlier or at the same time as your beet variety, so you don't have to worry about disturbing the roots of companions when you harvest the beet roots.

# Broccoli

*Brassica oleracea* (Italica Group)
**Family: Brassicaceae, the cabbage family**

Given that you can easily find high-quality, reasonably priced broccoli in grocery stores, you

# CHARD'S NOT HARD

Beautiful and productive, Swiss chard is essentially a beet without a thickened root, and you grow it the same way. Both the thick, colorful stems and the green leaves are edible, tasting a bit milder than beet greens. Chard is cold tolerant (it may even live through the winter), and you can harvest it anytime, cutting the leaves as needed. 'Bright Lights' includes vividly colored red-, orange-, yellow-, pink-, and white-stemmed varieties. It's a highly ornamental mix that would be too pretty to harvest if it weren't so tasty.

may not choose to give it high priority if space is limited. But it's a fun vegetable to grow, and it adores cool weather, so it's a useful crop for warm-climate gardeners who want to make efficient use of their containers or raised beds in winter. In cool climates, gardeners can choose

fast-maturing varieties to get a couple of harvests in between March and late May/June. For extra interest, try some of the lesser-known types or taste-alikes, such as Chinese broccoli (a hybrid that produces a baby-broccolilike crop), sprouting broccoli (with long, thin, elegant stems tipped with tasty tufts of the familiar broccoli buds), or broccoli raab (a turnip relative with broccoli-flavored leaves). They all have similar growing needs, taste, and texture but offer that "something different" factor.

**Habit:** Broccoli is a tall, spreading plant with stiff stems, making it pretty inflexible in terms of the space it consumes. It needs plenty of room, but you can pair it with low-growing or trailing crops.

**How to start:** One option is to sow broccoli seeds $1/4$ to $1/2$ inch deep in the garden: in early spring in warm climates and in midspring (about a month before your last frost date) in cool climates. But if you want to get the longest possible harvest period before the weather becomes intolerably hot—broccoli prefers temperatures between 55° and 75°F—give it a 4- to 5-week head start indoors. For the broccoli alternatives described above, check the seed packet for specific recommendations for your climate.

**Season:** Spring through early summer; fall; winter in warm climates.

**When to harvest:** Cut the central head while the tender flower buds are still tightly closed and dark green. The remaining stem will produce many side shoots topped with smaller but equally tasty heads.

**Water requirements:** High. Don't allow the soil to dry out.

**Light requirements:** Full sun is best, but broccoli may tolerate light shade, especially in warm climates.

**Pests and diseases:** Like all cabbage relatives, broccoli is likely to fall prey to aphids and cabbage worms. Neither is likely to destroy the plant, but both cause unappetizing damage and can spoil what would otherwise be a lovely meal of homegrown broccoli. Wash aphids off your plants with a hose. Pick off any visible cabbage worms by hand, and soak harvested broccoli heads in cold water for an hour or so before you use them to drown any hidden caterpillars. To prevent problems with both pests, protect growing plants with floating row cover.

**Recommended varieties:** The best way to choose a broccoli variety is by its days to maturity. 'Blue Wind' is a very early variety, maturing in just under 50 days, which makes it adaptable to many different weather conditions and ensures at least one harvest. Heat-tolerant varieties, such as 'Green Magic' and 'Imperial', are good choices in hot climates with unpredictable weather and in areas that experience short springs.

**Space-to-yield ratio:** Low to medium. Because of its ability to continue producing side shoots after you harvest the main stem, broccoli can potentially produce for a long time. However, its productivity is highly weather dependent, making it difficult to predict how much you'll be able to harvest from a single plant.

**Plot-free pointers:** Broccoli prefers soil more on the basic (alkaline) side, which can be problematic for container growing, because most potting mixes tend to be acidic. Instead of using peat-based mixes, use soil heavily amended with compost. Though compost is slightly acidic, it improves the soil to meet the other conditions (high nitrogen, moisture retaining) that make broccoli and broccoli-related crops thrive. Alternatively, mix a bit of lime into the soil, if you have it on hand.

# MEET THE CABBAGE CLAN

The genus *Brassica,* which includes broccoli, Brussels sprouts, cabbage, cauliflower, kale, kohlrabi, mustard greens, rutabaga, and turnip, is one of the largest single genera of edibles you can grow in your garden. Centuries of breeding and selection have created unique maintenance requirements for each crop, but their basic needs and the pests and diseases that prey on them overlap considerably.

As a group, these crops are commonly referred to as cabbage-family plants or brassicas. You may also hear them referred to as crucifers, a now-outdated outdated term that came from Cruciferae, the former name of their botanical family. This appellation derives from the distinctive cross or X shape made by their four petals—something gardeners rarely see unless they forget to harvest at the right time!

**Garden role:** Broccoli is a thriller, if for no other reason than its stiff stems make it a bold presence compared to that of many other vegetables.

# Carrot

*Daucus carota* var. sativus
**Family: Apiaceae, the carrot family**

The carrot world is so much more varied and interesting than the selection at grocery stores would lead us to believe! Elegant and thin, well proportioned and thick, round, cylindrical, or pyramidal; orange, red, purple, yellow, and white: All of these carrot shapes and colors are possible when you grow your own. Carrots are particularly handy for maximizing yields from small spaces, because you can harvest them at a wide range of sizes. Pull them when they're small to make room for warm-weather crops, or leave them in place for another month or so and then follow them with a fall crop.

**Habit:** Carrots produce an upright spray of tall, elegant, dill-like foliage indicating where the tasty root is developing below.

**How to start:** Sow carrot seeds outdoors every few weeks from early spring until the weather gets hot, then again when the weather starts to cool. Scatter the seeds as evenly as you can, not too thickly, and cover them with about ¼ inch of soil. Once the seedlings are up, snip out the weaker ones to leave 1 to 2 inches between the rest. If you want to combine carrots with other crops, sow a few seeds here and there among the other plants or in a ring around the perimeter of a container planting. Carrot seeds are tiny, so they're usually sold in a pelleted form, which makes it easier to sow them earlier and more accurately.

**Season:** Spring through early summer—carrots become pithy and bitter in hot weather—and then in fall. In mild climates, you may even get a winter or early-spring crop.

**When to harvest:** Start pulling your crop as early as 5 weeks after the seedlings emerge for true baby carrots. These tender, sweet roots are nothing like those nasty, pared-down nubs sold as baby carrots in the grocery store, and it is worth devoting at least some portion of your crop to these tasty treats. If you want full-size roots, refer to the days to maturity indicated on the seed packet for the variety you've chosen.

**Water requirements:** Moderate. Water frequently from sowing time until the seedlings are an inch or two tall. After that, carrots are relatively modest in their water needs, especially if they're not growing very close to other crops; just make sure that their soil doesn't dry out.

**Light requirements:** Full sun is best, but carrots can tolerate light shade.

**Pests and diseases:** Though several insects and diseases can bother carrots, they're usually not a serious problem in the home garden. You can help to ensure a healthy crop by thinning crowded patches to the correct spacing and watering regularly in dry weather to keep the plants growing vigorously. It's also smart to avoid planting carrots in the same spot season after season.

**Recommended varieties:** Choose varieties based on your preferences for thick or thin carrots, or try some of the more unusual colors. 'Napoli', with cylindrical orange roots, has good cold resistance, extending the season earlier into spring and later into fall and winter in all climates.

**Space-to-yield ratio:** Medium. Though each seed produces only one root, carrots don't take up a lot of room. They're quick to grow, too, so they make great early- and late-season fillers when other crops aren't using the space.

**Plot-free pointers:** Carrots are eminently suited to edible spots and pots, where loose, rock-free soil allows them to form long, perfectly shaped roots. Growing carrots this way also means fewer weeds than traditional inground growing, which translates into less work for you and less competition for the plants.

**Garden role:** The delicate, fernlike foliage of carrots is a soft, wispy filler in a container or raised bed.

# Collard

*Brassica oleracea* **(Acephala Group)**
**Family: Brassicaceae, the cabbage family**

If you love collard greens, as my family does, you could probably devote all of your garden space to them and still not have enough to satisfy your appetite for this delicious, nutrient-

rich green. Collards are relatively easy to grow and produce for a long time: as a summer crop in cool climates and as a spring and fall-to-winter crop in hot-summer areas. You can continue harvesting collard greens until the plants bolt (form a flowerstalk), which indicates the end of their life cycle.

**Habit:** Tall and upright, with large, paddle-like, dark green leaves sticking out from all sides.

**How to start:** Sow seeds $1/2$ inch deep in the garden around the date of your last frost, or give them a head start indoors about 4 weeks before your last frost date.

**Season:** Summer; fall and possibly even winter in areas with mild winters. Collards tolerate cold better than they do heat.

**When to harvest:** Don't let the way collards are sold at the grocery store fool you—you don't have to harvest the entire bunch at once. Instead, clip off the largest leaves on each plant as needed. If you have several plants, you should be able to harvest enough greens for at least one meal a week this way.

**Water requirements:** Moderate. Though their waxy foliage prevents them from losing lots of water, it is difficult for collard plants to recover if they dry out completely, and they'll produce fewer new leaves.

**Light requirements:** Full sun is best, but a bit of afternoon shade is not a problem.

**Pests and diseases:** Though closely related to cabbage and broccoli, collards seem to be less attractive to cabbage loopers and cabbage worms. Aphids can be a problem, particularly on lush, well-watered and -fertilized plants, but it's easy to crush them with your fingers or knock them off with a strong spray of water.

**Recommended varieties:** There aren't many collard varieties out there, but you won't go wrong with any of them. 'Flash' is an early (55-day) variety that is slow to bolt. 'Georgia Green' is an excellent choice for southern gardens but can be grown in the north as well.

**Space-to-yield ratio:** High. Collards produce a continuous supply of leaves over a long period.

**Plot-free pointers:** Growing collards in a container lets you to move them to optimal conditions: plenty of sun in cooler weather, a bit of shade during the hottest summer months, and a sheltered spot when cold weather settles in. Protecting the plants with floating row cover helps to extend your harvest into frosty weather.

**Garden role:** Thriller. Collard plants get quite large (even to the point of needing staking) and offer a bold presence in a container or raised bed.

# Corn

*Zea mays*
**Family: Poaceae, the grass family**

If you don't like corn on the cob, it's probably because you've never had the chance to enjoy it really fresh. The stories of people bringing a pot to a boil before picking and shucking the ears, and then running back inside to get them into the water right away aren't just made up! The second you remove corn from its stalk, the sugars begin converting to starches, and the taste and texture change considerably. Newer varieties are bred to retain their sugar content longer, but corn connoisseurs will nonetheless know the difference.

Besides planting sweet corn for fresh eating, you can grow many beautiful and historically interesting varieties of flint and dent corn for flour or cornmeal. I can only touch on the very basics of these fascinating crops here, so I highly recommend referring to your favorite seed catalogs and your local Cooperative Extension Service for advice on growing corn successfully in your particular area.

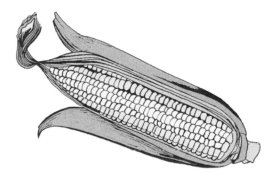

**Habit:** Tall and lanky, corn plants closely resemble their botanical relatives, bamboo and sugarcane. Most corn varieties typically reach 6 to 8 feet in height.

**How to start:** Sow corn seeds $1\frac{1}{2}$ to 2 inches deep outdoors, when the danger of frost has passed and nighttime temperatures are consistently in the 60s. Plant in very fertile soil that's heavily amended with compost, and provide supplemental fertilizer through the season. Thin the seedlings to stand 12 to 15 inches apart.

**Season:** Summer in most areas; late spring and early summer in very hot climates.

**When to harvest:** Pick sweet corn when the silks turn brown and shrivel and the kernels are well formed, large, and bursting with juice. Let field and dent corn plants stand past a few frosts so the ears dry on the stalks.

**Water requirements:** Moderate to high. Field and dent corns may have some drought resistance, especially ancient varieties like those available from Native Seeds/SEARCH, but sweet corn needs frequent irrigation to produce succulent ears.

**Light requirements:** Full sun.

**Pests and diseases:** Various insects affect corn, but most gardeners find that raccoons and squirrels are their most destructive pests. These critters love to eat sweet corn, and they'll damage the plants by climbing them to try to get the developing ears; a good fence is the best defense. Corn smut, a fungal disease, can infect the kernels and cause a misshapen gray mushroom to emerge from them. It is extremely alarming to see it on your ears of corn, but it is a choice ingredient in Mexican cuisine known as huitlacoche (weet-la-ko-chay).

I've tried it at Mexican restaurants, and it is actually delicious, tasting almost exactly like a corn-flavored mushroom. While I wouldn't wish for it to form, if it does, try looking for an authentic Mexican recipe calling for it and cook it that way.

**Recommended varieties:** First, consider which type of corn you'd like to grow—sweet, dent, field, or popcorn (which is a type of flint corn)—and if you want a hybrid or an heirloom variety. Then, look at the days to maturity information in the catalog description to make sure that type is suitable for your area. Flint and dent corns take a long time to mature and may not be suitable in regions with short summers. Sweet corn comes in early-, midseason-, and late-ripening varieties; in short-season areas, look for an early variety such as 'Spring Treat' or 'Precious Gem'.

**Space-to-yield ratio:** Low to medium. Though each plant produces only a couple of ears, you need to grow a fair number of them in a block to ensure good pollination (see below), so you'll end up with a pretty good harvest overall.

**Plot-free pointers:** Most corn varieties are too tall to grow easily in containers, but breeders are working on more compact varieties, such as 'On Deck'. Corn is generally better suited to raised beds than containers. You'll need enough space to put in at least four rows, with as many seeds as your raised bed's width will allow. Corn is wind pollinated, and block planting like this helps ensure that some pollen will fall from the tassels onto the ears instead of being whisked away by the slightest breeze. Even with a four-row minimum, it's still a good idea to gently bend the tassels downward to the ears on neighboring corn plants once they begin bearing pollen (look for tiny rectangles dangling from the tassels at the top) to help ensure complete pollination. Each strand of silk emerging from the ears runs down to an individual kernel, and each strand must receive some pollen to allow its kernel to swell and become edible; otherwise, the ears will be misshapen, with missing kernels.

**Garden role:** Thriller.

# Cucumber

*Cucumis sativus*

**Family: Curcubitaceae, the squash family**

Is there any food more suited to summer than a cool, refreshing cucumber? For productivity, versatility, and edibility, it's hard to beat this enthusiastically vining vegetable. Cucumbers are so easy to grow that even a child can do it (I ought to know: I was 5 or 6 years old the first time I grew them, and I filled our refrigerator with the fruits I harvested off my two plants). Their highly productive nature is probably what led to their frequent use in pickling. Regular cucumbers are so abundant and inexpensive in season that it's smart to save your space for more unusual kinds, such as the round yellow lemon cucumber or the more refined Asian types, which take well to being grown on trellises.

**Habit:** Long, scrambling vines.

**How to start:** Sow cucumber seeds 1 inch deep right in your garden after all danger of frost has passed and the soil is warm.

**Season:** Summer.

**When to harvest:** Pick your cucumbers anytime the fruits are large enough to handle, from tiny baby fruits to those at full size. Over the course of the season, you may well end up doing both, if only because the fruits can be difficult to find in a vigorous patch and may escape your eye, swelling to enormous proportions before you find them.

**Water requirements:** High. The plants need plenty of water to produce succulent fruits. Cucumber foliage wilts readily when the soil is dry.

**Light requirements:** Full sun.

**Pests and diseases:** Cucumber beetles are the worst pest, turning the flowers to tatters and chewing and stippling the leaves. Pick off and crush the black-spotted or -striped adults (be sure to check the flowers, where they especially like to hide), and rub their orange-yellow egg masses off the undersides of the leaves to prevent further damage. Cucumber beetles can spread cucumber diseases like bacterial wilt, which will cause the foliage to look wilted, but affected plants do not revive when you water them. If your plants get wilt, remove and destroy them. (If it's still early in the season, try a second sowing of a fast-maturing variety to get a later crop.)

Powdery mildew, along with a host of other

fungal diseases, is also widespread. Look for resistant varieties and site plants in areas with full sun and good air circulation. Avoid wetting the foliage when you water to reduce the chance of infection.

**Recommended varieties:** Choose varieties depending on whether you plan to use the fruits for fresh eating or pickling. Spineless varieties make harvesting easier, as the tiny prickles on the fruits can be surprisingly painful when touched. Also pay attention to the days to maturity: Some, such as 'Diamant' and 'Rocky', are extremely fast cropping (ready in as little as 48 days), while others, such as 'Bella' and 'Striped Armenian', take 60 days or more.

**Space-to-yield ratio:** High. Though the rambling vines do take up a lot of space, a single cucumber plant can be unbelievably prolific, bearing several pounds of fruit over the season.

**Plot-free pointers:** Be sure to choose varieties that are described as "parthenocarpic." That means they set fruit without pollination, so you can get a good harvest from just one plant. Before you put cucumbers in your garden, think about how you'll manage them: Will you let them sprawl and scamper over the soil surface, or will you provide a trellis to coax them to grow upward rather than outward, saving ground space? If you want to encourage them to climb, check your plants frequently so you can direct the growth of their vine tips before they head in unwanted directions.

**Garden role:** Spiller, usually, though a well-trellised specimen would venture more into thriller territory.

# Eggplant

*Solanum melongena*
**Family: Solanaceae, the tomato family**

Growing eggplant for the first time is a kind of revelation—not just because its flavor and texture are so much better when fresh picked but also because the plant is so shockingly beautiful. Its large, oaklike foliage is covered in fine hairs, creating a soft, felted texture, and its flowers are bold, deep purple, and dramatic. It's surprising to discover that eggplants bear small but sharp thorns on their calyxes (the green bit at the top of the fruit) and, on some varieties, the leaf surfaces as well.

Eggplants like hot weather and can be extremely productive when conditions are right. As with so many other vegetables, the

# TRAINING TIPS FOR CUCUMBER, SQUASH, AND MELON

Cucurbits—cucumbers, melons, and squash—are all vining plants, and their stems can grow several feet. You can let them cascade over the edge of the container or bed, wind them around in a spiral from their growth point, or trellis them. Trellising makes it easier to spot, remove, and destroy cucumber beetles and their egg masses on the underside of the leaves.

**Support structures.** There are many different options for the trellis itself, from store-bought items to the copper trellis I show you how to build on page 137. You can even do something as simple as criss-crossing garden twine between two stakes to form a makeshift ladderlike trellis. It must be strong enough to support the vines, though, which are heavy when the fruit develops. This is more important in the case of squash or melons, which will remain on the vine growing heavier for several weeks, as opposed to cucumbers, which mature quickly and are most productive when you harvest them frequently.

**Trellising tips.** Cucurbit vines usually produce tendrils that spiral around nearby plants or structures to support the plants. Once they find something to grow on, they will secure themselves to it. However, they may require a little help getting up on the trellis or structure to start. Go out in the morning and afternoon to check the plants as they begin growing, and once there is a bit of stem there, help it onto the trellis. Repeat the process until the plant is well established and growing vigorously on the structure; after that, the plant will continue to spread on its own.

varieties available to gardeners are far more numerous and more interesting than what you'll find in your average grocery store: long, slender Asian types (much easier to cook evenly than the big, bulbous Italian varieties); pure white, pale purple, and striped varieties; and the amazing small, round types that resemble mutant tomatoes.

**Habit:** Upright and bushy, with heights anywhere from 2 to 4 feet.

**How to start:** Eggplant is a good candidate for starting indoors 6 to 8 weeks before your last frost date. By giving it a head start inside and growing the seedlings at a very cozy 70°

to 80°F, you'll enjoy a longer harvest. You can, however, sow the seeds directly in your garden if your area has a long growing season. Plant the seeds about $\frac{1}{2}$ inch deep.

**Season:** Summer.

**When to harvest:** You can start picking as soon as the fruits are large enough to be worth eating, but don't be in too much of a rush: Some varieties are bred to be enjoyed at full size. Cut off the fruits, rather than try to pull them off, to avoid damaging the plant and to protect your fingers from the tiny spines on their fruit stems.

**Water requirements:** Medium to high.

Mulching goes a long way to keeping the soil around the roots moist and weed free: conditions that eggplants very much enjoy.

**Light requirements:** Full sun.

**Pests and diseases:** The two biggest pests you're likely to encounter are flea beetles and Colorado potato beetles. Flea beetles chew tiny, round holes in the leaves, but mild infestations won't severely affect productivity. Colorado potato beetles will tatter the foliage and flowers alike. Pick off the adult beetles by hand and crush them or drop them into soapy water, and rub their orange egg cases off the undersides of the leaves with your fingers. Even better, prevent damage from both pests by protecting the plants with a floating row cover.

**Recommended varieties:** Choose a variety based on the type of recipes you're most likely to prepare with your crop. The traditional large, oblong, purple types are a must for classic Italian dishes; long, thin Asian types are perfect for stir-fries; and smaller round types are best for Indian and Thai curries. Short days to maturity and tolerance of cool conditions are also desirable traits to look for. 'Gretel' is a prolific white variety that grows on a compact plant and is ready to harvest in about 55 days. 'Mangan' in a nicely sized Asian variety with dramatic, dark purple calyxes for extra ornamental appeal.

**Space-to-yield ratio:** High, as long as the growing conditions are ideal.

**Plot-free pointers:** Eggplant's good looks make it an excellent choice for container combinations and handsome raised beds. Just be sure to provide it with the highly fertile, compost-enriched soil it needs for vigorous growth, and give it a liquid fertilizer such as compost tea or fish emulsion when the flowers begin forming. Ample water and nutrients are especially important if you're growing eggplant close to other high-needs plants.

**Garden role:** Filler (when combined with taller plants) or thriller (when it's with shorter companions).

# Garlic

*Allium sativum*
**Family: Alliaceae, the onion family**

Garlic is inexpensive at market and reliably tasty, so why devote space in your raised beds or containers to this crop? Well, if you're a garlic lover, you'll thrill at the enormous number of varieties that are available when you shop from seed purveyors instead of grocers. Unique heirloom varieties from countries around the globe tempt the aficionado with their unique colors (white, purple, red violet) and varied aromas ranging from delicately nuanced to sharply pungent. Another good reason to grow garlic is because its growing season is different from that of most other crops—from fall through spring—making use of space that might otherwise be empty. Its tall, narrow habit means you can tuck a spring crop, such as spinach or arugula, in between the garlic plants and finish up both crops in

# THE LURE OF SHALLOTS

Shallots seem like a luxury when you buy them in the grocery store, where they are very expensive if you can find them at all. However, they are easy to grow, behaving just like garlic. Their habit is a bit different—shallots more closely resemble a small chive clump than a tall, single-stemmed garlic—but you plant and harvest them around the same time as garlic. As with garlic, I recommend purchasing shallots for planting from a seed supplier, if you can, rather than popping grocery store bulbs in the ground, so you can get the kind best suited to your area.

early summer, leaving enough time to plant a crop for fall harvest, such as kale or carrots. Home-grown garlic also provides you with a unique late-spring treat: Its scapes (flower stems and buds) are beautiful and tasty as a pesto or sauté.

**Habit:** Very upright and narrow, with long, thin leaves and spiraling scapes in spring.

**How to start:** Buy garlic heads for planting from a farmers' market or seed catalog, not from the grocery store (those sold there may not be right for your climate). Separate the heads into individual cloves and poke them

into the soil so the tip of each clove is 1 to 2 inches below the surface. The larger the clove, the larger the head it will form, so you may want to plant only the bigger cloves and save the small ones for eating.

**Season:** Early to midsummer.

**When to harvest:** Clip the flowering stems once they've emerged well above the plant and have begun to bend and spiral. Harvest garlic heads once the plants turn brown and wither, indicating that they've taken in all the energy from the leaves.

**Water requirements:** Low to moderate. You won't need to go out of your way to water garlic if it is planted among your other crops.

**Light requirements:** Full sun.

**Pests and diseases:** Nothing of note, though garlic doesn't appreciate competition from weeds.

**Recommended varieties:** Avail yourself of some of the more interesting varieties you aren't likely to encounter at the store, like 'Spanish Roja', a large-cloved red type, or 'Siberian' for those in areas with cold climates.

**Space-to-yield ratio:** Moderate. You get two products from each garlic plant, and each clove you put in the ground yields a head of anywhere from 5 to 12 cloves of varying sizes.

**Plot-free pointers:** Gathering the heads involves some digging and can damage nearby roots, so avoid pairing garlic with crops that will be actively growing in early to midsummer. Instead, pair it with early crops, such radishes, peas, spinach, or lettuce, which will be gone or nearly done by garlic harvesttime.

**Garden role:** Filler. Garlic forms a strong vertical line in the garden, providing structure to more wild plantings.

# Kale

*Brassica oleracea* (Acephala Group)
**Family: Brassicaceae, the cabbage family**

Many American gardeners have grown ornamental or flowering kale as an autumn garden accent, but we're just catching up to the Europeans in appreciating the tastier types meant for harvest. There are three main types: curly kale, with densely ruffled leaves; Russian kale, with flat, oaklike leaves; and strappy-leaved Tuscan kale (also known as lacinato, black kale, cavolo nero, and dinosaur kale). All of these can make a striking, leafy accent in the vegetable garden—you might say they're the hosta of edibles!

**Habit:** Upright, bushy, and leafy.

**How to start:** Sow seeds $1/2$ inch deep right in the garden in midspring or give them a head start indoors a few weeks earlier. Kale begins to yield usable leaves fairly quickly, but starting it inside will let you get a crop sooner and harvest for a longer period.

**Season:** Spring and fall, mainly, but summer, too, in cool climates (especially for Tuscan kale) and winter in hot climates.

**When to harvest:** Most kales are bred to be harvested as an entire head, but you can clip individual leaves as needed. Try Tuscan kale at baby size (roughly 30 days after transplant-

ing), let it mature (60+ days), or pick it anytime in between.

**Water requirements:** Low in cool weather; medium in hot spells. Kale is most productive when it gets ample water and soil nutrition.

**Light requirements:** Full sun to partial shade.

**Pests and diseases:** Aphids are the primary threat, and though they don't cause much actual damage, they can make kale unappetizing to consume. It's especially hard to control them on the curly varieties. Cabbage loopers and cabbage worms can also be an issue, though less so on kale than on other cabbage-family crops. Soak harvested leaves in cold water for an hour or so before eating to remove any hidden pests. Better yet, prevent damage by protecting your plants with a floating row cover.

**Recommended varieties:** If you have room for only one type of kale, I recommend a Tuscan kale, such as 'Toscano'. Beautiful and easy to grow, the plants are both cold and heat tolerant, and you can use the leaves raw or cooked. Tuscan kale also tends to be more expensive to buy than curly kale, if you can even find it at the grocery store.

'Winterbor' is the standard for curly kale. Red varieties, such as 'Redbor', are lovely in the garden but lose their color when cooked, giving it off to any onions or garlic being cooked in the same pan and giving the whole meal a rather unappetizing grayish cast.

**Space-to-yield ratio:** Moderate to high. Tuscan

types, especially, produce leaves over a long period, and even those that are bred for a single harvest are fairly quick to crop (50 to 55 days) and bear heavily.

**Plot-free pointers:** Kale is an excellent crop for containers. It looks good with anything, is not extremely greedy for water and nutrition, and can grow well into autumn or even winter. It's one of the best vegetables to grow if you want to put something home grown on your Thanksgiving table!

**Garden role:** Filler morphing to thriller as the season wears on. If you harvest the individual leaves of Tuscan kale, the plant continues to grow as a long, tall stalk topped with a tuft of leaves, easily becoming the focal point of any planting.

# Kohlrabi

*Brassica oleracea* (Gongylodes Group)
**Family: Brassicaceae, the cabbage family**

If you've never tried eating this truly alien-looking vegetable, you probably can't imagine growing it in your garden, but it's worth considering. Kohlrabi is a bit like a round, swollen broccoli stem, with crunch, succulence, and a slightly cabbagey flavor, but it is much easier to grow than broccoli. You can harvest kohlrabi in as little as 6 weeks from direct seeding, making it a very fast crop, and it is versatile in the kitchen, lending itself to being shredded raw for slaws, cut into sticks for snacking, or cubed and cooked in almost any way you can imagine. It is widely incorporated into curry dishes in India. The leaves are edible, too: Try them steamed, boiled, or in soups.

**Habit:** A round, bulblike base with widely spaced leaves emerging from the center and all around.

**How to start:** Kohlrabi grows quickly and enjoys cool (but not cold) weather, so you can plant the seeds ½ inch deep right in your garden as soon as the soil is thawed and dried out a bit and the really cold weather has passed. If you want an even earlier harvest, start the seeds indoors in early spring. Consider sowing again every few weeks to get a continuous supply of kohlrabi through the growing season.

**Season:** Spring and fall, mainly; summer as well in cold climates.

**When to harvest:** Most varieties take 38 to 45 days to reach full size, but you can harvest them earlier for baby kohlrabi.

**Water requirements:** Moderate. Plenty of water yields a tasty, crispy harvest very quickly.

**Light requirements:** Full sun to partial shade (especially when the weather gets warm).

**Pests and diseases:** As a member of the cabbage family, kohlrabi is subject to many of the same pests and diseases, but it is much less likely to be bothered by them. If aphids or caterpillars are especially abundant, rub or pick them off the plants.

**Recommended varieties:** Three main types are available: white, purple, and storage. The storage varieties are very large (about the size of a rutabaga) and much slower to yield a crop than the white and purple are, so I recommend sticking to the fast-turning white varieties like 'Quickstar' or slightly slower (but more dramatic-looking) purple varieties like 'Kolibri'.

**Space-to-yield ratio:** Moderately high. Besides the crunchy "bulb," kohlrabi produces leafy growth that you can harvest and cook like kale.

**Plot-free pointers:** With such a quick time to maturity, kohlrabi is a great seed to have on hand for filling in little spaces left when you harvest other crops. Its highly unusual look makes it an unexpected addition to containers.

**Garden role:** Filler in a large pot with larger plants; thriller in a small pot as the centerpiece and underplanted with smaller companions, such as lettuce.

# Lettuce

*Lactuca sativa*

**Family: Asteraceae, the daisy family**

Deliciously fresh and tender, just-picked lettuce is a true luxury. Growing your own means that a salad is always just a few steps away and always special. I am a big fan of growing "cut and come again" mixes, which include a variety of colors, textures, and sizes of leaf-lettuce types, as these can produce all season long in cool summers. In hot summers, you can sow them multiple times to have a steady supply of top-quality greens in all but the hottest and

coldest periods. A single-harvest head lettuce here and there can be a pretty and unique accent to a container, taking up just a few square inches of room.

**Habit:** A loose rosette of glossy foliage. Textures range from smooth to ruffled to jagged.

**How to start:** Sow lettuce seeds $1/8$ to $1/4$ inch deep right in the garden in early spring, as soon as the soil is thawed and dry enough to dig. Hot weather often causes the plants to bolt, or go to flower, making the greens bitter; when this happens, pull out the plants and sow again. If your season is mild, you may be able to harvest all season long.

**Season:** Spring through summer; fall; even winter, too, in mild areas.

**When to harvest:** Gather leaf lettuces anytime there are enough leaves to harvest. Cut above the central growing point of each plant so it can produce more topgrowth for the next harvest. Cut head lettuces just above the soil when the head is well formed and firm.

**Water requirements:** Moderate to high.

The warmer and sunnier the weather, the more water you'll need to provide.

**Light requirements:** Full sun to shade. More shade means a longer growing period in hot weather, but the plants may not produce as much leafy growth in the early part of the season there.

**Pests and diseases:** If slugs are a problem, dust the plants and the area around them with diatomaceous earth. Squash aphids with your fingers or wash them off the plants.

**Recommended varieties:** Seed catalogs offer a dizzying selection of lettuces. I like the varied textures and flavors of the mixes produced by Renee's Garden Seeds and Johnny's Selected Seeds, and I recommend them above all. If you prefer a more uniform harvest, however, you can't go wrong with classic, reliable varieties like 'Black Seeded Simpson', 'Deer Tongue', and 'Dark Lollo Rossa'.

**Space-to-yield ratio:** High for leaf lettuces; low to moderate for head lettuces.

**Plot-free pointers:** One of the major advantages to growing lettuce in a container is that the leaves stay very clean, especially if you cover the surface of the potting mix with a mulch. Container growing also lets you move just-harvested pots of leaf lettuce to an out-of-the-way spot while the plants regrow, so they don't detract from your pretty display of edible pots.

**Garden role:** Paired with other plants, lettuce is a filler that verges into spiller, as its foliage dips gently over the edge of the pot or bed. However, I prefer to devote entire pots to a planting of mixed salad greens, which makes harvesting easier and still looks good except for the few days right after cutting.

# ONE-MONTH CROPS

Want homegrown food superfast? Sow seeds of these speedy crops right in your garden and enjoy a harvest about a month after germination (even sooner, in some cases). To get the very quickest results from these express-lane edibles, compare seed packets or catalog descriptions to find varieties with the fewest days to maturity. Also, look for those particularly recommended for early harvesting as "baby" vegetables.

- ☼ Arugula
- ☼ Basil
- ☼ Beet
- ☼ Carrot
- ☼ Chervil

- ☼ Cilantro
- ☼ Lettuce
- ☼ Kohlrabi
- ☼ Radish
- ☼ Spinach

# Malabar Spinach

*Basella alba* 'Rubra'
**Family: Basellaceae, the basella family**

You may not have eaten Malabar spinach yet, but there's a very good chance you've seen this stunningly beautiful climbing plant in ornamental plantings at public gardens, and it will look just as good in your garden. Also known as climbing spinach, it has extremely glossy foliage, brilliant magenta stems, and clusters of pinkish white flowers that resemble lily-of-the-valley. The fact that it's grown extensively as a spinachlike vegetable in the Philippines, India, and Southeast Asia is a good clue that this unusual edible is very well suited to continuous production in hot climates. Cold-climate gardeners, too, can enjoy Malabar spinach as a summer crop, though they won't get quite as long a harvest.

**Habit:** Climbing, twining vine with highly succulent leaves and stems.

**How to start:** Sow seeds ¼ to ½ inch deep in the garden when all danger of frost has passed and the soil is warm, or give them a head start indoors 4 weeks before your last frost date.

**Season:** Summer, extending into spring and autumn in warm climates.

**When to harvest:** Clip off shoots or individual leaves as needed once the plant is established and growing vigorously.

**Water requirements:** Moderate to high. The plant loves hot, humid weather but requires ample water to keep producing those juicy leaves.

**Light requirements:** Full sun.

**Pests and diseases:** None of note. Probably the biggest problem you'll have with Malabar spinach is harvesting it—it's so beautiful, you may not be able to bear to cut it!

**Recommended varieties:** The very ornamental 'Rubra' is the most widely available type of Malabar spinach, but you may sometimes find green-stemmed species.

**Space-to-yield ratio:** High. Fast growing and undeterred by summer heat, Malabar spinach provides a steady harvest over a period of several weeks or even months.

**Plot-free pointers:** This vigorous vine needs a large, strong support, such as a bean tepee. Try it as an edible cover for an arbor or archway.

**Garden role:** Thriller. In a container, allow some shoots to grow downward over the edge of the pot for an attractive spiller effect as well.

# Okra

*Abelmoschus esculentus*
**Family: Malvaceae, the hibiscus family**

With its mucilaginous (some might say slimy) texture and relatively regional popularity, okra is a crop you might be tempted to overlook. However, okra is an absolutely beautiful plant, with tall, straight stalks that bear large yellow flowers with a dark burgundy center. It's also an indispensable crop for hot-climate gardeners, as it adores warm temperatures. Okra tends to bruise easily and toughen as it sits after harvest, so it really is worth growing your own if you want to taste it at its best. If you find the flavor still isn't to your liking, you can always find a homesick Southerner who will gratefully take your harvest, and you can simply enjoy the beauty of the plants.

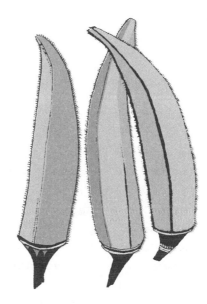

**Habit:** Tall, upright, and leafy. The edible portion is the immature seedpod, which sticks straight up from the leaf axils.

**How to start:** Sow okra seeds $1/2$ to 1 inch deep indoors about 4 weeks before your last frost date. Or sow them in the garden after your last frost date if you live in an area with a long, hot growing season.

**Season:** Summer.

**When to harvest:** Harvest the pods when they are small and tender. Keep okra plants well picked for continuous production. If the pods begin to mature, production may slow or stop, and the large pods tend to be stringy and unpalatable.

**Water requirements:** Moderate.

**Light requirements:** Full sun.

**Pests and diseases:** None serious. Aphids may be a problem if you are providing ample amounts of the water and the fertile soil okra loves, but you can easily wash them off the plants with a strong spray of water.

**Recommended varieties:** All okra plants bear tiny spines, but "spineless" varieties have fewer spines on the pods, making harvesting easier. While 'Clemson Spineless' is the classic standard, most modern varieties also have this trait. (It's still a good idea to wear gloves and long sleeves when harvesting to avoid skin irritation.) In short-season areas, consider early-maturing varieties like 'Jambalaya', which begins producing 50 days after transplanting.

**Space-to-yield ratio:** High. As long as the weather is warm and the soil's not too dry, okra will keep producing pods. You can eat the flowers, too, though if you pick them, then they can't produce a pod.

**Plot-free pointers:** Okra becomes quite a large plant as it matures, so it's best in raised beds and large containers. Look for red varieties such as 'Red Burgundy' for an extra dash of ornamental value.

**Garden role:** Thriller. Tall and upright with large showy flowers, okra is a centerpiece to any planting.

# Pea

*Pisum sativum*

**Family: Fabaceae, the bean family**

Peas are a classic spring crop. Besides producing a tasty harvest, they're interesting, attractive plants with pretty flowers, and planting the seed is a perfect cure for spring fever. Though peas are not nearly as productive as beans, their close relative, they make use of your garden space early in the season and are typically ready to give up the ghost about the time your warm-weather crops are getting established. You can plant again later in the season to fit in another harvest in the cool weather of fall.

**Habit:** Upright vines with fine tendrils that allow them to cling to one another or to a support stake to remain upright.

**How to start:** Sow pea seeds 1 inch deep outdoors in early spring, as soon as the soil is completely thawed and has dried out a bit. Traditionally, peas are planted on either the Ides of March (March 15) or St. Patrick's Day (March 17), though this isn't always possible every year for all gardeners.

**Season:** Spring, possibly into early summer if the weather is mild and heat is limited. You can make a second sowing in mid- to late summer for a fall crop as well.

**When to harvest:** Pick shelling peas when the peas inside are fully formed (open one pod to check before you harvest a bunch). Gather snap peas when they are crisp, fat, and succulent, and snow peas as soon as they are large enough to be worth taking (usually at least 2

inches long). The shoot tips and flowers are edible, too.

**Water requirements:** Moderate. Do not let the soil get too dry. Because of their early nature, peas usually do not require a lot of supplemental water, but it depends on the weather and your climate.

**Light requirements:** Full sun or partial shade.

**Pests and diseases:** None serious.

**Recommended varieties:** First, choose which type of pea you'd like. Shelling peas are the beautiful, classic peas-in-a-pod that are so difficult to find fresh. Sugar snap peas are known as *mange tout* in French (which translates to "eat all") because both the fat, crisp pod and the seeds within are sweet and delicious. And then there are snow peas, the flat, edible-podded type used so often in Chinese cuisine and stir-fries. Among these, look at days to maturity so you can harvest as much as possible while the weather is relatively cool. Hot-climate gardeners should choose fast-maturing varieties; cool-climate gardeners can opt for slower-maturing types.

**Space-to-yield ratio:** Low to moderate, depending on how long ideal conditions persist.

**Plot-free pointers:** In containers, I like to sow peas in a large ring around the edge of the pot and plant another spring crop, like spinach, in the middle, or else leave the center space free for a slightly later planting of tomatoes, peppers, or another warm-season crop that will fill in once the peas are done.

**Garden role:** Filler. Combine peas with other pretty cool-weather plants like parsley, pansies, or spinach for a pleasing seasonal display.

# Pepper

*Capsicum* spp.
**Family: Solanaceae, the tomato family**

Peppers, especially hot peppers, are quickly gaining on tomatoes as a must-have summer crop for even the most casual gardener. Thanks to the rise in popularity of heirloom vegetables and the American mania for hot sauce, more and more people who don't even consider themselves "gardeners" opt for a pot or two of an interesting hot pepper among their patio plantings. Peppers are easy to grow and highly productive, as long as the weather is warm (even hot) and sunshine is abundant.

**Habit:** Strong, bushy plants ranging from 8 to 12 inches tall for some small hot peppers up to 3 to 4 feet tall for some bell peppers.

**How to start:** To give peppers the head

start they need to be productive, sow the seeds ¼ inch deep indoors 6 to 8 weeks before your last frost. They do not germinate well in soil mixes that contain peat, which means that most commercial seed-starting mixes are not a good option; instead, use a blend of equal parts sand and compost, or a peat-free mix. The seeds take a very long time to sprout—often 2 weeks or more—and benefit greatly from the use of a germination mat.

**Season:** Summer.

**When to harvest:** People are often surprised to hear that green peppers are merely unripe red peppers, but it's true: Peppers go through a range of colors on their way to ripening. Though you can eat them at any stage from green to red (or yellow or orange or purple or brown), most varieties are bred to be at their best at a certain stage. For example, I wouldn't think of harvesting my beloved cherry hot peppers anytime but when they're bright, blazing red—but have you ever even seen a jalapeño pepper offered in any color but green?

**Water requirements:** Moderate. Peppers should not dry out, but if they get too much water, their flavor (and in the case of hot peppers, their heat) will be diluted. This is

especially a concern for gardeners using drip irrigation, so arrange the emitters so that pots containing peppers do not get too much water.

**Light requirements:** Full sun.

**Pests and diseases:** Peppers are subject to leaf spot diseases, but these are unlikely to be a problem for most home gardeners. Good air circulation and dry foliage will go a long way toward keeping pepper plants healthy. Spider mites can be a problem as well, but healthy, vigorous plants can outgrow their damage.

**Recommended varieties:** It's always a good idea to opt for unusual varieties that you won't typically find in stores. For bell peppers, that may mean one of the unique new "chocolate" varieties, with brown-purple skin, or a vibrant orange like 'Sweet Sunrise'. Hot peppers are a fascinating world unto themselves, and there are many beautiful, interesting varieties to try. My must-haves include hot cherry peppers for stuffing (hot but extremely flavorful), highly productive Thai peppers, scorching but florally flavorful red Scotch bonnets, and a beautiful heirloom variety known as lemon pepper. Whether you're growing bells or hots, it's important to choose a variety that is adapted to your climate. Most peppers like very long, very hot seasons, so extreme northern gardeners may get little or no harvest from long-season types.

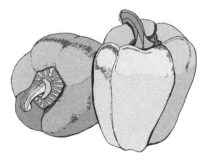

**Space-to-yield ratio:** High. When the weather is warm and plants are well fertilized, you'll have more peppers than you know what to do with. Find some chile-head friends and make their day with a basket of gleaming fruit.

**Plot-free pointers:** Hot pepper plants tend to be smaller and more compact than bell or sweet peppers, so you can tuck them in wherever space allows. If you grow bell peppers, give them plenty of room. Keep plants well fed with a tomato fertilizer (do not use high-nitrogen fertilizer) all season long.

**Garden role:** Bell peppers are thrillers, while hot peppers can be either thrillers or fillers, depending on the variety.

# Potato

*Solanum tuberosum*
**Family: Solanaceae, the tomato family**

If you're used to thinking of potatoes as a bland kitchen staple, homegrown potatoes will turn your culinary world upside down! You'll be amazed by the interesting shapes, colors, and national origins, and the flavor and texture are an absolute revelation. Potatoes are easy to grow in both containers and raised beds, but they need a bit of regular attention to produce a good crop. Most potatoes produce their tubers very close to the soil surface, and as they swell, they may be exposed to sunlight. If this happens, you need to cover them with soil to keep them from turning green and to encourage their further development. Mound soil around the base of the plant to keep the

two or three), as well as some flesh to sustain the buds while they sprout. Cut the pieces a day or so before your planting day so the surfaces can "cure," or dry out. You'll know they're ready for planting when a crystalline sheen forms on the cut surfaces: usually in 12 to 24 hours.

**Season:** Mid- to late summer, depending on variety.

**When to harvest:** When your potato plants begin to bloom, you can root around in the soil with your fingers to start harvesting some baby tubers as "new" potatoes. For the biggest harvest, wait until the stems have browned and withered to dig up the full-size tubers.

**Water requirements:** Low to moderate. Potatoes are far from the most demanding garden crop in terms of water, but they won't produce as well if the soil is kept very dry.

**Light requirements:** Full sun.

**Pests and diseases:** Colorado potato beetle is the number one threat to your potato crops. Begin scouting for the orange egg masses on the undersides of leaves in late May, as soon as the plant is growing well, and rub off any you find. Once the plants start flowering, the plant can withstand pretty severe defoliation and still produce a crop, so pest patrol is less critical—simply hand-pick the black-striped, yellow-orange adult beetles as you see them. Tiny, black flea beetles can also be an issue, chewing tiny holes in the foliage, but their presence is unlikely to severely affect your harvest. Potatoes can get a host of blights and fungal diseases, but these are mostly only problematic when weather is cool and wet all summer. If the foliage turns black or gets severe leaf spot, remove the plants and discard them. In a container, discard the soil, too; in a raised bed,

tubers buried, or plant in a trench or furrow in a raised bed and push soil into it as the plant grows. Or plant your potatoes in a container half filled with soil, then keep adding more soil as the stems grow upward.

**Habit:** Upright and bushy. Potato plants look very much like tomato plants, except with less lacy-looking foliage and purple or white flowers instead of yellow.

**How to start:** Plant potatoes 3 to 4 inches deep in spring, as soon as the soil is thawed out and not soggy. Even though you may have purchased something labeled "seed potatoes," these are not actually seeds: They are tiny, whole potatoes that will sprout and grow into a plant. Some varieties are sold as larger potatoes that you cut into pieces to plant. Each piece needs at least one bud or "eye" (ideally

# SOURCING SEED POTATOES

There is some question as to whether you can use grocery-store potatoes for planting. Some store-bought potatoes intended for eating have been treated to delay sprouting, which gives them a longer shelf life but makes them unsuitable for planting. If, however, you have sprouted potatoes in your pantry, they were either untreated or the treatment wore off, and they will probably grow successfully. Ultimately, though, since these are the same varieties you can buy any day at the grocery store, why settle? Visit a garden center or purchase seed potatoes from a good mail-order source and indulge in something more interesting.

Curing seed potatoes (see page 245)

avoid planting potatoes again in that spot for at least 3 years.

**Recommended varieties:** There are four main types of potatoes you can grow: yellow, red, baking, and fingerling. Yellow and red are the most productive and tastiest fresh from the garden; they're also suitable to early harvest if you're impatient. Baking or russet potatoes are best for storage, but they produce big plants that can take up a lot of space. Fingerlings are the least productive but the most interesting and special: perfect for growing at home. You can also experiment with blue or pink varieties for something really different. You're best off chatting with growers at your local farmers' market to find out which particular potato varieties do best in your area.

**Space-to-yield ratio:** Moderate to high, depending on the variety.

**Plot-free pointers:** Potatoes appreciate very fertile soil and regular fertilizing up until flowering. They are most productive in a raised bed where they have ample room to spread their roots and create tubers, and they're easy to harvest there, too. Potatoes are also great candidates for growing in grow rings (page 143). You can raise them in a very large container, too, though they prefer to have the space all to themselves.

**Garden role:** A potato plant could potentially fill any of the three roles, but with its upright, thick stem, showy flowers, and interesting globular fruits, it is most often a thriller. Keep in mind, though, that you'll need to dig up the tubers to harvest them, so don't plant companions too close by.

# Radish

*Raphanus sativus*

**Family: Brassicaceae, the cabbage family**

There's a good reason that radishes are the first edible plant that children grow in preschool or kindergarten: They're one of the fastest and easiest crops anywhere. No matter how old you are, it's absolutely magical to pull a brightly colored, perfectly shaped radish out of the earth in as little as 3 weeks after you plant the seed. Not only is the root edible, but so are the greens and, if you let the plant bloom, the seedpods. With all of these great traits, you'd think everyone would grow radishes, but some folks don't care much for the peppery but watery taste of common radishes. If you're one of them, check your favorite seed catalogs for more unusual varieties and give those a try. It's worth experimenting, because radishes are one of the very best edibles for maximizing your harvest season.

**Habit:** A tuft of lightly haired foliage marks the location of the developing rounded, oblong, or tapering root.

**How to start:** Sow radish seeds ½ inch

# DOUBLY DELICIOUS

Top-notch edibles are more than pretty faces: They're extra-productive, too. The very best of these yield even more of a harvest, giving you two or even three different parts to pick from every plant. If you're not sure which crops to try first, or if your gardening space is really limited, give these elite edibles a try.

- Arugula: leaves and flowers
- Beets: roots and leaves
- Chives: leaves and flowers
- Cilantro: leaves, flowers, and seeds (seeds are the spice coriander)
- Dill: leaves, flowers, and seeds
- Fennel: leaves, flowers, and seeds
- Garlic: bulb and flower stems (scapes)
- Kohlrabi: leaves and swollen stems
- Nasturtium: leaves and flowers
- Parsley: leaves and stems
- Peas: shoot tips, flowers, and fruits
- Radishes: roots, leaves, and seedpods
- Rosemary: leaves and flowers
- Summer squash: flowers and fruits

deep outdoors in early spring; if the seed is not planted deeply enough, the radish will not form. This crop can tolerate cold and will grow as long as the soil is not completely sodden.

**Season:** Spring to early summer; fall; and even winter in warm climates. Heat makes them unpalatably peppery and pithy.

**When to harvest:** Refer to the seed packet or catalog description for the days to maturity to get an idea of the target harvest date. Look for the top of the root at the base of the leaves to estimate the root's size and determine if it's big enough to harvest.

**Water requirements:** Low to moderate. Early-season radishes don't need much supplemental water, simply because the weather is cool and rain tends to be more regular at the times of year that radishes like to grow. However, if dry conditions prevail, watering will help keep your radishes succulent and mild.

**Light requirements:** Full sun in spring; partial shade for later crops.

**Pests and diseases:** Flea beetles will feed on the foliage, leaving tiny, round holes but usually not affecting your harvest. If you want to prevent the damage, protect the plants with a floating row cover. A pest known as a root maggot can burrow along and into developing radishes. These are less of a problem in containers than in the ground and are more likely to occur in soils where related plants grew the previous year; reduce the chance of problems by growing cabbage-family crops in different sites each year.

**Recommended varieties:** Packets of mixed varieties are fun for an array of colors, and the long French-type radishes, such as 'French Breakfast', are a nice alternative to the standard round grocery-store varieties. Watermelon radishes and black radishes take longer to mature than standard radishes and must be sown later in the season (in late spring to midsummer) to prevent them from going to flower before you can pick them. They're definitely worth considering, though—especially the delicious, you-won't-believe-it's-a-radish watermelon type, which has white skin and a pink-to-red center.

**Space-to-yield ratio:** Moderate to high. Though each seed produces only a single root, radishes are so fast to grow and take so little space that you can harvest a lot of them with very little effort.

**Plot-free pointers:** Keep a packet of radish seed handy through the season—it's easy to tuck in a seed or two in wherever there is a little opening to produce another crop.

**Garden role:** Filler.

# Scallion

*Allium fistulosum*
**Family: Alliaceae, the onion family**

Regular round onions are so inexpensive and readily available that there's not much point in growing them in a spot better taken up by a more interesting crop. Scallions—also known as green onions—are another matter. They take little effort, grow quickly, and provide a long season of harvest: from early summer clear through frost and possibly even beyond, in mild climates. In fact, in my USDA Zone 6 garden, scallions overwinter easily in containers for an early-spring harvest. To maximize the white portion of scallions, you can mound soil around the base of the plant as it develops, but this isn't necessary to produce a good, tasty crop.

**Habit:** Upright, narrow fans of tubular foliage.

**How to start:** Sow seeds ¹⁄₂ inch deep directly in the garden starting in early to midspring. Sow again every 2 weeks or so through early August in cold climates and through midto late fall in mild climates.

**Season:** Early summer through fall; early spring for any that were allowed to overwinter.

**When to harvest:** You can pick scallions at any stage, finishing up around the maturity date suggested for whatever variety you're growing.

**Water requirements:** Moderate. In good soil that's enriched with organic matter, they won't need much watering; just don't let the ground get very dry.

**Light requirements:** Sun.

**Pests and diseases:** None serious.

**Recommended varieties:** Try a beautiful purple variety, like 'Deep Purple', for an interesting alternative to the standard scallion. Though it is primarily only the outer layer that shows the rich purple color, it is particularly ornamental in the garden and on the table.

**Space-to-yield ratio:** Medium. Each plant is almost entirely edible, and though scallions take about 2 months to mature, they can grow fairly close together, and you can sow them continuously for a steady harvest.

**Plot-free pointers:** Scallions are an easierto-grow and more-productive alternative to leeks and onions, making them an excellent choice for onion-loving gardeners with limited space. Plant an entire container's worth, grow them in a row in a raised bed, or strategically sow clusters of seeds in areas where there is a bit of open space.

**Garden role:** Filler.

# Spinach

*Spinacia oleracea*
**Family: Chenopodiaceae, the beet family**

Cold tolerant and fast to grow, spinach will be one of the first crops you harvest every season. It can be among the last you'll pick into fall, too, if you sow seeds for an autumn crop in late summer. Though some varieties are more heat tolerant than others, none thrive in hot weather. You'll have to plant a hot-weather substitute, like Malabar spinach (see page 240) or New Zealand spinach (*Tetragonia tetragonoides*), to get your spinach fix in the summer.

**Habit:** Rosettes of dark green foliage.

**How to start:** Sow spinach seeds about ¹⁄₄ inch deep in the garden once the soil is completely thawed and dried out a bit in early spring. You can sow again every few weeks up until about 2 weeks

before the weather starts to get really warm (in the low 80s), then resume sowing in early to mid-August for a fall and winter crop.

**Season:** Spring, fall, and winter.

**When to harvest:** Start picking individual outer leaves anytime they are large enough to handle, or let the plants reach full size and cut the whole top.

**Water requirements:** Low to moderate. Though conditions tend to be cool and moist during its preferred growing times, spinach may need watering during dry spells.

**Light requirements:** Full sun is best, but it's all right if the plants get some shade as the weather warms up.

**Pests and diseases:** Spinach is mostly problem free. If you are having trouble growing it, your soil is probably too acid or too alkaline (check the pH and correct it to near 7.0, if needed), or your weather is too warm.

**Recommended varieties:** Smooth-leaved varieties tend to be the fastest cropping and the easiest to clean. Try 'Red Cardinal', which is ready to harvest in as little as 3 weeks for baby spinach. Savoyed varieties have strongly crinkled leaves, which are beautiful but can hold soil in their crannies, making it difficult to remove the grit. Choose a savoyed variety only if you can mulch your plants to keep soil from splashing up on them or if you are growing in a soilless mix.

**Space-to-yield ratio:** High.

**Plot-free pointers:** There are several advantages to growing spinach in containers: The leaves stay cleaner, and it's much easier to sow and pick them when you don't have to bend down to ground level.

**Garden role:** Filler, if you don't mind taking extra care when harvesting it to avoid damaging closely packed companions. For quicker picking, give your spinach plants a whole pot or an entire row to themselves.

# FLOWER POWER

Summer squash has separate male and female flowers on every plant. It's easy to tell them apart: The female flowers have a tiny fruit at their base; male flowers, simply a narrow stem. When the plant first begins to blossom, most of those flowers will be male, which don't set fruit. You can pick and eat these: They make tasty, colorful accents on salads especially. Female flowers, once they appear, are edible as well, and they are what's preferred in the classic Italian stuffed zucchini blossom dishes. However, harvesting female flowers removes the possibility of their producing fruit, so do this only if you are willing to sacrifice some of your crop.

# Summer Squash

*Curcubita pepo*
**Family: Curcubitaceae, the squash family**

Squash comes in two main categories: summer squash, which produces succulent, thin-skinned fruits that are eaten fresh, and winter

deep right in the garden, a week or two after all danger of frost has passed. The plants emerge and grow quickly, and their fleshy taproots greatly prefer direct sowing to being transplanted from an indoor start.

**Season:** Summer into fall.

**When to harvest:** You can pick summer squash fruits at any size, but you'll get the best flavor and highest yields if you regularly pick the fruits when they are about 6 inches long. They ripen quickly, so check your plants every day or two to make sure you don't miss any. Overlarge fruits get tough and seedy and aren't good for eating.

**Water requirements:** Moderate to high. If a summer squash plant needs water, its foliage wilts severely. It can recover, but frequent drought stress slows the production of more fruits.

**Light requirements:** Full sun.

**Pests and diseases:** Those who joke about their overabundance of zucchini have likely (and luckily) never encountered the pests and diseases that can affect these plants. Of particular note is the squash vine borer, which usually kills plants outright as it burrows

squash, with hard-skinned fruits intended for storage for winter eating. Winter squash plants take up too much space to be practical for most containers and smaller raised beds, but summer squash, with a bushier habit and prolific yield, is a great crop to consider. Zucchini is the best known type of summer squash, but it's not the only one: Many other shapes, colors, and sizes are available.

**Habit:** Summer squash is a large plant, with enormous leaves sprouting from the central point on strong, tubular stems to create a rather fountainlike habit. As the plant matures, it may begin to creep or spread a bit, but it is in no sense a vine like cucumber or winter squash.

**How to start:** Sow the seeds ¹/₂ to 1 inch

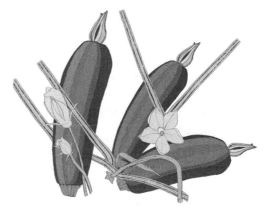

through the main stem, eating all around it and severing it from the ground. It is the larval stage that is responsible for this damage, and it begins life as a tiny egg laid by a moth at the base of the plant. Most gardeners find out they have squash vine borer when they go to harvest a fruit and find the whole plant is detached from the roots. If you manage to catch it before then—look for small piles of brown sawdustlike powder on the stems at the base of the plant—you can carefully cut open the stem with a sharp knife, remove and destroy the larva, and then heap soil over the cut stem section encourage it to form new roots. A better way to deal with squash vine borer, however, is to prevent the damage by protecting the plants with a floating row cover. (You'll have to remove the cover once the plants start to bloom, though, so insects can get in to pollinate the flowers.)

Squash bugs are another squash-specific pest, and they can be quite harmful to your plants. Pick off and destroy the gray-brown adult bugs, and rub the coppery orange egg masses off the undersides of the leaves with your fingers.

Summer squash seems to be a magnet for powdery mildew, even when you take the precautions of planting in full sun, avoiding wetting the leaves, and providing good air circulation. You can't cure it once your plants are affected, but you might be able to prevent it with kaolin clay (see page 106).

If you are growing summer squash and aren't getting any fruit, it's probably a cultural issue and not related to pests or diseases, especially if it is the beginning of the season. Summer squash plants bear both male and female flowers on the same plant, and both need to be present at the same time for pollination to occur. Once the plant grows a bit more, it will produce ample quantities of both flowers.

**Recommended varieties:** Select for color, shape, size, and productivity. For classic green zucchini, try 'Dunja' or another disease-resistant type. Then expand your horizons with a yellow, striped, or crookneck variety, all of which share the flavor and productivity of zucchini but are more ornamental on the vine because they contrast with the foliage. Pattypan and round varieties are especially unusual choices, and children love them. 'Ronde de Nice' is an heirloom French variety with small, round fruits; 'Flying Saucer' is a colorful and unique-looking pattypan type that yields in 50 days.

**Space-to-yield ratio:** High, as long as the plants get plenty of water and you protect them from pests.

**Plot-free pointers:** Summer squash is a large plant and requires a large container—no smaller than 18 inches in diameter—or a fair share of a raised bed. However, as long as plants stay healthy, they will be as productive as cherry tomatoes, providing you with an abundant harvest every week for months. Fortunately, summer squash has a wide range of uses in the kitchen and keeps for several days in the refrigerator. If you have the space, grow more than one plant to encourage pollination and to have a backup in case one gets affected by vine borers.

**Garden role:** Thriller. The large, dramatic leaves and colorful fruits make summer squash the center of attention. Its large habit makes it unsuitable for pairing with most anything else anyway.

# Sweet Potato

*Ipomoea batatas*

**Family: Convolvulaceae, the morning glory family**

Ever since sweet potato vine became a popular ornamental plant for summer containers and hanging baskets, gardeners everywhere (especially those outside the South who were unfamiliar with the plant) have been shocked to discover their pots full of plump tuberous roots at the end of the season. So are these sweet potatoes? Yes, they are, and they're edible, too, although they may not be especially tasty since they were bred for their ornamental foliage and not the flavor and nutrition of their roots. But this provides ample evidence of how easy sweet potatoes are to grow yourself and what a pretty companion they can make for your planting combinations. Don't be fooled by the word *potato* in the name—they aren't remotely related botanically to regular potatoes, and they're very different in the way they grow and taste, too.

**Habit:** Long, trailing vines with broad, heart-shaped or lacy leaves. The sweet potatoes form underground.

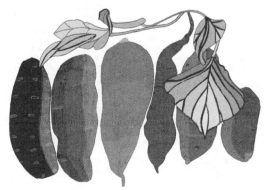

**How to start:** Sweet potatoes grow from slips, which are young stems that sprout up from the tuberous root. You can grow your own by suspending a sweet potato over a glass of water with toothpicks, with its narrow end just touching the surface of the water below. After several weeks, clusters of sprouts will emerge at the top—these are the slips. Carefully break these off and plant the individual stems outdoors when nighttime temperatures are consistently above 55°F, and the soil has warmed completely. Set them about 1 foot apart.

Grocery store varieties of this heat loving crop tend to be suited for production in the South, so they may not produce high yields for cold-climate gardeners, though they'll probably form some usable roots. If you live in an area with a short season, it's better to purchase varieties bred for your climate from a mail-order supplier or your local garden center or feed store. You can also purchase sweet potatoes from your farmers' market in autumn, keep them over winter, and use them to start your own crop the following spring.

**Season:** Late summer to fall.

**When to harvest:** In cool climates, dig the roots after the first frost blackens the foliage or when you're ready to clean up your containers for winter. In warm climates, dig after the first frost or when the plant begins to wither and go dormant.

**Water requirements:** Moderate.

**Light requirements:** Full sun.

**Pests and diseases:** None to speak of. Keep your slips free of weeds while they are getting established; once they're settled in and growing vigorously, they can tolerate some competition.

**Recommended varieties:** 'Centennial' and 'Beauregard' are two widely available varieties that are adapted to northern climates, though they should perform well most anywhere.

**Space-to-yield ratio:** Moderate to high, especially when conditions are warm. Sweet potatoes require little work or attention and will provide several large tubers at the end of any reasonably long season.

**Plot-free pointers:** Sweet potatoes are one of the prettiest, most useful, and lowest mainte-nance vines for your edible garden. Stick slips almost anywhere—except near other large root crops, such as potatoes, rutabagas, or onions, because harvesting those earlier root crops will likely damage the sweet potato roots.

**Garden role:** You'd be hard pressed to find a more ornamental, made-for-just-this-purpose edible spiller, but it is also a good candidate for a solo perfomer.

## THE BEST OF BOTH WORLDS

Heirloom tomatoes have a devoted following for their rich flavors and interesting stories, but they may lack the disease resistance and high-yielding potential that hybrid varieties have to offer. In an attempt to combine the best of both heirloom and hybrid tomatoes, many companies are now offering grafted tomatoes, with the topgrowth of an heirloom variety, such as 'Brandywine', grafted onto a roots of a hybrid variety. The rootstock contributes increased vigor and disease resistance to the plant, making it perform more like a hybrid but with the flavor of an heirloom in the fruit. Some trials have shown as much as a 50 percent increase in productivity over nongrafted heirlooms—a big deal! You can purchase grafted tomato plants by mail order or at garden centers that carry a large selection of vegetable plants.

# Tomato

*Solanum lycopersicum*
**Family: Solanaceae, the tomato family**

Tomatoes embody every good reason why you'd want to grow your own vegetables: Instead of spending money on tasteless grocery-store tomatoes, you get to enjoy a long harvest of delightfully tasty fruits from very ornamental plants that are satisfying and easy to grow and harvest from. For most of us, it simply isn't summer without a tomato plant or two somewhere in our yard, and this is true even among those who don't consider themselves gardeners.

**Habit:** Bushy and vigorous. There is a reason that some gardeners refer to the plants' stems as vines: In Mexico and South America, where tomato relatives grow wild, they are sprawling plants that generally creep along the ground.

**How to start:** It's usual to start the seeds of this warm-weather crop indoors 6 to 8 weeks before your last frost date, sowing them about $1/4$ inch deep. If you'd rather plant the seeds in your garden, you'll have to wait longer but you'll still get a harvest—just ask anyone who has had tomato plants come up on their own in the compost pile or last year's tomato patch.

**Season:** Summer into early autumn in most areas; spring into early summer in very hot climates.

**When to harvest:** Harvest when the fruit is richly colored more or less all over (the shoulders of some varieties remain green) and yields a bit to the touch. Tomatoes will ripen off the vine but are tastiest and sweetest when you let them mature on the plant.

**Water requirements:** Moderate to high. It takes a lot of water to produce succulent, smooth-skinned fruits, but too much may result in bland fruit that is likely to crack or burst, especially if the water comes too quickly. A consistent supply of moisture is ideal; tomatoes are excellent on drip irrigation!

**Light requirements:** Full sun.

**Pests and diseases:** A number of insects and diseases can affect tomatoes, depending on your region and the overall vigor of your plants. Your local Cooperative Extension

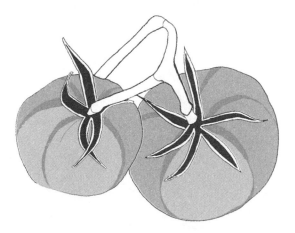

office is the best resource for learning about which pest problems can afflict tomatoes in your area.

A number of things can happen to a tomato plant or its fruit that are related not to pests or diseases but to issues with the growing conditions. Moving the seedlings outdoors too suddenly, for instance, can cause them to develop silvery white patches on the leaves: a symptom that looks like a fungal disease but is simply sunburn, a condition that the plants usually grow out of in a few days. Uneven watering heavy rain or irrigation after a dry spell—is another problem that can cause a number of diseaselike symptoms, including cracking (corky lines on the "shoulders" of the fruits or actual splits in the skin), catfacing (a weird sort of misshapen growth, usually on the bottom of the fruit), and blossom-end rot (blackening on the bottom of the fruits).

**Recommended varieties:** There are hundreds, maybe thousands, of tomato varieties available to home gardeners, so it's tough to narrow them down to just a few top performers for all parts of the country. Look for colors that you find appealing and fruit types that suit what you plan to do with your harvest (large fruits for slicing into sandwiches, cherry and grape varieties for salads, and paste types for sauces, for example). If you have enough space, I suggest choosing a couple of different sizes— say, two types of cherry or grape tomatoes, one or two different small- to medium-fruited varieties, and one or two kinds of large slicers—to enjoy the most versatile harvest.

Then, narrow your options by searching for varieties that are well suited to the growing conditions in your region, especially if you live

# TRAINING TIPS FOR TOMATOES

Tomatoes, even the determinate or "bush" types, benefit from staking to save space, to make their fruit more available, and to keep it off the ground and out of the way of slugs. These plants are naturally weak stemmed and sprawling, so it is best to have a staking plan in place at planting time. Tomatoes grow quickly in warm weather and can grow beyond control in a matter of days.

**Commercial supports.** Most gardeners who grow tomatoes have their own personal preferences and methods for staking tomatoes. There are the time-honored tomato rings and their many variants, like tomato cages and tomato towers. They are good because you can install them at planting time and the tomato simply grows up through them. When the plant begins to branch, bear, and lean, the cage or ring supports it. This method relies on the purchase of a ready-made item, and they vary considerably in quality. Poor-quality tomato cages can bend or break under the weight of a healthy plant, so make sure anything you purchase feels sturdy and is crafted with wire that doesn't bend easily.

**Homemade ring supports.** You can make your own form of a tomato ring using a wire wreath form and bamboo stakes. Full instructions are on page 143. This is an inexpensive DIY alternative to commercial tomato rings and will generally be longer lasting, too. This method is especially good for container-grown tomatoes, because wreath forms are available in a range of diameters, so you can match them to the diameter of your container for a sleek, unified look.

**A combined approach.** My favorite way to train tomatoes in a container involves a combination of pruning and staking. Beginning when the plant is young, pinch out the suckers—the little sprouts that come up in the angle formed where the stem meets an individual leaf. These are what cause the plant to branch wildly, making it a big, top-heavy mess, and pinching them out helps the plant develop a single, strong stem instead of multiple weak ones.

It's easy to secure the main stem to a strong stake as it grows. When the tomato vine reaches the top of the stake, head it back down the stake and resecure it in that direction. This method results in a streamlined, narrow plant that allows lots of light and air circulation to reach the foliage and fruit, encouraging each fruit to develop fully and minimizing pests like spider mites and fungal diseases, too. While it does result in a bit less fruit than allowing the suckers to grow, the ease of maintenance and higher fruit quality more than makes up for this approach, especially when growing several plants.

It is possible to use this method with purchased transplants, but inspect plants carefully and choose those that do not already have well-established suckers. Sometimes, a sucker will emerge quite low on the plant and grow very large; removing it would result in severe damage to the plant. In this case, the plant could be grown in a ring or a cage, but the single-stake method may be inadequate to support it.

in a particularly cool, hot, dry, or rainy area. In the far North, for example, look for the short-season "Siberian" tomatoes, which can put out a crop in as few as 50 to 55 days. In very hot climates, consider medium-season varieties, which can produce fruit in 65 to 75 days—quick enough to give you a harvest before the plants are harmed by an extended period of high night temperatures. Shopping with a regional seed company, such as Southern Exposure Seed Exchange, Native Seeds/SEARCH, or Denali Seed Company for Alaska, is the best way for gardeners in more extreme conditions to find satisfying varieties.

**Space-to-yield ratio:** Medium to high, depending on the variety. The smaller the fruit, the more you'll harvest off the plant. Large-fruited tomatoes may put out only 10 to 15 fruits per plant, while cherries and other small types will give you a harvest every day during the height of the season.

**Plot-free pointers:** See the staking and sucker-pruning methods on the opposite page to find strategies for growing high-quality tomatoes in the least amount of space possible. If you want to grow tomatoes in pots, choose large containers (16-inch diameter and up) to give the roots plenty of room.

**Garden role:** Thriller (for most tomatoes) or spiller (for trailing types, such as 'Tumbling Tom', which were developed to cascade over the edges of pots or baskets); solo performer for heirloom and large-fruited types.

# PERENNIAL *Vegetables*

Perennial vegetables are gorgeous, garden-worthy plants that just happen to be edible. They make dramatic design elements in a landscape, and they have a place in edible spots, too. While you **could** grow them in a large container, these long-lived plants are better suited to raised beds, where they can grow happily for years without being moved and where they have lots of room to form the extensive root systems needed to support lush topgrowth. Artichoke, horseradish, and rhubarb can be successful with half or a quarter of a raised bed; asparagus and Jerusalem artichokes, however, will require a good deal more space.

Whether or not these crops can survive winter in your climate depends on your hardiness zone, a number based on the average lowest temperature observed in your area. If you don't know yours, you can find it on the USDA's Web site (http://planthardiness.ars.usda.gov/PHZMWeb/). The microclimate created by raised beds (especially stone ones, which stay a bit warmer) and containers (which can be moved to more protected locations) can give you a little flexibility in growing plants that are rated for a zone warmer than yours. You can also edge your zone a little warmer through the use of mulch—a good 2- to 3-inch-thick layer helps protect the roots so they can withstand winter's chill. With the exception of artichokes, however, all of the perennial vegetables described here can be grown throughout most of North America.

# Artichoke

*Cynara scolymus*
**Family: Asteraceae, the daisy family**

Stately and dramatic, artichoke plants produce large, scaly flower buds that are typically steamed and enjoyed with melted butter or Hollandaise sauce. This Mediterranean native is perennial in milder areas (USDA Zone 6 or 7 and warmer), but you can grow it as an annual in colder areas. To get a harvest in areas with short growing seasons, you'll need to give the plants an early start indoors and treat them to plenty of water and fertilizer to encourage fast growth.

**Habit:** The large, blocky plants look like giant thistles, with spiny leaves and stems. A single specimen in a container or in the center of a raised bed makes a unique aesthetic statement that no other vegetable can match.

**How to start:** Unless you know you can buy artichoke plants locally, you're best off starting your own indoors. They need plenty of growing time, so start them early—about 3 months before your last frost date. Sow them ¼ inch deep in moist potting soil and keep them in a warm spot.

**Season:** Mostly summer; possibly into fall.

**When to harvest:** Artichokes are ready to harvest anytime their flower buds are large enough to handle. Pick them small (baby artichokes are an in-demand gourmet item) or let them get larger; just make sure you get them before the scales begin to spread, indicating that the gorgeous but inedible purple flower is about to appear.

# A Close Cousin

Cardoon (*Cynara cardunculus*) plants look much like artichokes, but instead of harvesting the flower buds, you eat the thick leaf stems. They look something like celery but share artichoke's pleasingly complex flavor. Plant and care for cardoon just as you would for artichokes.

Harvest time for this gourmet treat is mid- to late autumn, but you'll need to prepare the stems 4 to 6 weeks before that, on a dry day. This process, known as blanching, involves bringing all of the leaf stems up to the center of the plant, wrapping them with twine to hold the bundle together, wrapping them with heavy brown paper or flexible cardboard, and then wrapping again with twine. This keeps sunlight away from the stalks, making them much more tender and easier to cook. To prepare them for eating, cut the stems close to the ground, remove the leafy parts, and peel the stems to remove the fibrous outer coat before you steam or use them in other recipes. Cut portions will discolor so rub them with half a lemon.

**Water requirements:** High. Though the plants are drought tolerant, they produce well only when supplied with abundant water and very fertile soil.

**Light requirements:** Full sun.

**Pests and diseases:** Artichoke plants are more or less trouble free, though the lush growth they produce with ample water and fertility can encourage aphids. Smash these tiny pests with your fingers or wash them off with a strong spray of water.

**Recommended varieties:** In cold-climate areas, look for artichoke varieties bred for use as annuals, such as 'Imperial Star'. Warm-climate gardeners can indulge in classic Italian varieties like the gorgeous purple 'Violetto'.

**Space-to-yield ratio:** Low to moderate where the plants are annuals; moderate to high where the plants are perennial. In Mediterranean-like climates, a single artichoke plant will bear about two dozen buds a year for 6 to 8 years. The rest of us are likely to have the plant only for a season and harvest perhaps 5 to 10 buds from each plant.

**Plot-free pointers:** If growing in containers, choose very large pots to keep them in scale with the plants and provide plenty of room for their long taproots.

**Garden role:** These bold beauties are definitely thrillers. Artichoke plants look great all summer long (or all year long in areas where they thrive), so you can enjoy their beauty even if you aren't able to grow a successful harvest.

# Asparagus

***Asparagus officinalis***
**Family: Liliaceae, the lily family**

The crisp new shoots of asparagus are a delicious spring treat, and the plants are a delight for the eye, too. Their feathery, fernlike foliage blends easily with other plants during the summer, and then it turns an eye-popping cadmium yellow in autumn, adding a splash of late-season color to your garden. Asparagus is a very long-lived vegetable, with a single planting remaining productive for 25 years or longer, so choose its site carefully; the plants can be slow to recover if you have to move them. This perennial crop is hardy to USDA Zone 4 and heat tolerant to about Zone 8. It does not do well in areas with relatively mild winters, because it needs a cool rest period every year to grow properly.

**Habit:** Clump forming with tall, graceful foliage and thick, fleshy roots.

**How to start:** It's possible to grow asparagus from seed, but starting with roots (known as crowns) means that you can begin harvesting a year or two sooner. Plant the crowns about 6 inches deep and 12

# GROCERY SHOPPING FOR CROPS

You expect to find seeds and starts of veggies and herbs in seed catalogs or at your local garden center—but what about the grocery store? The produce section can provide a variety of unexpected options.

**Garlic and shallot.** Though you're probably better off starting with bulbs from a garden supplier to make sure you get the kinds best suited to your region, you may be able to grow garlic and shallots from those you find at the store.

**Herbs.** Sometimes you can root the herbs that are sold in plastic containers in the produce section. Basil and mint, especially, produce roots readily if you stand the pieces in a glass of water, with at least one leaf joint (with the leaves removed) below the surface. Rosemary, too, may root, but you need to plant the lower half of the stem piece in moist potting soil rather than water.

**Horseradish.** If you can't find horseradish roots elsewhere, look for them in the produce section at your favorite grocery. Sometimes they're too dried out to grow well, but they're worth a try.

**Jerusalem artichoke.** Look for these knobbly tubers in ethnic markets, particularly those that sell Central European foods. Plant just a few of them whole and you'll likely have all you can use in just a year or two.

**Potato.** Though most store potatoes have been treated to delay shoot formation, those you bought a while back and have stored at home for a while often form shoots, and you can plant them. Not all varieties are equally well suited to growing in all climates, but there's little harm in trying.

**Sweet potato.** Buy one of the tuberous roots, set it in a drinking glass with the narrow end just touching water, and set it on a sunny windowsill. Remove the leafy shoots that emerge and plant them outdoors to produce a new crop of roots.

inches apart in early spring, once the soil is completely thawed and no longer soggy.

**Season:** Spring for harvest; foliage remains attractive through winter.

**When to harvest:** Asparagus needs time to become established, so wait until the third spring after planting the crowns to start harvesting. You can pick the spears anytime after they've emerged and before the scales around the buds begin to open (they're usually about 8 inches tall at this point). Continue harvesting for 6 to 8 weeks, then let the remaining shoots develop fully so the plant can build its energy for next year.

**Water requirements:** Moderate. Asparagus needs regular watering during dry spells but demands perfectly drained soil to thrive.

**Light requirements:** Full sun is best, but asparagus can tolerate light shade.

**Pests and diseases:** Asparagus beetles and Japanese beetles may appear on the plant—their damage is difficult to notice on the fine foliage, though. Pick them off individually or gently shake the insect-laden stems over a bucket of soapy water. Fusarium wilt and rust can be a problem in some areas, but newer varieties are resistant.

**Recommended varieties:** The most prevalent varieties have "Jersey" in their name, indicating their development at Rutgers University. These are vigorous, disease-resistant selections that were developed as male-only varieties. (Male-only plants do not produce fruit, so they put more energy into producing leaves and strong roots, and you don't end up with unwanted seedlings.)

**Space-to-yield ratio:** Very high, once the plants have settled in.

**Plot-free pointers:** Give asparagus a large raised bed all to itself, because the mature plants take up a good bit of space.

**Garden role:** Solo performer.

# Horseradish

*Armoracia rusticana*
**Family: Brassicaceae, the cabbage family**

For fans of this pungent root, nothing can match the intense flavor and powerful scent of homegrown horseradish, making it a worthwhile choice. More of a seasoning than a vegetable, horseradish is easy to grow and can be prolific when it is happy. Its pungency is related to its growing conditions: Well-watered, well-fertilized horseradish tends to be far less pungent than that growing in less-predictable conditions. Horseradish is hardy to USDA Zone 3 and heat tolerant up to about Zone 9.

**Habit:** Clumps of elegant, oblong leaves arrayed over a very large edible root.

**How to start:** Horseradish doesn't produce seeds that are capable of sprouting, so you must start it from whole, pencil-thin roots or 6- to 8-inch-long sections of thicker roots (let the cut pieces dry for a few days before planting). Plant the pieces vertically, with the thicker end up and about 2 inches below the soil surface.

**Season:** Fall.

**When to harvest:** Dig the roots in mid- to late autumn, before the soil freezes, leaving some in place so the plant can grow again next year. Horseradish isn't a crop that you can snatch small harvests from through the season.

**Water requirements:** Low to moderate.

**Light requirements:** Full sun. Horseradish can tolerate light shade but is less vigorous and less flavorful there.

**Pests and diseases:** None serious.

**Recommended varieties:** No varieties available.

**Space-to-yield ratio:** Moderate to high, especially if growing in a permanent location and allowed to mature. Some gardeners characterize horseradish as prolific bordering on invasive; this probably depends on how much horseradish your family can use each year!

**Plot-free pointers:** Of all the perennial vegetables, horseradish is the one best suited for

container use. It needs a very large, deep pot, though, and you'll have to dump the entire thing in fall to collect your harvest. Store the remaining roots in your refrigerator for winter or replant them immediately in the container (in a pot that can stay outside all winter).

**Garden role:** Thriller, when its giant leaves are allowed to reach full size on mature roots; filler when they emerge from small, young roots.

# Jerusalem Artichoke

*Helianthus tuberosus*
**Family: Asteraceae, the daisy family**

Jerusalem artichoke grows in a spreading clump of 6- to 10-foot-tall stalks topped in cheery, chocolate-scented, sunflower-like blooms from late summer into autumn; a big surprise to people who expect vegetable plants to be basically green and leafy. Besides looking so pretty, it's productive as well, yielding an abundance of crunchy tubers. Luckily, it's fine to harvest heavily from this tasty crop—in fact, it's the best way to keep it from getting too big for its space. Jerusalem artichoke is increasingly known as "sunchoke," a more correct name, since "Jerusalem" is thought to be a corruption of the Italian word for sunflower, *girasole*. It is hardy to USDA Zone 3 and heat tolerant to Zone 8.

**Habit:** Tall, leafy stems, forming large colonies very quickly.

**How to start:** The easiest way to get started

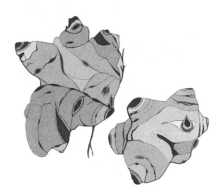

is with tubers from a mail-order supplier or your local farmers' market. Plant them 4 to 6 inches deep and about 1 foot apart.

**Season:** Fall, mainly.

**When to harvest:** The tubers will be large and well formed by late summer, so you can start harvesting a few here and there then or wait until the stems start to die back in fall and dig up the entire patch at once.

**Water requirements:** Low to moderate.

**Light requirements:** Full sun.

**Pests and diseases:** Pests are rarely a problem; in fact, the flowers attract beneficial insects (and butterflies as well).

**Recommended varieties:** There are few named varieties, though some sources are breeding for smoother, less knobby tubers, such as those of 'Red Rover'.

**Space-to-yield ratio:** High.

**Plot-free pointers:** The only problem with Jerusalem artichoke is that it can be so vigorous that it's hard to limit its spread. Planting it in a container is a good way to get around the problem, and harvesting will be much easier that way, too. It needs to be a very big pot, however, to be in proportion to their towering height. The Mesh Towers on page 140 are an excellent solution.

**Garden role:** Thriller or solo performer.

# Rhubarb

*Rheum rhabarbarum*
**Family: Polygonaceae, the buckwheat family**

In the Midwest, you can spot the site of an old farmstead by the persistence of a lilac bush and a clump of rhubarb, a testament to the longevity and low-maintenance nature of this perennial crop. The edible portion of rhubarb is its thick leaf stalks, which have a flavor and culinary uses that are more like a fruit than a vegetable. The leaves themselves are poisonous—they contain oxalic acid and cause the mouth and tongue to swell if chewed—but it's easy to remove the foliage completely as you harvest the stems. While rhubarb does flower, it's best to remove the emerging flower stalks to encourage more leaf production. Rhubarb plants are hardy to USDA Zone 3 and heat tolerant up to Zone 8 or 9.

**Habit:** Large clumps of enormous leaves; very dramatic.

**How to start:** Plant purchased rhubarb crowns (root divisions) in spring, with the buds about 1 inch below the surface. If you have room for more than one clump, space them 3 to 4 feet apart.

**Season:** Spring.

**When to harvest:** Cut the stalks when they're about 1 foot long. Take just a few the first year so the plant has a chance to settle in; after that, cut what you need though late spring or even into early summer. You'll know it's time to stop when the stalks become stringy and unpalatably bitter.

**Water requirements:** Low.

**Light requirements:** Full sun.

**Pests and diseases:** None.

**Recommended varieties:** You can choose from green- or red-stalked varieties, but the classic red ones (such as 'Canada Red' or 'Valentine') are prettiest. Some varieties are more heat tolerant than others, so it's best to shop locally for your rhubarb crowns to get one that is appropriate for your climate.

**Space-to-yield ratio:** Moderate based on space, but fairly high based on the very minimal maintenance requirements.

**Plot-free pointers:** Rhubarb can make a striking, permanent element in a raised bed. Or plant a pair of them at the entrance to your vegetable or flower garden for an unexpected edible accent.

**Garden role:** Thriller or solo performer.

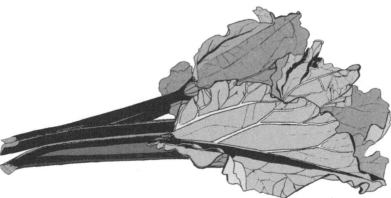

# HERBS and Edible FLOWERS

Neither edible pot nor spot can be complete without herbs and edible flowers. There is something incomparably luxurious about having an abundance of tasty herbs and pretty, safe-to-eat blossoms right at hand, and their prolific nature inspires culinary experimentation. Versatile and easy to grow, they're especially nice in containers so that they can be a part of your outdoor living spaces, perfuming the air during al fresco meals or providing sprigs of flavorful foliage to grace your drink of choice as you relax on your deck or patio.

Herbs and edible flowers may be annual or perennial, which is an important consideration when planning edible spots and pots. You can tuck in annuals just about anywhere there's enough room and light, but perennial herbs take a bit more thought. If you want to grow them in a container and leave them outside for the winter, you'll need to choose a pot that is weatherproof and select herbs that are hardier to at least one zone colder than where you live, or else plan to provide extra protection for them in winter. In raised beds, perennial herbs look best and are most productive when they can grow in the same spot for years, so you'll want to think carefully about where you'll plant them and give them plenty of space. (See page 276 for details on each.)

For the most part, herbs and edible flowers are pest and disease free. The occasional bug or leaf spot may occur, but if you give the plants the growing conditions they like best and don't crowd them, they'll be able to outgrow pretty much any kind of damage.

# Basil

For many, fresh basil is as much a part of summer as homegrown tomatoes. This annual herb is intensely fragrant and flavorful, and it's a fantastic culinary companion to most any summer vegetable. There are many varieties to choose from: heavily anise-scented Thai types; tiny-leaved and supercompact Greek types; giant lettuce-leafed Italian types; lemon-, cinnamon-, and licorice-scented varieties; and green- or purple-leaved selections, too, among other options. One of my favorite basils is 'Pesto Perpetuo', a unique, strongly upright variety that's variegated in shades of creamy white and cool, minty green. Best of all, it does not flower or set seed, so the flavor doesn't become unpleasantly strong and the leaf production doesn't decline as it tends to on flowering plants. 'Pesto Perpetuo' can be hard to find, so once you get it, it's worth bringing plants or cuttings indoors before the first frost and growing them as houseplants through the winter to keep them from year to year.

Fusarium wilt can afflict basil plants in some areas, causing wilted shoot tips, brown-spotted stems, and dropped leaves. If you have frequent problems with this disease, be sure to select a fusarium-resistant variety from a reputable seed source.

# Borage

The beautiful, Della Robbia–blue flowers of borage appear in profusion all summer long and taste like cucumber with a hint of sweet nectar. They're pretty as a garnish or on top of a salad. You can also float them on top of beverages or freeze them in ice cubes. Their light, delicate flavor is less discernible this way, but they add a delightful touch of charm and color. Borage flowers are beloved by bees, other pollinators, and beneficial insects, so they're a great choice for gardeners who want to bring these good guys to their plantings.

Plant borage once and this generously self-seeding annual will return year after year with no help from you. If any of the seedlings pop up where you don't want them, it's no trouble to remove them: They're large and easy to pull.

# Calendula

One of the oldest herbs in cultivation, this cheery, golden orange annual flower has long been valued for healing and dyeing. For most gardeners, though, its main attractions are its beauty, its ability to attract pollinators, and its edible petals (technically florets), which have a slightly spicy, pollen-y flavor. Calendula petals look and taste great when sprinkled over salads or chopped and incorporated into cream cheese or other spreads.

Also known as pot marigold, calendula comes in a number of varieties, with single or double flowers in shades of yellow, orange, and red. It self-sows in many areas, but not to the point of being a nuisance, and you can easily pull out or transplant excess seedlings.

# Chamomile

Chamomile flowers, which resemble miniature daisies, are a magnet for beneficial insects and pollinators, earning these dainty herbs a place in any garden of edibles. They have long been used in teas and in herbal medicine, though more recently it's been noted that people who are sensitive to ragweed may experience an allergic reaction to chamomile, too. While it's up to you if you wish to consume chamomile, there's no question this annual herb makes a nice addition to edible gardens.

# Chervil

Though chervil is an integral component of the classic French fines herbes, this annual or biennial herb is difficult to find at market or in garden centers. To enjoy its light, aniselike, herbaceous flavor, you'll have to grow your own. Fortunately, that's easy to do, and the plants produce useful leaves over a long period, especially if the weather doesn't get too hot. Chervil plants often survive over winter, so you may be able to harvest garden-fresh chervil all through the cold months if your raised beds or containers aren't covered in snow. If it does overwinter, its flowerstalk comes up quickly in spring, so plan to sow yearly to have a constant supply of tender, tasty leaves.

# Chives

Far easier to grow than onions or leeks, chives contribute the same flavor and return year after year. True, chives cannot withstand cooking as well as their allium cousins, but growing chives is the best way to get that savory taste from smaller spaces. Regular chives produce tubular leaves, flower with pretty purple pink tufts in early summer, and have a classic onion scent and flavor. Garlic chives have flat foliage, flower in white clusters later in the season, and feature a pungent, garlicky aroma and flavor. They're typically used cooked and are especially useful in Asian cuisine, where they make a delicious companion to stir-fried rice noodles, dumplings, or dipping sauces. Garlic chives are the "scallion" traditionally used in Chinese scallion pancakes.

I recommend growing both of these productive perennials if you have enough space, but if you must choose, go for traditional chives. Both benefit from spring division every 2 years or so (up to 4 years in cold climates). Common and garlic chives are hardy in USDA Zones 3 to 9.

# MAKE THE MOST OF EXTRA HERBS

It happens all the time: You go out to snip a few sprigs of herbs for cooking and end up bringing in way more than you can possibly use right away. Instead of tossing the extras in the compost pile, try these options.

**Butter them up.** Chop the surplus herbs and mix them into softened butter, then wrap in parchment paper and freeze. Herb butters are delicious as a topping for grill-baked potatoes or grilled fish or melted for making omelets.

**Chill them out.** Rinse excess herbs, pat them dry, roll them up in a paper towel, and place them in a plastic bag in your refrigerator, where they'll keep for several days longer.

**Freeze them for later.** For longer storage, toss the herbs into a bag and put them in your freezer for making stock, or freeze chopped herbs with water or oil in ice-cube trays and later add them to dishes while cooking.

# Cilantro

Growing your own cilantro is easy and rewarding. The leaves you pick at home from this cool weather annual may not be as large and lush as those you buy at the store, but you can't beat the convenience of having fresh-picked cilantro right at hand—and all for free! When the plants bolt, cut off the developing flowerstalks to encourage the plants to produce more leaves, or let the lacy white blooms form. Collect the seeds and save them to sow a new crop, or let them dry in the sun for a few days and store them in a tightly sealed glass jar on your spice rack. (In its seed form, cilantro is known as coriander.) The roots of cilantro are a common ingredient in Thai cuisine.

# Dill

Versatile, fragrant, flavorful, and beautiful, dill is an excellent herb to include in all types of gardens. The domed heads of yellow blooms are as pretty as any ornamental flowers—both in the garden and in bouquets—and they'll attract beneficial insects to your plantings. (Removing the flowers will extend your leaf harvest for a while, but I recommend letting the plants bloom eventually.) Keep a supply of dill seed on hand so you can sow it frequently and enjoy a steady supply of foliage, flowers, and seeds for your kitchen, too.

# Fennel

Fennel closely resembles dill, and it's equally useful in the garden and in the kitchen. The leaves, blooms, and seeds are all edible, and the flowers are pretty for arrangements. Fennel has a more licorice-like flavor, though. I particularly like using its flowers and foliage in salads and as a fragrant bed for grilled fish. Fennel tends to be perennial in USDA Zone 6 or 7 and warmer areas; in colder areas, it's easy to grow as a self-sowing annual. It self-sows so generously, in fact, that it grows wild in many states and is considered invasive in California. If you want to prevent its spread, simply clip off the developing flowers so they can't set seed.

# Johnny-Jump-Up

The adorable flowers of Johnny-jump-ups may look too pretty to eat, but I highly recommend trying them: They're surprisingly sweet tasting. Sprinkle them into salads or use them as a charming garnish for desserts. You can plant this undemanding spring beauty anywhere you wish the first year, but don't expect it to stay there: In future years, its seedlings will pop up in the most surprising places. Once summer's heat comes on, Johnny-jump-up usually dies back to the ground, but don't worry: They'll reemerge in fall and flower early in spring.

# Lavender

Lavender is most popular for its pretty flowers and distinctive fragrance, but it can have a place as an edible, too. It's often used as an ingredient in herbes de Provence, and it's appearing more frequently in chocolate and other sweets, too. Though any lavender is edible, English lavender (*Lavandula angustifolia*) is the best type for culinary purposes, because it offers the lightest, sweetest taste. It's also the hardiest species (USDA Zones 5 to 8). The key to long-term success with lavender is soil that's very well drained (especially in winter) with a slightly alkaline pH.

# Lemon Balm

Lemon balm is one of the few hardy perennial herbs with a true lemon scent. The fresh leaves add a light flavor to both savory and sweet dishes and combine nicely with many fruits. Fresh or dried lemon balm leaves are also popular for use in tea and other beverages. In the garden, the tiny flowers of this perennial herb are fantastic for attracting pollinators and beneficial insects. Lemon balm spreads freely by seed, though, so it's a good idea to clip the whole plant back to about 1 inch above the ground soon after it starts blooming if you want to control its spread. Lemon balm is hardy in USDA Zones 4 to 9.

# Lemon Verbena

Sweetly flavorful and intoxicatingly fragrant, lemon verbena is delicious in beverages, desserts, and seafood dishes. It's rarely available at the grocery store, so it's definitely worth making a place for a plant or two. Loose clusters of tiny, purplish white flowers appear near the shoot tips in late summer to fall. Lemon verbena is a perennial only in very warm climates (USDA Zones 10 and warmer), but the rest of us can grow it as an annual or houseplant and still enjoy an ample harvest.

# Lovage

Lovage is the perfect perennial herb for those who love celery's flavor but don't want to fuss with that vegetable's high maintenance requirements. The leaves, stems, and even roots are used to impart a celery flavor to soups, and the flowers and seeds are also edible. You can even use the hollow stem as a straw for vegetable juice or a bloody Mary. Lovage is hardy in USDA Zones 5 to 8.

# Marjoram

Marjoram is closely related to oregano, but these two herbs are surprisingly different, so consider growing both if you have the space. Marjoram forms a more well-behaved plant than oregano and offers a stronger flavor even when fresh. It is more cold sensitive than oregano, though, and usually doesn't survive the winter north of USDA Zones 8 or 9. Fortunately, it's easy to grow marjoram as an annual.

# Mint

With so many flavors and fragrances to choose from, the hardest part of growing mint is deciding which ones to try. If you're primarily interested in tasty teas, consider pungent peppermint (*Mentha × piperita*) or fruity orange mint (*M. × piperita* f. *citrata*). For good looks and fragrance in the garden, both pineapple mint (*M. suaveolens* 'Variegata'), with green-and-white leaves, and green-and-yellow ginger mint (*M. × gentilis*) are lovely. If you simply can't choose among these and the dozens of other mints, or if you have room for only one plant, go for spearmint (*M. spicata*): It's the most popular choice for its sweet-mint scent and flavor. Most mints are hardy in USDA Zones 4 to 9.

# Nasturtium

Nasturtiums just make you smile. Their intricate flowers in bright, saturated colors; their neat, round, water lily–like leaves; and the way their stems corkscrew into spirals as they set seed make them one of the most interesting annuals you can grow. While most people prize nasturtiums for the peppery flowers, which have an appealing texture and measure of delicious nectar in the long spur, the leaves and seeds are also edible. A homegrown salad sprinkled with nasturtium flowers never fails to delight. The intricate blossoms can host little insects who are after the sweet nectar, though, so to avoid shocking your dinner companions, you may wish to immerse flowers in a bowl of cool water briefly and allow them to drain and dry for an hour before the meal.

# Oregano

You can count on oregano to return year after year and provide more fresh foliage than you could possibly use—unless you own a pizzeria! Fortunately, oregano dries well and develops a stronger flavor that way, so you can easily enjoy it all winter. The key to getting the very best flavor is making sure you get the right plant, because many plants that are sold as "oregano" or that have "oregano" in the name are actually a completely different species and may or may not be good for kitchen use. Look for those labeled *Origanum vulgare* (the subspecies *hirtum* is known as Greek oregano and is especially suitable for culinary applications); *Origanum majoricum*, known as Italian oregano, is also a good choice. True oregano is hardy in USDA Zones 5 or 6 to 9.

# Parsley

With its fresh green foliage and strong stems, a parsley plant exudes health and goodness. The vitamin- and mineral-rich leaves are a flavorful addition to a variety of dishes, including vegetables, pastas, and homegrown salads. This biennial herb overwinters in most climates, so you will get a full season of harvest the first year and a month or two the next spring, until the plant goes to flower. Flat-leaved or Italian parsley, with ferny foliage, is the kind most often used for cooking. Curly-leaved parsley, with densely crinkled leaves, is more often used as a garnish, but it has a good flavor, too, and it's pretty enough to complement more floriferous companions.

# Rosemary

Rosemary is an exceedingly handsome plant, as evidenced by its frequent use in landscaping in climates where it is hardy. It can be difficult for those of us who have only experienced rosemary as a small container plant to believe that it gets enormous and requires frequent pruning in warm areas; however, it is by nature a true shrub. Rosemary is usually said to be hardy in USDA Zones 7 to 10, but it may not be as tender as widely believed: At Wave Hill in New York, a rosemary has been overwintering happily for decades, and even here in my town in west Michigan (Zone 6a), there is a sizable plant that must be at least 3 years old. If you'd like to experiment with overwintering rosemary in your garden, the key is excellent drainage, especially in winter.

# Sage

A single, mature clump of this dependable perennial herb can provide more pungent leaves than most of us could use in a lifetime. It's also a very attractive plant, with lovely purple-blue flowers. The leaves are commonly grayish green, but you can find varieties with foliage that's especially silvery (such as 'Berggarten'), purplish ('Purpurascens'), yellow variegated ('Icterina'), or multicolored ('Tricolor'). Some of the colored-leaf varieties aren't as intensely aromatic or as hardy as common culinary sage—it's usually recommended for USDA Zones 4 to 8—but they are so pretty that it's worth enjoying them as annual ornamentals.

# Salad Burnet

Salad burnet is pretty enough for any garden, but it has a bonus feature that earns it a place in edible spots and pots, in particular: The lovely leaves have a light cucumber flavor that's a treat in beverages, salads, and sandwiches. It looks dainty, but it's sturdy and prolific, providing an abundance of foliage all through the growing season and even in winter in mild climates. This perennial herb is hardy in USDA Zones 3 to 8.

# Shiso

Extremely easy to grow, shiso, also known as perilla or Japanese basil, is a close relative of regular basil, but it tastes much fruitier and does not have the powerful anise-y punch. Though this delicious herb is most commonly included in Japanese cuisine, it deserves to be more widely used: It's a delicious addition to salads, can be used in desserts, and creates a unique flavor when steeped with tea. I recommend growing the purple-leaved variety of this self-seeding annual so you can enjoy its good looks in between harvests.

# Stevia

Five years ago, few gardeners had heard of stevia. Now that it is a popular sweetener, however, garden centers everywhere are selling this easy-to-grow, unassuming herb. Instead of buying the refined extract at the store, you can enjoy its natural, sugar-free sweetness without any processing: Simply add the fresh or dried leaves to brewing tea or steep them in water or alcohol to make a sweetener you can add to recipes. Stevia is perennial in USDA Zone 9 and south (even into Zone 8 with winter protection); elsewhere, you can grow it as an annual or try your luck at overwintering it indoors.

# Summer Savory

There are two types of savory: winter savory, a perennial with a strong, resinous taste, and summer savory, an annual with a more delicate, lighter flavor that's reminiscent of thyme and oregano. I recommend summer savory, because it's easier to fit into a variety of spaces and its flavor is more versatile. Its tiny but abundant flowers are wonderful for attracting pollinators and other beneficial insects to your plantings. Summer savory is an annual and does not overwinter; winter savory is hardy to USDA Zone 6.

# Thyme

Beautiful in the garden and versatile in the kitchen, thyme is a can't-live-without-it perennial herb. The flavor of fresh thyme is incomparable, and you'll revel in the luxury of having an abundant supply just a few steps from your door. The secret to success with thyme is perfect drainage and plenty of sun. Choosing the right kind is also important: Many ornamental varieties, while still fragrant, are not well suited to culinary use. Besides the well-known common or English thyme, there are other edible varieties—lemon, orange, and silver thymes, to name a few—so it's worth smelling and tasting a few varieties before deciding which one(s) you'll grow. Most thymes are hardy in USDA Zones 5 to 9.

# Herbs at-a-glance

| HERB | THRILLER, FILLER, OR SPILLER | HABIT | HOW TO START |
|---|---|---|---|
| **BASIL**<br>*Ocimum basilicum*<br><br>Family: Lamiaceae, the mint family | Basil is usually a filler but can be a thriller if you pair it with smaller or trailing companions. Variegated and purple varieties offer special drama. | Basil is spreading and bushy, usually about 2′ tall, with strong square stems and dense foliage. | Basil is extremely easy to grow from seeds (sow outdoors ½″ deep after your last frost date), except in the case of 'Pesto Perpetuo', which grows only from cuttings. |
| **BORAGE**<br>*Borago officinalis*<br><br>Family: Boragina-ceae, the borage family | Filler or thriller | Borage produces an upright, branching stems up to about 2′ tall from a large, spreading rosette of lightly hairy leaves. | It's easy to grow borage from seeds—plant a few ½″ deep and 12″ to 18″ apart around the time of your last frost date. |
| **CALENDULA**<br>*Calendula officinalis*<br><br>Family: Asteraceae, the daisy family | Filler | Calendula starts as a tidy rosette of oblong leaves, then the flower stems emerge from the center of the plant and reach 1′ to 2′ tall. | Sow the seeds right in your garden after your last frost date, about ¼″ deep and 8″ apart. |
| **CHAMOMILE**<br>*Matricaria recutita* (German) and *Chamaemelum nobile* (Roman)<br><br>Family: Asteraceae, the daisy family | Filler or spiller | German chamomile is a bushy, upright annual up to about 2′ tall; Roman chamomile is a ground-covering perennial up to about 1′ tall. Both have ferny foliage with tiny daisy flowers borne on fine stems. | Sprinkle chamomile seeds right into your garden in early spring. Don't cover them: Just press them into the soil surface and keep the area moist until seedlings appear. |
| **CHERVIL**<br>*Anthriscus cerefolium*<br><br>Family: Apiaceae, the carrot family | Filler | Small rosettes of finely dissected leaves | Sow the seed directly on the surface of the soil or potting mix in early spring and cover very lightly. May self-sow if allowed to go to seed. |

| HARVESTING | WATER NEEDS | LIGHT NEEDS | PLOT-FREE POINTERS |
|---|---|---|---|
| Instead of taking individual leaves, snip off whole shoot tips, cutting just above a pair of big, healthy leaves. That will encourage new shoots to emerge, keeping the plants bushy and dense and extending your harvest. | Moderate. The soft, fleshy leaves of basil wilt dramatically, but the plants can recover from a bit of dryness. | Full sun. | Basil is so useful and ornamental that it's a must-have for any garden. Tuck seeds or seedlings into any small open spot, letting the plants wend their way through their companions to reach the sun. |
| Pick borage flowers whenever they are open. Each one lasts only a day, so take as many as you can use each day. | Moderate. While borage is not exactly drought tolerant, the plants don't demand frequent watering unless the weather is very dry. | Full sun to light shade | Borage becomes a large plant, easily reaching 18″ across, so be sure to give it plenty of room. In raised beds, let it pop up through your crops or plant it along the edges for a lovely edible accent. If you grow it in a container, consider trying leaf-pruning techniques (see page 100) to make room around it for companions. |
| Snip off entire flowers, cutting back to the leafy part of the stem. Regularly removing the blooms encourages the plants to keep producing more buds, so harvest as much as you like. | Low to moderate; drought stress will impede growth. | Full sun | Tuck calendula into raised beds or containers, anywhere there's a little space and a lot of sun. It's particularly pretty paired with colorful lettuces and other leafy greens in a salad combination. |
| Pick the flowers as needed when they are fully open. | Low | Full sun to light shade | One of the best places for Roman chamomile is in the pathways between raised beds, where it will release its pineapple scent when you step on or brush by the foliage. German chamomile looks cute mingling with other leafy or flowering edibles in a raised bed or container. |
| Pick chervil leaves anytime you need them. When the plants reach the flowering stage, collect and save the mature seeds for future plantings or let them drop to the ground to produce a new crop in the same spot. | Low | Full sun to partial shade. Plants growing in some shade are slower to flower in hot weather. | This delicate, diminutive herb can readily get lost in mixed plantings, so keep it on the edge of plant combinations, or dedicate a portion of a pot or window box to it. |

# Herbs at-a-glance–Continued

| HERB | THRILLER, FILLER, OR SPILLER | HABIT | HOW TO START |
|---|---|---|---|
| **CHIVES** <br><br> *Allium schoenoprasum* and *A. tuberosum* (garlic chives) <br><br> Family: Alliaceae, the onion family | Filler | Both types of chives form upright, grasslike tufts of foliage typically 1' to 2' tall. | Buy plants or grow your own from seed: Sow ¼" to ½" deep indoors in early to mid-spring or outdoors in mid- to late spring. |
| **CILANTRO** <br><br> *Coriandrum sativum* <br><br> Family: Apiaceae, the carrot family | Filler | Cilantro grows in loose, 18"- to 36"-tall clumps of rich green leaves topped with airy clusters of tiny white flowers. | Sow cilantro seeds about ½" deep garden in midspring, when the soil is workable and has warmed a bit. Sow more every few weeks until early summer and again in fall to get a steady supply of tender leaves. |
| **DILL** <br><br> *Anethum graveolens* <br><br> Family: Apiaceae, the carrot family | Filler, mostly. (Despite its tall stature, dill is generally too thin and wispy to be a thriller.) | Dill plants are narrow and upright, typically 3' to 4' tall, with very fine, featherlike foliage and large, glowing yellow flower heads. | Scatter the seeds directly in the garden in midspring and cover them with about ¼" of soil. Sow again every 2 to 3 weeks through midsummer to maintain a consistent supply. |
| **FENNEL** <br><br> *Foeniculum vulgare* <br><br> Family: Apiaceae, the carrot family | Filler | Fennel grows 4' to 6' tall and is upright and graceful, with feathery, green or bronze foliage and broad heads of tiny yellow flowers. | Sow the seeds ¼" to ½" deep outdoors in early spring. |
| **JOHNNY-JUMP-UP** <br><br> *Viola tricolor* <br><br> Family: Violaceae, the violet family | Filler or spiller | Johnny-jump-ups are small, loosely mounded plants up to about 8" tall, with flat-faced, purple-and-yellow flowers held above the bright green leaves. | Sow the seeds ⅛" deep outdoors in early spring, or buy started plants to get an earlier harvest. |

| HARVESTING | WATER NEEDS | LIGHT NEEDS | PLOT-FREE POINTERS |
|---|---|---|---|
| Clip the leaves anytime there are enough present to be worth harvesting, cutting a few inches above the ground. You can harvest the flowers, too: They're great in salads. | Low | Full sun. Chives tolerate a bit of shade but may be sparse and floppy if they don't get enough sun. | These perennial herbs can live a long time and form large, attractive clumps, so don't crowd them. Each one could easily fill an entire medium-sized container or a space 12″ to 18″ across in a raised bed over a season or two. |
| Harvest individual leaves as needed, or cut or pull the entire plant. | Moderate to high. Drought stress will encourage bolting. | Full sun (in cool climates) to partial shade | Grow cilantro on the edges of raised beds and containers so you can harvest regularly and sow new seeds as needed without disturbing nearby companion plants. |
| Clip leaves anytime. For bouquets or kitchen use, cut the flower heads just as the yellow color develops. Pick off the seeds while they are still green for use as a fresh seasoning, or let them turn brown first if you want them for replanting or to store as a spice. | Low to moderate | Best in full sun, but the plants can tolerate a bit of shade, especially in warm climates. | Dill produces lots of seeds and will make itself right at home in raised beds, but it can have a little trouble sowing itself within the confines of a container. To help it along, crumble the mature seed heads over the potting soil; the seedlings will come up wherever there's room. |
| Snip off the leaves any time; harvest the flowers when they're freshly opened. | Low | Full sun | Leaf fennel makes an excellent substitute for bulb fennel (also known as Florence fennel). While it lacks the succulent crunch of the bulb fennel's thickened leaf bases, it contributes the same flavor and is far easier to grow. |
| Pick the flowers when they are fully open. | Low to moderate, depending on weather | Full sun to partial shade | With their easy-care nature and cheerful good looks, Johnny-jump-ups deserve a place in any garden of edibles, even if you don't plan to eat them. If cool weather keeps your plants from dying back in summer, trim them back by half to encourage dense new growth. |

# Herbs at-a-glance–Continued

| HERB | THRILLER, FILLER, OR SPILLER | HABIT | HOW TO START |
|---|---|---|---|
| **LAVENDER**<br><br>*Lavandula* spp.<br><br><br>Family: Lamiaceae, the mint family | Filler | Lavenders have a compact, shrubby form anywhere from 1' to 3' tall, with narrow spikes of purple flowers hovering above the slender, silvery gray foliage. | Lavender grows very slowly from seeds, so it's easiest to start with purchased plants. Space them about 18" apart. |
| **LEMON BALM**<br><br>*Melissa officinalis*<br><br><br>Family: Lamiaceae, the mint family | Filler | Lemon balm grows in dense, gradually expanding mounds about 2' tall, with bright green leaves and white flowers. | Sow lemon balm seeds outdoors around your last frost date (barely cover them with soil), or start with a purchased plant. |
| **LEMON VERBENA**<br><br>*Aloysia triphylla*<br><br><br>Family: Verbenaceae, the verbena family | Thriller in a small pot; filler if paired with a larger plant in a raised bed or container | Lemon verbena grows into a large shrub or small tree where it's perennial; in cold climates, it's a small, sprawling shrub up to about 2' tall. | Purchase a lemon verbena plant from a garden center. |
| **LOVAGE**<br><br>*Levisticum officinale*<br><br><br>Family: Apiaceae, the carrot family | Filler (in leaf) or thriller (in bloom) | The plants start out mounded and bushy, then send up thick, tubular, 5'- to 7'-tall stems topped with lacy heads of yellow flowers in summer. | Sow lovage seeds about ¼" deep in mid- to late spring, once the soil has warmed up and dried out a bit. Or start with a purchased plant to get a quicker harvest. |
| **MARJORAM**<br><br>*Origanum majorana*<br><br><br>Family: Lamiaceae, the mint family | Spiller | Marjoram forms upright, bushy plants that grow 12" to 18" tall, with small leaves and tiny purplish pink to white flowers. | Marjoram seeds are slow to germinate and may not produce a large crop, especially in areas where it is not hardy, so it's best to start with purchased plants. |
| **MINT**<br><br>*Mentha* spp.<br><br><br>Family: Lamiaceae, the mint family | Filler or spiller | Mints grow in upright, spreading clumps usually 12" to 18" tall, with rounded to oblong leaves and clusters of tiny purplish or white flowers. | It's best to buy starter plants, so you can make sure you get the scents and flavors you like best. One plant of each type is plenty. |

| HARVESTING | WATER NEEDS | LIGHT NEEDS | PLOT-FREE POINTERS |
|---|---|---|---|
| Pick the bloom spikes the morning that the first flowers open from the buds. Use them fresh, or dry them thoroughly and store for later. | Low | Full sun | Lavender particularly appreciates the excellent drainage a container can provide; use a light, fast-draining soil mix. In a raised bed, plant lavender along the edge as a low hedge or in the corners as accents. |
| Pick the leaves anytime the plant is actively growing. | Low to moderate | Full sun to partial shade. (Shade is particularly beneficial in hot climates.) | Lemon balm doesn't produce runners like mints, but a single clump can quickly fill a space 18" to 24" across, so give it plenty of room in a raised bed or plant it by itself in a medium to large container. |
| Pick leaves anytime you need them. | Moderate | Full sun | Lemon verbena adapts well to life in a small pot of its own. Set it outside during your frost-free season and enjoy it as a houseplant over winter to keep it from year to year. |
| Gather lovage leaves whenever you need them. | Low to moderate | Full sun to light shade, especially in warm climates | Lovage doesn't look like much at the beginning of the growing season, but it can easily reach 6' tall and 2' wide in summer. Use it in a large container, or give it plenty of room in a raised bed. |
| Snip the leaves as needed. | Low | Full sun | Marjoram is a pretty little plant, but it can get lost among bigger, showier companions in a large raised bed. Try it instead at the edge of a container or in a window box or hanging basket. |
| Pick the leaves anytime during the growing season. | Moderate to high | Full sun | As a group, mints are well known for their tendency to spread far and wide by creeping roots. That's not a problem when you grow them in containers, though: They'll happily fill a small to medium-size pot, and they're wonderful in window boxes, too. |

# Herbs at-a-glance–Continued

| HERB | THRILLER, FILLER, OR SPILLER | HABIT | HOW TO START |
|---|---|---|---|
| **NASTURTIUM**<br>*Tropaeolum majus*<br><br>Family: Tropaeolaceae, the nasturtium family | Filler (mounding types) or spiller (climbing/trailing types) | "Climbing" nasturtiums produce 6'-long stems that may trail along the ground, scramble up short trellises, or cascade out of containers. "Mounding" types form tidy clumps usually 8" to 12" tall. | Plant the seeds 1/2" deep and about 10" apart in spring, when the soil has warmed. |
| **OREGANO**<br>*Origanum vulgare*<br><br>Family: Lamiaceae, the mint family. | Filler or spiller | Oregano plants are bushy and upright, usually 12" to 18" tall, with a woody base, deep green, hairy leaves, and clusters of pinkish white flowers. | Buy starter plants locally so you can rub a leaf with your fingers to experience its scent, and maybe nibble on it to check its flavor, to ensure you're getting the proper oregano. Or buy only from reputable mail-order suppliers of culinary herbs to get the best varieties for cooking. |
| **PARSLEY**<br>*Petroselinum crispum*<br><br>Family: Apiaceae, the carrot family | Filler | Parsley forms a rosette of leaves the first year, taking on a vaselike shape when it sends up its flower stems. | Sow parsley seeds outdoors in midspring, barely cover them with soil, and keep the area evenly moist until seedlings appear (it may take a month or more). Or start with a purchased seedling for a quicker harvest. |
| **ROSEMARY**<br>*Rosmarinus officinalis*<br><br>Family: Lamiaceae, the mint family | Thriller, spiller, or filler, depending on the variety and maturity | Rosemary can be upright and bushy or spreading to trailing, depending on the variety, with needlelike, green to grayish leaves and blue flowers. | It is best to start with plants. Though it's possible to grow rosemary from seeds, they take a long time to sprout. You could also try rooting cuttings, even of the stems sold in plastic packs in the herb section of your grocery store. |
| **SAGE**<br>*Salvia officinalis*<br><br>Family: Lamiaceae, the mint family | Filler | Sage forms a shrubby clump up to about 2' tall and wide, with woody stem bases, oblong to oval leaves, and spikes of pretty flowers in late spring to early summer. | It's possible to grow common sage from seed, but it's much easier and quicker to buy a plant, especially if you want one of the more colorful varieties. |

| HARVESTING | WATER NEEDS | LIGHT NEEDS | PLOT-FREE POINTERS |
| --- | --- | --- | --- |
| Collect leaves anytime. Flower production may slow or stop in hot weather but resumes when cooler temperatures return. | Moderate | Full sun is best, but light shade is acceptable in hot climates. | Fertilizing encourages nasturtiums to produce more leaves than blooms, so if you want lots of flowers, avoid pairing them with partners that need frequent feeding, such as corn or eggplant. |
| Some say oregano tastes best before flowering, so you could cut the whole plant at this point and bundle the stems for drying. I typically just take what I need, as I need it, and harvest several stems at the end of the season to dry for winter use. | Low | Full sun | Where the plant is hardy, oregano will expand quickly to form a sizable clump—to 18″ or more wide—so don't plant any companions too close. Let it trail over the edge of a raised bed or over the rim of a large pot or window box. |
| Snip off the leaves anytime before the plant goes to flower. When the bloom stalks appear, pull out the plant to make room for a new planting (consider keeping the stalks for making soup). | Low to moderate | Full sun to light shade | Parsley can grow back even if you harvest almost all of the leaves at one time, but it will take a few weeks to fill out again, so pair it with companions that can carry the show while the parsley recovers. |
| Use the leaves anytime: Pick them off individually or snip off the shoot tips. The flowers are also edible, with a milder flavor than the foliage. | Low | Full sun | Rosemary is an outstanding garden accent on its own but also combines beautifully with other foliage and flowering edibles in raised beds and container plantings. If you live where rosemary isn't hardy, keep one in a pretty pot by itself so you can easily bring it indoors for winter. |
| Pick the leaves anytime from spring well into fall, when very cold weather arrives. Or harvest some of the shoot tips in late spring, before the flowers open, and dry them for winter use. The blossoms are edible, too. | Low | Full sun | Tuck small sage plants into mixed container plantings for summer color, then move them to a raised bed or give them to a friend in early fall so the plants will have room to fill out and reach full size. |

| HERB | THRILLER, FILLER, OR SPILLER | HABIT | HOW TO START |
|------|------------------------------|-------|--------------|
| **SALAD BURNET**<br><br>*Sanguisorba minor*<br><br><br>Family: Rosaceae, the rose family | Filler, or possibly spiller if it's near an edge where the foliage can arch over the side | The neat, toothed leaves of salad burnet form a dense, ferny mound of grayish green foliage, with intriguing pinkish flowers on 12″- to 18″-tall stems in summer. | Sow the seeds outdoors in midspring, barely covering them with soil. |
| **SHISO**<br><br>*Perilla frutescens*<br><br><br>Family: Lamiaceae, the mint family | Filler | Shiso plants are upright and usually reach 2′ to 3′ tall, with large leaves that have strongly toothed edges and spikes of tiny white flowers in fall. | Sow the seeds outdoors in midspring, pressing them into the soil surface and keeping the area moist until the seedlings appear. |
| **STEVIA**<br><br>*Stevia rebaudiana*<br><br><br>Family: Asteraceae, the daisy family | Filler | The 1′- to 3′-tall plants have oblong, scalloped-edged leaves on upright stems topped with tiny white flowers in fall. | Purchase a plant from the herb section of your local garden center and set it outside after all danger of frost has passed. |
| **SUMMER SAVORY**<br><br>*Satureja hortensis*<br><br><br>Family: Lamiaceae, the mint family. | Filler | Summer savory forms small, upright plants that are 12″ to 18″ tall, with tiny green leaves and pinkish white flowers in summer. | Sow the seeds outdoors in midspring and barely cover them with soil. Summer savory may self-sow, so you may not need to plant it every year if you want it to grow in the same place. |
| **THYME**<br><br>*Thymus vulgaris*<br><br><br>Family: Lamiaceae, the mint family | Spiller usually, but possibly filler depending on the variety | Thyme generally grows in low, bushy mounds that are 6″ to 12″ tall, with small, gray, green, yellow, or variegated leaves and clusters of tiny pinkish or white flowers. | Buy one or more plants from a local source or a reputable supplier of culinary herbs. |

| HARVESTING | WATER NEEDS | LIGHT NEEDS | PLOT-FREE POINTERS |
|---|---|---|---|
| Cut the leaves anytime you need them. The young foliage has the most delicate flavor and best texture. | Moderate | Full sun | Grow salad burnet as a space-saving alternative to fruiting cucumbers, or enjoy it as a handsome foliage accent at the edge of a container or around raised beds. |
| Pick individual leaves anytime, or clip the shoot tips—which encourages the plants to branch out and develop a handsome, bushy shape. | Moderate | Full sun | Purple-leaved shiso looks very much like a coleus (its close relative) and makes an excellent foliage accent in raised beds and container combinations. Just be sure to keep the flower spikes clipped off, because the plant can self-sow prolifically, to the point of becoming invasive. |
| Take individual leaves as needed or clip the shoot tips, which encourages branching and increased leaf production. Or cut the entire plant in early fall and dry it for later use. | Moderate | Full sun | Stevia is a great choice for container growing, particularly if you'd like to bring it indoors before any frost to extend the harvest through winter. |
| Start clipping the tender shoot tips once the plants are at least 6" tall. Toward the end of the growing season, cut the entire plant and dry it for winter use. | Moderate | Full sun | Where space is limited, consider growing summer savory as an alternative to perennial relatives like thyme, rosemary, and oregano. It provides an abundant harvest in short time while not taking up a permanent spot. |
| Clip thyme shoots any time of the year, though they're the most flavorful before flowering, and pick off the leaves for cooking. Thyme stores well for future use, so consider cutting the whole plant back by one-third to one-half just before bloom and drying your harvest. | Low | Full sun | Containers are ideal for providing the well-drained conditions that thyme thrives in. Plant it on the edge of a pot or window box and let it cascade over the side. |

# resources

## Containers

Different materials, formats, and ideas in garden containers are emerging as quickly as radish seeds these days. This is a small sampling of resources that I have had experience with; it is by no means exhaustive, and the exclusion of a brand or type herein does not necessarily imply that such a type shouldn't be used. Most containers can be mail-ordered, though I encourage you to support your local garden centers. If they do not carry a product you are interested in, let them know you are looking for it. Chances are someone else in your area will be searching for that product as well.

### Basic Containers

**FoodMap Container**
foodmapdesign.com

**Gardener's Supply Company**
gardeners.com

**GeoPot Aerated Fabric Pots and Planters**
geopot.com

**Haxnicks**
haxnicks.co.uk
*Based in the United Kingdom, but most products are available in the United States*

**LiveWall Green Wall Systems**
livewall.com

**Pacific Home & Garden**
pacifichomegarden.com

**Smart Pots**
smartpots.com

**UrBin Grower**
naturesfootprint.com

### Self-Watering Containers

You'll encounter a pretty startling range of price and aesthetics when shopping for self-watering containers. Not surprisingly, the least expensive way is to make your own (there are dozens of videos and tutorials on line demonstrating different methods), but you can also keep your eye out for these brands. Though not the cheapest way to start an edible container garden, they're effective, durable, and attractive.

**Lechuza**
lechuza.us
*These German-made planters are stylish, durable, and effective.*

**Earth Box**
earthbox.com

**The Grow Box**
agardenpatch.com

# Manure Tea

Compost and manure teas make excellent liquid fertilizers for those who garden organically. As a liquid, these provide a good dose of nitrogen and other nutrients at application so you see results immediately. While most of us don't have enough surplus compost (or manure, for that matter!) to make our own, there are ranchers out there who make manure or compost tea "bags" so you can brew your own at home. Look also at your farmers' markets and garden centers for local brands.

**Authentic Haven Brand Natural Brew Tea**
ahavenbrand.com

# Pest Control

Truly nontoxic pest control takes a creative approach, incorporating various methods, tools, and ideas to achieve a satisfactory result. Chances are, you'll need to look beyond your local garden center for some of the simplest and most effective options.

**A.M.Leonard**
amleo.com
*Professional-quality pest control, with a large selection of solutions for mammals.*

**Arbico Organics**
www.arbico-organics.com
*Beneficial insects, sticky traps, and more*

**Gempler's**
gemplers.com
*Pest control products used by the horticultural industry*

# Raised Beds

As with containers, there are hundreds of different products available to help you build a raised bed. These merely represent a few companies and products I have had positive experiences with; it is by no means exhaustive nor meant to imply that exclusion from this list means that product is not recommended.

**Art of the Garden**
artofthegarden.net
*M-brace raised bed corners*

**Eartheasy**
eartheasy.com
*Wide selection of raised beds*

**Easy Bed Raised Beds**
kinsmangarden.com
*Metal*

**Frame-It-All System**
frameitall.com
*Unique joints and composite timbers for raised beds*

**Gardener's Supply Company**
gardeners.com
*Wide selection of raised bed kits and corners*

## Seeds

There are dozens of seed companies around—I offer this sampling because their well-written catalogs provide extra information about varieties that are especially suited to growing in containers. They also offer enormous selections and regionally adapted varieties.

**Baker Creek Heirloom Seed Co.**
rareseeds.com

**Johnny's Selected Seeds**
johnnyseeds.com
*Excellent source for cover crop information and seeds*

**Native Seeds/SEARCH**
nativeseeds.org

**Renee's Garden Seeds**
reneesgarden.com

**Seed Keeper**
seedkeepercompany.com
*An all-in-one seed storage system*

**Seed Savers Exchange**
seedsavers.org

**Southern Exposure Seed Exchange**
southernexposure.com

## Tools

Good garden tools are well designed, well made, and a pleasure to use. Though the best ones tend to be a bit pricey, they are a long-lasting investment in your personal comfort and in the enjoyment you get out of your garden.

**Corona Tools**
coronatoolsusa.com
*Innovative telescoping-handle tools for containers and raised beds plus a huge selection of hand tools and cutting tools. I especially like their fine garden snips.*

**Pot Lifter**
potlifter.com
Clever, easy to use, and incredibly useful for container gardeners

**Sneeboer Tools**
sneerboer.com
*Heirloom quality, beautifully handmade tools from the Netherlands. I am never without my Sneeboer potting trowel when working in my container garden, especially.*

# Further Reading

Even with the abundance of information available online, every gardener needs to have a good library. These books are absolutely worth owning.

Bradley, Fern Marshall, Barbara W. Ellis, and Deborah L. Martin. *The Organic Gardener's Handbook of Natural Pest and Disease Control.* Rodale, 2010.
*An excellent companion to the Cranshaw book below, as it gives detailed information on resolving pest issues with nontoxic methods.*

Cranshaw, Whitney. *Garden Insects of North America.* Princeton University Press, 2004.
*A truly comprehensive guide to identifying backyard insects, whether friend or foe.*

Scott, Linda Chalker. *The Informed Gardener* and *The Informed Gardener Blooms Again.* University of Washington Press, 2008 and 2010.
*Professor and urban extension horticulturist Linda Chalker Scott shares honest, science-based advice on gardening's most contentious topics, from the sustainability of peat moss to releasing beneficial insects for pest control. She also maintains an excellent Web site,* puyallup.wsu.edu/~Linda%20Chalker-Scott/.

Soderstrom, Neil, *Deer-Resistant Landscaping.* Rodale, 2009.
*Don't let the title fool you—this is one of the best books available for any gardener who struggles with deer, woodchucks, squirrels, chipmunks, or any mammalian pest.*

# Web Sites

### Kitchen Gardeners International
kgi.org
*An online community of gardeners who grow their own food, this site offers inspiration from vegetable gardens around the world and ideas for using your harvest. Most of the information on the site is user-generated so may not always be reliable or relevant to your climate, but the thousands of photos and articles that people share make it a fun place to explore.*

### National Sustainable Agriculture Information Service
attra.ncat.org
*Though intended primarily for farmers, this site has a wealth of resources (including free downloadable pdfs) for home gardeners who wish to grow their crops with nontoxic methods.*

### *Organic Gardening* magazaine
organicgardening.com/learn-and-grow/raised-bed-gardening

# acknowledgments

As Sir Isaac Newton said, we all stand on the shoulders of giants, especially at this point in human history. Those before us did the hard work of figuring things out first, leaving us the considerably easier tasks of improving and perfecting. I am grateful to all of the gardeners, growers, horticulturists, plant scientists, breeders, and farmers whose collective experience and wisdom have been passed on to me through my teachers and in the books I've read. I couldn't have discovered, described, and shared the information in this book without their hard work.

An enormous, heartfelt thanks to Ethne Clarke, whose warmth and generosity was the initial spark for this book. Few of us get anywhere in life if someone doesn't give us a chance, and I have Ethne to thank for this one. Also at Rodale, thanks to Karen Bolesta and Nancy Ondra, the editors for this book. Editors don't get enough credit for their contributions to a work, but I assure you that this book wouldn't be half so useful without their ideas, insight, suggestions, and expertise. Thanks to art director Christina Gaugler and illustrator Lindsey Spinks, you're holding a book that is far more visually dynamic and fun to look at than it would have been without their talent and vision.

Much appreciation and gratitude goes to the dedicated, visionary gardeners who are profiled over the previous pages: Tom Palamuso and Carol Siracuse; Chris Untalan, Katie Parsons-Untalan, and Safia, Lio, and Stella; Gwen Meyers, Megan Heeres, and everyone who makes Lafayette Greens the beautiful and valuable presence it is in downtown Detroit; and Patti Jablonski-Dopkin and the rest of the staff at Urban Roots Community Garden Center in Buffalo. An extra special thanks to Jim Charlier (jcharlier.com) and Katie Foreman (katieforeman.com) for taking the portraits of the gardeners at Urban Roots and Lafayette Greens, respectively.

Writing a book does not happen in a vacuum—it happens within the reality of the author's life and has a residual effect on everyone he or she comes into contact with during the making of it. To the staff at my day job at Spring Meadow Nursery, who every day reaffirm my belief that some of the best people on earth work in horticulture: Thank you. Everyone should be so lucky as to work with people like you.

Thanks to my late grandmothers who, in their way, contributed to my love of gardening: Glenna Webb, who let me pick as many lilies of the valley as I wanted, and Marilyn Hirvela, whose tomato patch intrigued and terrified me as a child.

To my amazing mom, Susan Robinson, who let me pick up beans off the floor at the grocery store and plant them: Can you believe that that was when the seeds of this book were planted, too? Thank you, thank you, thank you for your unlimited love and support. I could fill this same volume and then some with my love and appreciation.

For the benefit of my late father, Douglas Hirvela, I would like to publicly admit: You were right, Dad. I do need math. The proof is in this book.

To my in-laws, Amos and Amy Golovoy: I owe you an enormous debt of gratitude for your support of my career and for raising an amazing son. I will never be able to properly thank or repay you for what you've contributed to my life, though I will never stop trying.

My husband, Adam, saw the potential for this book before anyone else did, when it was a mere outline that I handed him so I could rehearse my talk for the 2012 Colonial Williamsburg Garden Symposium. His ideas, suggestions, and hard work are as much a part of this book as mine are. Adam, thanks for all of the watering, fertilizing, cooking, and cleaning you did so I could have time to write, and thank you, most of all, for your enthusiasm for gardening.

# about the author

Stacey Hirvela is a lifelong gardener whose love for growing food began at the age of 3, when her mother told her that the dried bean she picked up from the grocery store floor would grow if she planted it in soil. In her senior year at the University of Michigan, Stacey realized that her gardening hobby promised a better career than her linguistics degree did, so she moved to New York City to attend the School of Professional Horticulture at the New York Botanical Garden. After completing the 2-year program, Hirvela worked as a rooftop gardener in Manhattan, served as the horticulturist at the former Tavern on the Green restaurant in Central Park, and spent 6 years as a garden editor for *Martha Stewart Living*. There, she cohosted a call-in garden program on Sirius satellite radio and wrote numerous features for the magazine. She is based in west Michigan and works as part of the marketing team for Proven Winners ColorChoice Flowering Shrubs. As their social media specialist and contact person for home gardeners, she can confidently answer just about any hydrangea question.

When she's not in the garden, Stacey is either in the craft room or the kitchen, sewing, knitting, crocheting, spinning wool, or reading about and cooking all types of food. Living on the coast of Lake Michigan in the largest freshwater dune system in the world affords amazing opportunities for hiking, exploring, and botanizing. She speaks frequently to garden clubs and master gardener groups around the Midwest and, like most gardeners, cannot leave a garden center or plant sale empty-handed. Hirvela dreams of the day when she finally has room to grow all the edibles she wants with enough space left over to exercise her passion for ferns, native plants, and unusual trees.

# photo credits

All photos courtesy of the author with the exception of the following:

Rob Cardillo: page 167

Jim Charlier: page 84 (bottom right)

Katie Foreman: page 56 (top)

Adam Golovoy: pages 15, 36

Saxon Holt: pages 44, 54

iStock: pages 2 (all), 3 (all), 4 (bottom right), 6, 10, 14, 16, 20, 26, 31, 48, 54 (top), 58, 62, 63, 66 (all), 69, 74, 76, 79, 83, 88, 92, 94 (all), 95, 97, 99, 101, 104, 105 (all), 107, 108

Tom MacDonald: page 166

Patrick Montero: pages 72, 88, 112

Rodale Images: pages 165, 210

The hanging salad garden shown top left on page 4 was photographed at Chanticleer Gardens, Wayne, Pennsylvania.

The photo on page 27 is courtesy of PotLifter.

# index

Boldface page numbers indicate photographs or illustrations. <u>Underscored</u> references indicated boxed text, charts, and graphs.

## A

*Abelmoschus esculentus* (okra), 240–41, **241**. *See also* Okra (*Abelmoschus esculentus*)
Accessibility
    paths in raised beds and, 62, **62**, 64–65
    site selection and, 17, 19
Allelopathy, 46, 170–71
    black walnuts and, 46, 47, 171
*Allium fistulosum* (scallion), 248–49, **248**. *See also* Scallions (*Allium fistulosum*)
*Allium sativum* (garlic), 234–35, **234**. *See also* Garlic (*Allium sativum*)
*Allium schoenoprasum* (chives), 268, **268**, <u>278</u>–<u>79</u>. *See also* Chives (*Allium schoenoprasum*)
*Allium tuberosum* (garlic chives), 268, **268**, <u>278</u>–<u>79</u>. *See also* Garlic chives (*Allium tuberosum*)
*Aloysia triphylla* (lemon verbena), 271, **271**, <u>280</u>–<u>81</u>. *See also* Lemon verbena (*Aloysia triphylla*)
*Anethum graveolens* (dill), 269, **269**, <u>278</u>–<u>79</u>. *See also* Dill (*Anethum graveolens*)
Animal pests
    combatting, 108
    raised beds as solution for, 45, <u>60</u>, 156, **157**
*Anthriscus cerefolium* (chervil), 267, **267**, <u>276</u>–<u>77</u>. *See also* Chervil (*Anthriscus cerefolium*)

Arbors, Bean Arbor, 118, 120–21, **121**
Archways, Bean Archway, 118–19, **119**
*Armoracia rusticana* (horseradish), <u>261</u>, 262–63, **262**
Artichoke, Jerusalem (*Helianthus tuberosus*), <u>261</u>, 263, **263**
    as solo performer, 214, **214**
Artichoke (*Cynara scolymus*), 259–60, **259**
    in large-pot thriller-filler-spiller combination, 177, **177**
    in small-area thriller-filler-spiller combination, 210, **210**
    as thriller plant, <u>165</u>
Arugula (*Eruca sativa*), 220–21, **220**, <u>239</u>
    designing with, <u>169</u>
    edible parts of, <u>247</u>
    in medium-pot thriller-filler-spiller combination, 191, **191**
    as self-sower, <u>64</u>
    in small-area thriller-filler-spiller combination, 207, **207**
    succession planting and, <u>78</u>
    wild (*Diplotaxis tenuifolia*), 220–21, **220**
Asiatic garden beetles, 104
Asparagus (*Asparagus officinalis*), 260–62, **260**

## B

Bamboo
    projects
        Bamboo Ladder Trellis, 116–17, **117**

        Bean Arbor, 118, 120–21, **121**
        Bean Archway, 118–19, **119**
        Try a Tripod, 122–23, **123**
    stakes, 97
    using in projects, 115
Bamboo Ladder Trellis, 116–17, **117**
Bark (wood chips), as potting soil component, 32, <u>34</u>–<u>35</u>
*Basella alba* 'Rubra' (Malabar spinach), 240, **240**. *See also* Malabar spinach (*Basella alba* 'Rubra')
Basil Blowout, 193, **193**
Basil (*Ocimum basilicum*), <u>239</u>, 266, **266**, <u>276</u>–<u>77</u>
    Asiatic garden beetles and, 104
    as grocery store plant, <u>261</u>
    Italian
        in small-area thriller-filler-spiller combination, 200, **200**
        in medium-pot thriller-filler-spiller combination, 187, **187**
    'Pesto Perpetuo'
        in small-area thriller-filler-spiller combination, 193, **193**
    purple
        in large-pot thriller-filler-spiller combination, 179, **179**
    'Purple Ruffles'
        in small-area thriller-filler-spiller combination, 193, **193**
Bay laurel, as winter house plant, <u>111</u>
Bean Arbor, 118, 120–21, **121**
Bean Archway, 118–19, **119**

Bean Scene, 185, **185**
Beans (*Phaseolus vulgaris*), 221–23, **221**, 222
  bush
    in large-pot thriller-filler-spiller combination, 180, **180**
    in medium-pot thriller-filler-spiller combination, 185, **185**
    in small-area thriller-filler-spiller combination, 201, **201**
  pole
    as solo performer, 213, **213**
    training, 222
  as spiller plant, 167
  Summer Braised Vegetables, 171
  as thriller plant, 165
Beet (*Beta vulgaris*), 223–24, **224**, 239
  edible parts of, 247
  as filler plant, 166
  'Gourmet Golden'
    in small-area thriller-filler-spiller combination, 207, **207**
  in large-pot thriller-filler-spiller combination, 176, **176**
  saving seeds of, 81
  in small-area thriller-filler-spiller combination, 207, **207**
  succession planting and, 78
Beneficial insects, 105–6, **105**
*Beta vulgaris* (beet), 223–24, **224**. *See also* Beet (*Beta vulgaris*)
Biochar (charcoal)
  as potting soil component, 34–35
Bold Statement, 186, **186**
Borage (*Borago officinalis*), 266, **266**, 276–77
  as self-sower, 64
  in small-area thriller-filler-spiller combination, 202, **202**
Botanical names, 218
Box of Crayons, 201, **201**

*Brassica oleracea*
  broccoli, 224–27, **225** (*See also* Broccoli)
  collard, 228–29, **228** (*See also* Collard)
  kale, 236–37, **236**, **237** (*See also* Kale)
  kohlrabi, 237–38, **237** (*See also* Kohlrabi)
Broccoli (*Brassica oleracea*), 224–27, **225**
  in large-pot thriller-filler-spiller combination, 183, **183**
  in medium-pot thriller-filler-spiller combination, 191, **191**
  succession planting and, 78
  transplanting temperature for, 80
Brussels sprouts, substitute for in container gardens, 28
Buckets
  characteristics of, 12–13
  plastic
    as containers, 6
    drilling holes in, 11
Buckwheat, as cover crop for raised beds, 68

## C

Cabbage family members, 226
  club root and, 105
Cachepots, 7
  ceramic containers as, 10
Calendula (*Calendula officinalis*), 267, **267**, 276–77
  as self-sower, 64
  in small-area thriller-filler-spiller combination, 196, **196**
*Capsicum* spp. (pepper), 243–44, **243**, **244**. *See also* Pepper (*Capsicum* spp.)
Cardoon (*Cynara cardunculus*), 259
  in small-area thriller-filler-spiller combination, 210, **210**
Carrots (*Daucus carota* var. *sativus*), 227–28, **227**, 239
  as filler plant, 166

in large-pot thriller-filler-spiller combination, 183, **183**
  succession planting and, 78
Cauliflower, substitute for in container gardens, 28
Celery, substitute for in container gardens, 28
Celery root, substitute for in container gardens, 28
Ceramic containers, 2, **2**
  as cachepots, 10
  characteristics of, 12–13
  drilling holes in, 11
  weather and, 14
Chamomile, German (*Matricaria recutita*), 267, **267**, 276–77
  in small-area thriller-filler-spiller combination, 209, **209**
Chamomile, Roman (*Chamaemelum nobile*), 267, **267**, 276–77
  in small-area thriller-filler-spiller combination, 209, **209**
Charcoal (Biochar), as potting soil component, 34–35
Chard (Swiss chard), 225, **225**
  'Bright Lights'
    in small-area thriller-filler-spiller combination, 195, **195**
  in large-pot thriller-filler-spiller combination, 176, **176**
  in medium-pot thriller-filler-spiller combination, 187, **187**
  succession planting and, 78
Cheerful Companions, 196, **196**
Chervil (*Anthriscus cerefolium*), 239, 267, **267**, 276–77
  as self-sower, 64
  in small-area thriller-filler-spiller combination, 202, **202**
Chives (*Allium schoenoprasum*), 268, **268**, 278–79
  edible parts of, 247
  in medium-pot thriller-filler-spiller combination, 187, **187**
  in small-area thriller-filler-spiller combination, 204, **204**

Chive Talk, 204, **204**
Cilantro (*Coriandrum sativum*),
    <u>239</u>, 269, **269**, <u>278</u>–<u>79</u>
  edible parts of, <u>247</u>
  in large-pot thriller-filler-spiller
    combination, 175, **175**
  in medium-pot thriller-filler-
    spiller combination, 185,
    **185**
  as self-sower, <u>64</u>
  in small-area thriller-filler-spiller
    combination, 197, **197**
  succession planting and, <u>78</u>
Clay (terra-cotta) pots
  characteristics of, <u>12</u>–<u>13</u>
  drilling holes in, <u>11</u>
  weather and, 14
Climate
  choosing containers and, 11,
    <u>12</u>–<u>13</u>, 14–15
  degree days, <u>103</u>
Clover
  mammoth red
    as cover crop for raised beds,
      <u>68</u>, **69**
  in paths for raised beds, 64–65
Club root, cabbage family members
    and, 105
Cocoa (cocoa hulls), <u>29</u>
Coco (coco fiber, coir, coconut
    fiber, coconut hulls)
  as potting soil component, <u>29</u>,
    32, <u>34</u>–<u>35</u>
Coir (coco, coco fiber, coconut
    hulls, coconut fiber)
  as potting soil component, <u>29</u>,
    32, <u>34</u>–<u>35</u>
Collard (collard greens) (*Brassica
    oleracea*), 228–29, **228**
  in large-pot thriller-filler-
    spiller combination, 178,
    **178**
  in small-area thriller-filler-
    spiller combination, 196,
    **196**
  succession planting and, <u>78</u>
Companion planting
  old adages about, 170, 171
  thriller-filler-spiller concept
    and, 170–71
Compost
  increasing soil fertility with, 93

  as potting soil component,
    <u>34</u>–<u>35</u>
  using in raised beds, 70–71, 96
Composting, <u>94</u>–<u>95</u>, **94**, **95**
  bins for, **95**
  building pile for, <u>95</u>
  materials for, <u>94</u>–<u>95</u>, **94**
Compost/sand mixture, as potting
    soil component, 32
Compost tea, 96
Concrete containers, 2, **2**
  characteristics of, <u>12</u>–<u>13</u>
  drilling holes in, <u>11</u>
Container garden design recipes
  large-pot thriller-filler-spiller
    combinations
      Cucumber Lovers Only, 174,
        **174**
      Low Rider, 175, **175**
      Nutrition Station, 183, **183**
      Potluck, 176, **176**
      Sophisticate, The, 177, **177**
      Southern Sprawler, 178, **178**
      Summer Delights, 179, **179**
      Summery Sides, 180, **180**
      Tempting Tripod, 181, **181**
      Vampire Repellent, 182, **182**
  medium-pot thriller-filler-spiller
    combinations
      Bean Scene, 185, **185**
      Bold Statement, 186, **186**
      Leafy Glade, 187, **187**
      Lunar Landing, 188, **188**
      Pepper Party, 189, **189**
      Provence Provenance, 190,
        **190**
      Spring Greens, 191, **191**
  small-area thriller-filler-spiller
    combinations
      Basil Blowout, 193, **193**
      The Bitter End, 194, **194**
      To Boldly Grow, 211, **211**
      Bollywood Bowl, 195, **195**
      Box of Crayons, 201, **201**
      Cheerful companions, 196,
        **196**
      Chive Talk, 204, **204**
      Dinner Bell, 197, **197**
      Green Lanterns, 198, **198**
      In a Pickle, 199, **199**
      Rhapsody in White, 205, **205**
      Roman Holiday, 200, **200**

      Sage Advice, 206, **206**
      Seasonal Salad, 207, **207**
      Silver Sophistication, 210, **210**
      Sow Easy, 202, **202**
      Sweet and Golden, 208, **208**
      Sweet Somethings, 203, **203**
      Tea Time, 209, **209**
  solo performers
    beans on a tripod, 213, **213**
    heirloom tomatoes, 213, **213**
    Jerusalem artichoke, 214, **214**
    rhubarb, 214, **214**
    sweet potato, 215, **215**
Container gardens
  benefits of, 1–2
  diseases and (*See* Diseases)
  insect pests in (*See* Insect pests)
  tools for, <u>26</u>–<u>27</u>, **26**, **27**
  watering (*See* Watering)
Containers
  alternate uses for, <u>10</u>
  buckets
    characteristics of, <u>12</u>–<u>13</u>
    plastic, 6, <u>11</u>
  cachepots, **7**
    ceramic containers as, <u>10</u>
  caddies for, 151–52, **151**
  ceramic, 2, **2**
    as cachepots, <u>10</u>
    characteristics of, <u>12</u>–<u>13</u>
    drilling holes in, <u>11</u>
    weather and, 14
  choosing, 10–18, <u>12</u>–<u>13</u>, <u>15</u>, **15**
    climate and, 11, <u>12</u>–<u>13</u>, 14–15
    drainage and, 10–11, <u>10</u>, <u>11</u>
    sizes of, 16–17
  classic, 2–4, **2**, **3**, **4**
    hanging baskets, 4, **4** (*See
      also* Hanging baskets)
    planter boxes, 3, **3**, <u>12</u>–<u>13</u>
    pots, 2–3, **2**, **3** (*See also* Pots)
    window boxes, 4, <u>12</u>–<u>13</u>, 37
  clay (terra-cotta)
    characteristics of, <u>12</u>–<u>13</u>
    drilling holes in, <u>11</u>
    weather and, 14
  concrete, 2, **2**
    characteristics of, <u>12</u>–<u>13</u>
    drilling holes in, <u>11</u>
  conventional
    ceramic (glazed), 2, **2**, <u>10</u>, <u>11</u>,
      <u>12</u>–<u>13</u>, 14

concrete, 2, **2**, 11, 12–13
fiberglass, 3, 11, 12–13, 14–15
resin, 3, **3**, 11, 12–13
terra-cotta (clay), 2, **2**, 11,
  12–13, 14
wood, 11, 15
drainage holes in, 36–37
  drilling, 11
Fabric Grow Bag, 125–27, **126**,
  127
fall tasks, 108, 109–10
"feet" for, 3, **3**, 20, **20**
fiberglass, 3
  characteristics of, 12–13
  drilling holes in, 11
  weather and, 14–15
filling with soil, 37, 40
grow bags, 4–5, **4**, 125–27, **126**,
  127
  characteristics of, 12–13
  weather and, 15
grow rings, 5, 143–45, **144**, 145
grow towers, 5, 140–42, **141**, **142**
  characteristics of, 12–13
hanging baskets
  characteristics of, 12–13
  filling with soil, 37
  hammock, 134–35, **134**
  modular, 130–33, **130**, **132**,
  **133**
  sling for, 128–29, **129**
  spillers in, 168
Hanging Basket Sling, 128–29,
  **129**
hayrack, 6, 37
  characteristics of, 12–13
  layering dry fertilizer in, 93
  light and, 17
livestock equipment
  characteristics of, 12–13
  hayracks, 6, 12–13, 37
  stock tanks, 6, 12–13
Mesh Tower, 140–42, **141**, **142**
metal, 7, 15
  drilling holes in, 11
  working with, 136
Modular Hanging Planter,
  130–33, **130**, **132**, **133**
options for, 2–9, **2**, **3**, **4**, 5, **6**, 7, 9
for overwintering crops, 15, **15**
planters (planter boxes), 3, **3**
  characteristics of, 12–13

Planting Hammock, 134–35, **134**
plastic containers, buckets and
  bins, 6
  characteristics of, 12–13
  drilling holes in, 11
  weather and, 14–15
projects
  Mesh tower, 140–42, **141**, **142**
  Modular Hanging Planter,
  130–33, **130**, **132**, **133**
  Planting Hammock Planter,
  134–35, **134**
  Stacked Pot Planter, 158–59,
  **159**
Raised Beds, 153–57, **154**, **156**–
  57, **157** (See also Raised
  beds)
raising, 20, **20**
  using saucers for, 3, **3**
resin, 3, **3**
  characteristics of, 12–13
  drilling holes in, 11
saucers for, 3, **3**
self-watering, 8–9, **9**
  characteristics of, 12–13
  filling with soil, 40
  in Palamuso/Siracuse roof
  garden, 22–23
  saving water with, 90
  sowing seeds in, 78
  vacations and, 86
shoe organizer as, 7, 130–33,
  **130**, **132**, **133**
size of
  measurements for large, 173
  measurements for medium,
  184
for sowing seeds, 79
space fillers in, 18, **18**
Stacked Pot Planter, 158–59, **159**
stock tank, 6
  characteristics of, 12–13
terra-cotta (clay), 2, **2**
  characteristics of, 12–13
  drilling holes in, 11
  weather and, 14
thriller-filler-spiller design
  concept and, 168, 169–70
  (See also Design; Thriller-
  filler-spiller design concept)
unconventional, 4–9, **4**, **6**, **9**
  food cans, 7

grow bags, 4–5, **4**, 12–13,
  125–27, **126**, 127
grow rings, 5, 143–45, **144**,
  145
grow towers, 5, 12–13, 140–42,
  **141**, **142**
gutters, 7
hayracks, 6, 12–13, 37
kitchenware, 6, **6**
livestock equipment, 6, 12–13,
  37
metal, 7, 11, 136
plastic buckets and bins, 6, 11
recycled items as, 6
self-watering (See Self-
  watering containers)
shoe organizers, 7, 130–33,
  **130**, **132**, **133**
stock tanks, 12–13
whiskey barrels, 6–7, 12–13
wine boxes, 7–8
wood pallets, 8
upside-down tomato planter, 5
volume of, 38–39, **38**, **39**
watering (See Watering)
whiskey barrels, 6–7
  characteristics of, 12–13
window boxes, 4
  characteristics of, 12–13
  filling with soil, 37
winterizing, 109–10
wood, 3, **3**
  drilling holes in, 11
  weather and, 15
Copper Trellis, 137–39, **138**, **139**
*Coriandrum sativum* (cilantro),
  269, **269**, 278–79. See also
  Cilantro (*Coriandrum
  sativum*)
Corn (*Zea mays*), 93, 229–31, **229**
  in raised beds, 66
  Summer Braised Vegetables, 171
Cover crops
  for raised beds, 68–69, 68, **69**
  sowing, 109
Crop rotation, 67
  diseases and, 104–5
  insect pests and, 104–5
Crops
  choosing for containers, 24–25,
  28, 28
  for raised beds, 65–69, **66**, 67, 68

Crops (*cont.*)
  self-sowing, 64
  substitutes for large plants, 28
Cucumber (*Cucumis sativus*),
      231–32, **231, 232,** 233
  'Endeavor' or 'Diamant'
    in small-area thriller-filler-
      spiller combination, 199, **199**
  floating row covers and, 106
  in large-pot thriller-filler-spiller
    combination, 174, **174**
  powdery mildew and, 102–3
  saving seeds of, 81
  as spiller plant, 167
  training, 233
Cucumber Lovers Only, 174, **174**
*Cucumis sativus* (cucumber),
      231–32, **231, 232,** 233. *See
      also* Cucumber (*Cucumis
      sativus*)
*Cucurbita pepo* (summer squash),
      250–52, **251.** *See also*
      Squash, summer
      (*Cucurbita pepo*)
*Cynara cardunculus* (cardoon),
      259. *See also* Cardoon
      (*Cynara cardunculus*)
*Cynara scolymus* (artichoke),
      259–60, **259**

**D**
Damping-off, seedlings and, 79
*Daucus carota* var. *sativus* (carrot),
      227–28, **227.** *See also*
      Carrots (*Daucus carota*
      var. *sativus*)
Deck Corner Shelf, 147–48, **148**
Decks
  corner shelf for, 147–48, **148**
  protecting from pot stains, 20, **20**
  as sites for containers, 19
Degree days, 103
Design. *See also* Container garden
      design recipes; Sample
      gardens
  basics of, 20–21, **21,** 24
  fillers in, 163–64, **166,** 166–67
  layout considerations, 168–70
  raised beds, 61–62, 168–69
    crop placement in, 66–67, **66**
    paths in, 64–65

for small beds, 192
for small containers, 192
solo performers in, 212
spillers in, 164, 167–68, **167, 167**
thriller-filler-spiller design
    concept in, 163–64, 164,
    201 (*See also* Thriller-
    filler-spiller design
    concept)
  advantages of, 164
thrillers in, 163, 165, **165**
Dill (*Anethum graveolens*), 269,
      **269,** 278–79
  edible parts of, 247
  as self-sower, 64
  in small-area thriller-filler-spiller
    combination, 199, **199**
  succession planting and, 78
Dinner Bell, 197, **197**
*Diplotaxis tenuifolia* (wild arugula),
      220–21, **220**
Diseases
  advantages of container
      gardening in fighting, 100,
      101
  club root, 105
  crop rotation and, 104–5
  damping off, 79
  garden sanitation as control
      measure for, 108
  plant selection for resistance,
      104
  potting soil and, 36
  powdery mildew, 102–3
Drainage, 10, 11, 36–37
  drilling holes for, 11
  pot selection and, 10–11, 10
  raised beds siting and, 59
Drip irrigation, 86, 88–90, **89**
  drawbacks of, 89–90
  in seedbeds, 78
  as water-saving strategy, 90

**E**
Edible pots, tips for success with, 41
Eggplant (*Solanum melongena*),
      232–34, **232**
  as filler plant, 166, **166**
  in medium-pot thriller-filler-
    spiller combination, 186,
    **186**

in small-area thriller-filler-
    spiller combination, 194,
    **194**
  Summer Braised Vegetables, 171
Eight Tips for Excellent Edible
    Pots, 41
*Eruca sativa* (arugula), 220–21,
    **220.** *See also* Arugula
    (*Eruca sativa*)

**F**
Fabric Grow Bag, 125–27, **126,** 127
Fabric projects
  Fabric Grow Bag, 125–27, **126,** 127
  Hanging Basket Sling, 128–29,
    **129**
  Modular Hanging Planter,
    130–33, **130, 132, 133**
  Planting Hammock, 134–35, **134**
  working with fabric in, 124
Fall tasks, 108, 109–10
Fast-growing plants, 239
Fence Net, 149–50, **150**
Fences
  as plant supports, 97–98
  Fence Net, 149–50, **150**
Fennel (*Foeniculum vulgare*), 269,
    **269,** 278–79
  bronze
    in large-pot thriller-filler-
      spiller combination, 177, **177**
  edible parts of, 247
  Florence
    substitute for in container
      gardens, 28
  as self-sower, 64
Fertilizer, 41
  applying to raised beds, 93
  choosing, 93
  dry (granular), 93
    layering in containers, 93
  liquid, 93, 93
  role of in plant growth, 92
  slow-release, 37
  time-release, 37
Fertilizing, 92–93, 93, 96
  of seedlings, 79
Fiberglass containers, 3
  characteristics of, 12–13
  drilling holes in, 11
  weather and, 14–15

Fillers, 163–64
    plants useful as, 166–67, <u>166</u>, **166**
Floating row covers
    as frost protector, 109
    as insect control measure, 101,
        **101**, 106
Flowers
    edible, <u>247</u>, 265, <u>276</u>–<u>85</u>
        summer squash, <u>250</u>
*Foeniculum vulgare* (fennel), 269,
        **269**, <u>278</u>–<u>79</u>. *See also*
        Fennel (*Foeniculum
        vulgare*)
Frost
    frost-free date
        seed sowing and, 77
    protecting plants from, 109

## G

Garden sanitation
    as disease control measure, 108
    as insect pest control measure,
        108
Garlic (*Allium sativum*), 234–35,
        **234**
    edible parts of, <u>247</u>
    as grocery store plant, <u>261</u>
    in large-pot thriller-filler-spiller
        combination, 182, **182**
    in Summer Braised Vegetables,
        <u>171</u>
Garlic chives (*Allium tuberosum*),
        268, **268**, <u>278</u>–<u>79</u>
    in medium-pot thriller-filler-
        spiller combination, 186,
        **186**
Geraniums, scented
    as winter house plants, <u>111</u>
Glazed ceramic containers, 2, **2**, <u>10</u>
    characteristics of, <u>12</u>–<u>13</u>
    drilling holes in, <u>11</u>
    weather and, 14
Grass, as paths for raised beds, 64
Gravel, as paths for raised beds,
        65
Green Lanterns, 198, **198**
Grocery store plants
    basil, <u>261</u>
    garlic, <u>261</u>
    horseradish, <u>261</u>
    Jerusalem artichoke, <u>261</u>

mint, <u>261</u>
potato, <u>261</u>
potatoes, <u>246</u>
rosemary, <u>261</u>
shallots, <u>261</u>
sweet potato, <u>261</u>
Groundcovers, edible as paths for
    raised beds, 65
Grow bags, 4–5, **4**, 125–27, **126**,
    <u>127</u>
    characteristics of, <u>12</u>–<u>13</u>
    weather and, 15
Growing medium (soilless potting
        medium). *See also* Soil
    components of
        bark (wood chips), 32,
            <u>34</u>–<u>35</u>
        charcoal (Biochar), <u>34</u>–<u>35</u>
        coir (coco, coco fiber, coconut
            fiber, coconut hulls), 32,
            <u>34</u>–<u>35</u>
        compost, <u>34</u>–<u>35</u>
        compost/sand mix, 32
        manure, <u>34</u>–<u>35</u>
        peat moss (sphagnum moss),
            29–32, <u>34</u>–<u>35</u>
        perlite, <u>34</u>–<u>35</u>
        rice hulls, <u>34</u>–<u>35</u>
        sand, <u>34</u>–<u>35</u>
        sawdust (wood shavings), 32,
            <u>34</u>–<u>35</u>
        Styrofoam, <u>34</u>–<u>35</u>
        vermiculite, <u>34</u>–<u>35</u>
        water retaining crystals
            (hydrogel), <u>34</u>–<u>35</u>
    determining how much to buy,
        <u>38</u>–<u>39</u>, **38**, **39**
    diseases and, 36
    filling containers with, 37, 40
    homemade, 33
    nutrients in, 33, 36
    organic label and, <u>30</u>
    peat-based (sphagnum moss)
        mixes, 29–32
        alternatives to, 32
    recycling old, 33, 36, **36**
    selecting, 29–36, <u>30</u>, <u>33</u>, <u>34</u>–<u>35</u>
    using space fillers with, <u>18</u>, **18**
Grow rings, 5
Grow towers, 5, 140–42, **141**, **142**
    characteristics of, <u>12</u>–<u>13</u>
Gutters, as containers, 7

## H

Hand-picking, of insect pests, 106
Hand-watering, tools for, **83**, 87–88
Hanging baskets, 4, **4**
    characteristics of, <u>12</u>–<u>13</u>
    filling with soil, 37
    hammock, 134–35, **134**
    modular, 130–33, **130**, **132**, **133**
    sling for, 128–29, **129**
    spillers in, 168
Hanging Basket Sling, 128–29, **129**
Hardening off, of transplants, 80
Hayracks
    characteristics of, <u>12</u>–<u>13</u>
    as containers, 6
    filling with soil, 37
*Helianthus tuberosus* (Jerusalem
        artichoke), 263, **263**. *See
        also* Jerusalem artichoke
        (*Helianthus tuberosus*)
Herbs, 265, <u>276</u>–<u>85</u>
    fast-growing, <u>239</u>
    fertilizing, 93
    as filler plant, 166
    self-sowing, <u>64</u>
    with two or more edible parts,
        <u>247</u>
    using extra, <u>268</u>
    as winter house plants, <u>111</u>
Horseradish (*Armoracia
        rusticana*), <u>261</u>, 262–63,
        **262**
Hoverflies (syrphid flies), 105
Hydrogels (water retaining
        crystals)
    as potting soil component,
        <u>34</u>–<u>35</u>, <u>91</u>

## I

In a Pickle, 199, **199**
Insect pests
    advantages of containers is
        combatting, 100–101
    advantages of raised beds in
        combatting, 100–101
    in container gardens, 102–4
    controlling
        beneficial insects and, 105–6,
            **105**
        in container gardens,
            100–101, 102–4

crop rotation and, 104–5
floating row covers for, 101,
  **101**, 106
hand-picking, 106
kaolin clay sprays for, 106–7
physical barriers for, 101, **101**,
  106–7
plant selection for resistance,
  104
sticky traps for, 107–8, **107**
water sprays for, 107
creativity in combatting, 104
crop rotation and, 104–5
degree days and, <u>103</u>
garden sanitation and, 108
identifying, 103
raised beds and, <u>60</u>, 100–101,
  102–4
scouting for, 100
slugs, <u>101</u>
tolerating, 102
Insects. *See also* Insect pests
beneficial, 105–6, **105**
importance of properly
  identifying, 103–4
*Ipomoea batatas* (sweet potato),
  253–54, **253**. *See also*
  Potato, sweet (*Ipomoea
  batatas*)

## J

Jerusalem artichoke (*Helianthus
  tuberosus*), <u>261</u>, 263, **263**
as solo performer, 214, **214**
Johnny-jump-up (*Viola tricolor*),
  <u>64</u>, 210, **210**, 270, **270**,
  <u>278</u>–79
Juglone, 171
in soil from black walnuts, 46, 47

## K

Kale (*Brassica oleracea*), 236–37,
  **236**, **237**
succession planting and, <u>78</u>
Tuscan
  in large-pot thriller-filler-
    spiller combination, 181,
    **181**
Kaolin clay sprays
as insect control measure, 106–7

Kitchenware
as containers, 6, **6**
Kohlrabi (*Brassica oleracea*),
  237–38, **237**, <u>239</u>
edible parts of, <u>247</u>
in medium-pot thriller-filler-
  spiller combination, 188,
  **188**

## L

*Lactuca sativa* (lettuce), 238–39,
  **238**, **239**. *See also* Lettuce
  (*Lactuca sativa*)
Lafayette Greens garden, **56**,
  56–57, **57**
Lavender (*Lavandula* spp.), 270,
  **270**, <u>280</u>–81
in medium-pot thriller-filler-
  spiller combination, 190,
  **190**
Lawns, as sites for containers, 20
Leafy Glade, 187, **187**
Leek, substitute for in container
  gardens, <u>28</u>
Lemon balm (*Melissa officinalis*),
  270, **270**, <u>280</u>–81
in small-area thriller-filler-spiller
  combination, 209, **209**
Lemon verbena (*Aloysia triphylla*),
  271, **271**, <u>280</u>–81
in small-area thriller-filler-
  spiller combination, 203,
  **203**
as winter house plant, <u>111</u>
Lettuce (*Lactuca sativa*), 238–39,
  **238**, <u>239</u>, **239**
designing with, <u>169</u>
germination requirements of, 75
as self-sower, <u>64</u>
succession planting and, <u>78</u>
*Levisticum officinale* (lovage), 271,
  **271**, <u>280</u>–81. *See also*
  Lovage (*Levisticum
  officinale*)
Light
raised beds siting and, 58–59
seedlings and, 79–80
site selection and, 17
Livestock equipment
characteristics of, <u>12</u>–13
as containers, 6

hayracks, 6, <u>12</u>–<u>13</u>, 37
stock tanks, 6, <u>12</u>–<u>13</u>
Lovage (*Levisticum officinale*), 271,
  **271**, <u>280</u>–81
in medium-pot thriller-filler-
  spiller combination, 186,
  **186**
Low Rider, 175, **175**
Lumber (plastic and composite).
  *See also* Lumber
  (wood)
for raised beds, <u>52</u>, **52**, 53–54,
  **54**
framing kits for, 51
Lumber (wood). *See also* Lumber
  (plastic and composite)
for raised beds, 48–49, 51–53,
  <u>52</u>, **52**
durability of, 53
framing kits for, 51
maintenance of, 53
reusing old, 53
sealers for, 53
size of, 61
treated, <u>49</u>, 51–52
Lunar Landing, 188, **188**

## M

Maintenance
raised beds and, 45
  wood, 53
of thriller-filler-spiller plantings,
  171–72
Malabar spinach (*Basella alba
  'Rubra'*), 240, **240**
in large-pot thriller-filler-spiller
  combination, 181, **181**
as thriller plant, <u>165</u>
Manure
applying composted to raised
  beds, 96
composted, 96
as potting soil component, <u>34</u>–<u>35</u>
Marigolds, nematodes and, 170
Marjoram (*Origanum majorana*),
  271, **271**, <u>280</u>–81
in large-pot thriller-filler-spiller
  combination, 179, **179**
in medium-pot thriller-filler-
  spiller combination, 189,
  **189**

Masonry
    designing raised beds with, 62
    raised beds
        size of materials and, 61
    for raised beds, 52, **52**, **54**,
        54–55
*Matricaria recutita* (German
        chamomile), 267, **267**,
        <u>276–77</u>
    in small-area thriller-filler-
        spiller combination, 209,
        **209**
*Melissa officinalis* (lemon balm),
        270, **270**, <u>280</u>–81. *See also*
        Lemon balm (*Melissa
        officinalis*)
Melons
    saving seeds of, <u>81</u>
    as spiller plant in raised beds,
        <u>167</u>
    substitute for in container
        gardens, <u>28</u>
    training, <u>233</u>
*Mentha* spp. (mint), 272, **272**,
        <u>280–81</u>. *See also* Mint
        (*Mentha* spp.)
Mesh Tower, 140–42, **141**, **142**
Metal
    designing raised beds with, 62
    drilling holes in, <u>11</u>
    food cans as containers, 7
    in Lafayette Greens garden,
        56–57, **56, 57**
    projects
        Copper Trellis, 137–39, **138**,
            **139**
        Mesh Tower, 140–42, **141**,
            **142**
        Tomato Ring, 143–45, **144**,
            <u>145</u>
    for raised beds, 52, **52**, 55, <u>56–57</u>,
        **56, 57**, 58, **58**
    stakes, 97, <u>123</u>
    weather and, 15
    working with, 136
Millet, as cover crop for raised
        beds, <u>68</u>
Mint (*Mentha* spp.), <u>261</u>, 272, **272**,
        <u>280–81</u>
    in small-area thriller-filler-
        spiller combination, 203,
        **203**

Modular Hanging Planter, 130–33,
        **130, 132, 133**
Mulch
    as paths for raised beds, 65
    use of as water-saving strategy,
        90

# N

Nasturtiums (*Tropaeolum majus*),
        272, **272**, **282–83**
    edible parts of, <u>247</u>
    in small-area thriller-filler-
        spiller combination, 201,
        **201**
    trailing
        in large-pot thriller-filler-
            spiller combination, 181,
            **181**
        in medium-pot thriller-filler-
            spiller combination, 190,
            **190**
    as spiller plant, <u>167</u>, **167**
Nematodes, marigolds and, 170
Nutrition Station, 183, **183**

# O

*Ocimum basilicum* (basil), **239**,
        <u>261</u>, 266, **266**, <u>276–77</u>. *See
        also* Basil (*Ocimum
        basilicum*)
Okra (*Abelmoschus esculentus*),
        240–41, **241**
    in large-pot thriller-filler-spiller
        combination, 176, **176**
    in small-area thriller-filler-
        spiller combination, 195,
        **195**
    Summer Braised Vegetables,
        <u>171</u>
    as thriller plant, <u>165</u>
Onions
    longevity of seeds, <u>81</u>
    substitute for in container
        gardens, <u>28</u>
Oregano (*Origanum*), **272**, 272–73,
        <u>282–83</u>
    golden
        in small-area thriller-filler-
            spiller combination, 208,
            **208**

Organic, understanding the term,
        <u>30</u>
*Origanum majorana* (marjoram),
        271, **271**, <u>280–81</u>. *See also*
        Marjoram (*Origanum
        majorana*)

# P

Palamuso/Siracuse garden, 22–23,
        **22, 23**
Parsley (*Petroselinum crispum*),
        273, **273**, <u>282–83</u>
    edible parts of, <u>247</u>
    in large-pot thriller-filler-spiller
        combination, 180, **180**, 183,
        **183**
    longevity of seeds, <u>81</u>
    in medium-pot thriller-filler-
        spiller combination, 186,
        **186**
    in small-area thriller-filler-
        spiller combination, 194,
        **194**
    succession planting and, <u>78</u>
Parsnips
    longevity of seeds, <u>81</u>
    substitute for in container
        gardens, <u>28</u>
Paths
    in raised beds, 62, **62**
    materials for, 64–65
Paved surfaces, as sites for
        containers, 19, **19**
Paving stones, as paths for raised
        beds, 65
Peas (*Pisum sativum*), 242–43,
        **242**
    edible parts of, <u>247</u>
    as filler plant, <u>166</u>
    hot weather and, <u>78</u>
    in large-pot thriller-filler-spiller
        combination, 182, **182**
Peat moss (sphagnum moss)
    disadvantages of in containers,
        31–32
    as potting mix base, 29–32
        alternative to, 32
    as potting soil component,
        <u>34–35</u>
    potting soils based on, 29–32
        alternatives to, 32

Pepper (*Capsicum* spp.), 243–44, **243**, **244**
  bell
    in large-pot thriller-filler-
      spiller combination, 180,
      **180**
    in small-area thriller-filler-
      spiller combination, 197,
      **197**
    Summer Braised Vegetables,
      <u>171</u>
  as filler plant, <u>166</u>
  hot
    in small-area thriller-filler-
      spiller combination, 198,
      **198**
  hot lemon
    in medium-pot thriller-filler-
      spiller combination, 189,
      **189**
  Thai hot
    in medium-pot thriller-filler-
      spiller combination, 189,
      **189**
  transplanting temperature for,
    80
  white
    in small-area thriller-filler-
      spiller combination, 205,
      **205**
Pepper Party, 189, **189**
Perennials, in raised beds,
  67–68
*Perilla frutescens* (shiso), 274, **274**,
  <u>284</u>–<u>85</u>. *See also* Shiso
  (*Perilla frutescens*)
Perlite, as potting soil component,
  <u>34</u>–<u>35</u>
Pest control. *See* Animal pests;
  Insect pests
Pesticides
  container gardening and, 102
  rotenone, <u>30</u>
*Petroselinum crispum* (parsley),
  273, **273**, <u>282</u>–<u>83</u>. *See also*
  Parsley (*Petroselinum
  crispum*)
*Phaseolus vulgaris* (bean), 221–23,
  **221**, <u>222</u>. *See also* Beans
  (*Phaseolus vulgaris*)
Pinching back, 100

*Pisum sativum* (pea), 242–43, **242**. *See
  also* Peas (*Pisum sativum*)
Planning
  garden records and, <u>41</u>
  reflection as part of, 110
  in winter, <u>111</u>
Planters (planter boxes), 3, **3**
  characteristics of, <u>12</u>–<u>13</u>
  wooden and weather, 15
Planting Hammock, 134–35, **134**
Planting medium
  components of
    bark (wood chips), 32, <u>34</u>–<u>35</u>
    charcoal (Biochar), <u>34</u>–<u>35</u>
    coir (coco, coco fiber, coconut
      fiber, coconut hulls), <u>29</u>,
      32, <u>34</u>–<u>35</u>
    compost, <u>34</u>–<u>35</u>
    compost/sand mix, 32
    manure, <u>34</u>–<u>35</u>
    peat moss (sphagnum moss),
      29–32, <u>34</u>–<u>35</u>
    perlite, <u>34</u>–<u>35</u>
    rice hulls, <u>34</u>–<u>35</u>
    sand, <u>34</u>–<u>35</u>
    sawdust (wood shavings), 32,
      <u>34</u>–<u>35</u>
    Styrofoam, <u>34</u>–<u>35</u>
    vermiculite, <u>34</u>–<u>35</u>
    water retaining crystals
      (hydrogel), <u>91</u>
    water retaining crystals
      (hydrogels), <u>34</u>–<u>35</u>
  determining how much to buy,
    <u>38</u>–<u>39</u>, **38**, **39**
  diseases and, 36
  filling containers with, 37, 40
  homemade, 33
  nutrients in, 33, 36
  organic label and, <u>30</u>
  peat-based mixes, 29–32
    alternatives to, 32
  recycling old, 33, 36, **36**
  selecting, 29–36, <u>30</u>, <u>33</u>, <u>34</u>–<u>35</u>
  using space fillers with, <u>18</u>, **18**
Plants
  buying for transplanting, <u>74</u>, **74**
  selection of
    for disease resistance, 104
    for drought tolerance, 92
    for insect pest resistance, 104

Plant supports
  Bamboo Ladder Trellis, 116–17,
    **117**
  Bean Arbor, 118, 120–21, **121**
  Bean Archway, 118–19, **119**
  commercial for tomatoes, <u>256</u>
  Copper Trellis, 137–39, **138**,
    **139**
  Fence Net, 149–50, **150**
  homemade for tomatoes, <u>256</u>
  materials for, 97–98
  stakes, 97–98, **98**
    bamboo, 97
    metal, 97
    for tomatoes, <u>256</u>
    wood, 97
  systems of, 97–99, **97**, **98**, **99**
  Tomato Ring, 143–45, **144**, <u>145</u>
  tripods, 122–23, **123**
  Window-Frame Trellis, 160–61,
    <u>161</u>, **161**
Plastic buckets, bins, and pots, 6
  characteristics of, <u>12</u>–<u>13</u>
  drilling holes in, <u>11</u>
  weather and, 14–15
Potato, sweet (*Ipomoea batatas*),
  253–54, **253**, <u>261</u>
  in large-pot thriller-filler-spiller
    combination, 178, **178**
  purple sweet
    in small-area thriller-filler-
      spiller combination, 206,
      **206**
  as solo performer, 215, **215**
  as spiller plant, <u>167</u>
Potato, white (*Solanum tuberosum*),
  244–46, **245**, <u>246</u>, **246**,
  <u>261</u>
  growing cylinder for, 140–42,
    **141**, **142**
  in small-area thriller-filler-
    spiller combination, 204,
    **204**
Pot Caddy, 151–52, **151**
Potlifters, <u>27</u>, **27**
Potluck, 176, **176**
Pots, 2–3, **2**, **3**
  ceramic (glazed), 2, **2**
    characteristics of, <u>12</u>–<u>13</u>
    drilling holes in, <u>11</u>
    weather and, 14

classic, 2–3, **2**, **3**
concrete, 2, **2**
    characteristics of, <u>12</u>–<u>13</u>
    drilling holes in, <u>11</u>
fiberglass, 3
    characteristics of, <u>12</u>–<u>13</u>
    drilling holes in, <u>11</u>
    weather and, 14–15
glazed ceramic, 2, **2**
    characteristics of, <u>12</u>–<u>13</u>
    drilling holes in, <u>11</u>
    weather and, 14
resin, 3, **3**
    characteristics of, <u>12</u>–<u>13</u>
    drilling holes in, <u>11</u>
size of
    measurements for large, 173
    measurements for medium, 184
terra-cotta (clay), 2, **2**
    characteristics of, <u>12</u>–<u>13</u>
    drilling holes in, <u>11</u>
    weather and, 14
Potting soil (soilless growing medium)
    components of
        bark (wood chips), 32, <u>34</u>–<u>35</u>
        charcoal (Biochar), <u>34</u>–<u>35</u>
        coir (coco, coco fiber, coconut fiber, coconut hulls), 29, 32, <u>34</u>–<u>35</u>
        compost, <u>34</u>–<u>35</u>
        compost/sand mix, 32
        manure, <u>34</u>–<u>35</u>
        peat moss (Sphagnum moss), 29–32, <u>34</u>–<u>35</u>
        perlite, <u>34</u>–<u>35</u>
        rice hulls, <u>34</u>–<u>35</u>
        sand, <u>34</u>–<u>35</u>
        sawdust (wood shavings), 32, <u>34</u>–<u>35</u>
        Styrofoam, <u>34</u>–<u>35</u>
        vermiculite, <u>34</u>–<u>35</u>
        water retaining crystals (hydrogel), <u>91</u>
        water retaining crystals (hydrogels), <u>34</u>–<u>35</u>
    determining how much to buy, <u>38</u>–<u>39</u>, **38**, **39**
    diseases and, 36
    filling containers with, 37, 40

homemade, 33
nutrients in, 33, 36
organic label and, <u>30</u>
peat-moss (sphagnum moss) based mixes, 29–32
    alternatives to, 32
recycling old, 33, 36, **36**
selecting, 29–36, <u>30</u>, <u>33</u>, <u>34</u>–<u>35</u>
using space fillers with, <u>18</u>, **18**
Powdery mildew, 102–3
Projects
    bamboo
        Bamboo Ladder Trellis, 116–17, **117**
        Bean Arbor, 118, 120–21, **121**
        Bean Archway, 118–19, **119**
        Try a Tripod, 122–23, **123**
    fabric
        Fabric Grow Bag, 125–27, **126**, **127**
        Hanging Basket Sling, 128–29, **129**
        Modular Hanging Planter, 130–33, **130**, **132**, **133**
        Planting Hammock, 134–35, **134**
    metal
        Copper Trellis, 137–39, **138**, **139**
        Mesh Tower, 140–42, **141**, **142**
        Tomato Ring, 143–45, **144**, **145**
    wood
        Deck Corner Shelf, 147–48, **148**
        Fence Net, 149–50, **150**
        Pot Caddy, 151–52, **151**
        Raised Beds, 153–59, **154**, <u>156</u>–<u>57</u>, **157**
        Stacked Pot Planter, 158–59, **159**
        Window-frame Trellis, 160–61, <u>161</u>, **161**
Provence Provenance, 190, **190**
Pruning, 100
    tools for, 100
Pumpkins
    as spiller plant in raised beds, <u>167</u>
    substitute for in container gardens, <u>28</u>

R

Radishes (*Raphanus sativus*), <u>239</u>, 247–48, **247**
    edible parts of, <u>247</u>
    hot weather and, <u>78</u>
Rainwater, collecting, 90, 92, **92**
Raised beds, **44**, **46**, **47**, **48**
    advantages of, 45, 48
    animal pests and, 45, <u>60</u>, 108, 156, **157**
    basic mounded soil, 48
    building, 153–57, **154**, <u>156</u>–<u>57</u>, **157**
    cover crops for, 68–69, <u>68</u>, **69**
    creating, 71
    crops for, 65–69, **66**, **67**, <u>68</u>
    custom features for, <u>60</u>
    design of, 61–62, 64–65
    extras for, <u>156</u>–<u>57</u>, **157**
    fall tasks in, 108, 109–10
    fertilizing
        with dry fertilizer, 93
        with manure, 96
    framing
        kits for, 51
        treated wood and, <u>49</u>, 51–53
        with wood, 48–49, **48**, <u>52</u>, **52**
    getting started, 43–44
    grouping together, 62
    insect pests and, <u>60</u>, 100–104, 156, **157**
    lumber for (wood), 48–49, <u>49</u>, 51–53, <u>52</u>, **52**
        durability of, 53
        maintenance of, 53
        reusing old, 53
        sealers for, 53
        size of, 61
        treated, <u>49</u>, 51–52
    maintenance and, 45
    masonry, <u>52</u>, **52**, 54–55, **54**
        designing with, 62
        size of materials and, 61
    materials for
        masonry, <u>52</u>, **52**, 54–55, **54**, 61, 62
        metal, <u>52</u>, **52**, 55, **56**, 56–57, **57**, 58, **58**
        plastic and composite lumber, <u>52</u>, **52**, 53–54, **54**

Raised beds (*cont.*)
    materials for (*cont.*)
        treated wood and, 49, 51–52
        wood, 48–49, 51–53, 52, **52**,
            53, 61
    metal
        designing with, 62
        in Lafayette Greens garden,
            56–57, **56, 57**
    paths in, 62, **62**, 64–65
    perennial crops in, 67–68
    plastic and composite lumber,
        52, **52**, 53–54, **54**
    shape of, 62
    site selection for
        drainage and, 59
        light and, 58–59
        slopes and, 59, **59**
    sizing of, 60–61
    soil for, 69–71, 70
        increasing fertility of, 93, 96
    as solution for poor soil, 44,
        45
    thriller-filler-spiller design
        concept and, 168, 169–70
    tools for working in, 63, **63**
    in Untalan Family garden,
        46–47, **46, 47**
    in Urban Roots Community
        Garden Center, 84–85, **84,
        85**
    watering, 83, 156, **157**
*Raphanus sativus* (radish), 247–48,
    **247**. *See also* Radishes
    (*Raphanus sativus*)
Recipes
    for container designs
        See also Container garden
        design recipes
    culinary
        Summer Braised Vegetables,
        171
Recycling
    used items as containers, 6
    water, 92
Resin containers, 3, **3**
    characteristics of, 12–13
    drilling holes in, 11
Rhapsody in White, 205, **205**
Rhubarb (*Rheum rhabarbarum*),
    264, **264**
    as solo performer, 214, **214**

Rice hulls, as potting soil
    component, 34–35
Roman Holiday, 200, **200**
Roof gardens
    Palamuso/Siracuse garden,
        22–23, **22, 23**
Rosemary (*Rosmarinus officinalis*),
    273, **273**, 282–83
    edible parts of, 247
    grocery store plant, 261
    prostrate
        as spiller plant, 167
    topiary
        as thriller plant, 165
    trailing
        in large-pot thriller-filler-
            spiller combination, 175,
            **175**
    as winter house plants, 111
Rotenone, 30
Rutabaga, substitute for in
    container gardens, 28
Ryegrass, as cover crop for raised
    beds, 68

## S

Sage Advice, 206, **206**
Sage (*Salvia officinalis*), 274, **274**,
    282–83
    tricolor
        in small-area thriller-filler-
            spiller combination, 206,
            **206**
Salad burnet (*Sanguisorba minor*),
    274, **274**, 284–85
    in medium-pot thriller-filler-
        spiller combination, 188,
        **188**
    purple
        in large-pot thriller-filler-
            spiller combination, 174,
            **174**
        in small-area thriller-filler-
            spiller combination, 211,
            **211**
Salad greens
    designing with, 169
    fertilizing, 93
*Salvia officinalis* (sage), 274, **274**,
    282–83. *See also* Sage
    (*Salvia officinalis*)

Sample gardens
    Lafayette Greens garden, 56–57,
        **56, 57**
    Palamuso/Siracuse garden,
        22–23, **22, 23**
    Untalan Family garden, 46–47,
        **46, 47**
    Urban Roots Community
        Garden Center, 84–85, **84,
        85**
Sand, as potting soil component,
    34–35
Sand/compost mixture, as potting
    soil component, 32
*Sanguisorba minor* (salad burnet),
    274, **274**, 284–85. *See also*
    Salad burnet (*Sanguisorba
    minor*)
Sanitation, as disease and insect
    control measure, 108
*Satureja hortensis* (summer
    savory), 275, **275**, 284–85.
    *See also* Summer savory
    (*Satureja hortensis*)
Saucers, 3, **3**
Sawdust (wood shavings), as
    potting soil component,
    32, 34–35
Scallions (*Allium fistulosum*),
    248–49, **248**
    in large-pot thriller-filler-spiller
        combination, 178, **178**
    in medium-pot thriller-filler-
        spiller combination, 185,
        **185**
Seasonal Salad, 207, **207**
Seedlings
    damping off and, 79
    fertilizing, 79
    handling, 81
    hardening off, 80
    keeping healthy, 78–79
    light requirements of, 79–80
    planting depth, 81–82
    protecting roots during
        transplanting, 82
    supporting newly transplanted,
        82
    temperature requirements of, 79
    watering, 79, 82
Seeds
    advantages of using, 74–75

buying basics, 75–76
growing plants from, 73–80, **76**, **79**, **81**
longevity of, 81
organic, 76
pelleted, 76
planting depth for, 77
reading packets of, 75–76
saving, 81
self-sowing, 64
shopping for in winter, 111
sowing, 77, **79**
  indoors, 78, 79–80
  outdoors (direct sowing), 79
special germination needs, 75
starting in winter, 111
succession plantings and, 78
testing viability of old, 81
treated, 76
watering newly sown, 77–78
Self-watering containers, 8–9, **9**
characteristics of, 12–13
filling with soil, 40
homemade in Palamuso/
    Siracuse roof garden,
    22–23, **22**, **23**
saving water with, 90
sowing seeds in, 78
vacation watering and, 86
Shallots, 235, 261
Shiso (*Perilla frutescens*), 274, **274**, 284–85
  germination requirements of,
    75
  growth habit of, 168
  purple
    in large-pot thriller-filler-
      spiller combination, 174,
      **174**
Shoe organizers
  as containers, 7, 130–33, **130**,
    **132**, **133**
Silver Sophistication, 210, **210**
Site selection, 17, 18
  convenience and, 17, 19
  light and, 17, 58–59
  for raised beds, 45, 48
    drainage and, 59
    light and, 58–59
    slope and, 59, **59**
  for roof gardens, 22–23, **22**, **23**
  septic systems and, 55

surfaces for, 19–20
  decks, 19
  lawns, 20
  paving, 19, **20**
  water access and, 17
Slopes, raised beds and, 59, **59**
Slugs, 101
Soaker hoses, 88, **88**
Soil. *See also* potting soil
  buying topsoil for raised beds,
    70, **70**
  filling raised beds with, 71
  increasing fertility of, 93, 96
  as paths for raised beds, 64
  for raised beds, 69–71, **70**
  raised beds as solution for poor,
    44, 45
Soilless potting mix. *See* Potting
  soil
*Solanum lycopersicum* (tomato),
    254–57, 254, **255**, **256**, **257**.
    *See also* Tomatoes
    (*Solanum lycopersicum*)
*Solanum melongena* (eggplant),
    232–34, **232**. *See also*
    Eggplant (*Solanum
    melongena*)
*Solanum tuberosum* (potato),
    244–46, **245**, 246, **246**. *See
    also* Potato, white
    (*Solanum tuberosum*)
Sophisticate, The, 177, **177**
Southern Sprawler, 178, **178**
Sow Easy, 202, **202**
Space fillers, 18, **18**
Sphagnum (sphagnum moss, peat
    moss)
  disadvantages of in containers,
    31–32
  as potting mix base, 29–32
    alternative to, 32
  as potting soil component,
    34–35
  potting soils based on, 29–32
    alternatives to, 32
Spillers, 164
  plants useful as, 167, **167**
Spinach, Malabar (*Basella*), 240,
    **240**
  in large-pot thriller-filler-spiller
    combination, 181, **181**
  as thriller plant, 165

Spinach (*Spinacia oleracea*), 239,
    249–50, **249**
  designing with, 169
  hot weather and, 78
  in large-pot thriller-filler-spiller
    combination, 182, **182**
Squash
  summer (*Cucurbita pepo*),
    250–52, **251**
    edible parts of, 247
    floating row covers and,
      106
    growing cylinder for, 140–42,
      **141**, **142**
    in large-pot thriller-filler-
      spiller combination, 175,
      **175**
    in small-area thriller-filler-
      spiller combination, 211,
      **211**
    training, 233
  winter
    substitute for in container
      gardens, 28
Stacked Pot Planter, 158–59, **159**
Stakes, 27
  bamboo, 97
  materials for, 123
  metal, 97
  securing plants to, 98, **98**
  for tomatoes, 256
  wood, 97
Staking, 96–99, **97**, **98**, **99**
  advantages of, 96–97
  disadvantages of, 97
  systems for, 97–99, **97**, **98**, **99**
  of transplants, 82
Stevia (*Stevia rebaudiana*), 275,
    **275**, 284–85
  in small-area thriller-filler-
    spiller combination, 208,
    **208**
Sticky traps, for insect pest control,
    107–8, **107**
Stock tanks, 6
  characteristics of, 12–13
Straw-bale gardening, 50
Styrofoam, as potting soil
    component, 34–35
Succession plantings, 78
Summer Braised Vegetables, 171
Summer Delights, 179, **179**

Summer savory (*Satureja hortensis*), 64, 275, **275**, 284–85
Summery Sides, 180, **180**
Support systems, 97–99, 97–98, **98**, **99**
  arbors and archways
    Bean Arbor, 118, 120–21, **121**
    Bean Archway, 118–19, **119**
  materials for, 97–98
  stakes, 97, 98, **98**, 123, 256
  for tomatoes, 143–45, **144**, 145, 256
  Tomato Ring, 143–45, **144**, 145
  trellises, 98–99, **99**
    Bamboo Ladder Trellis, 116–17, **117**
    Copper Trellis, 137–39, **138**, **139**
    Fence Net, 149–50, **150**
    Window-Frame Trellis, 160–61, **161**, 161
  tripods, 122–23, **123**
Swallowtail butterflies, larvae of, 104, **104**
Sweet and Golden, 208, **208**
Sweet potato (*Ipomoea batatas*), 253–54, **253**
  grocery store plant, 261
  in large-pot thriller-filler-spiller combination, 178, **178**
  purple
    in small-area thriller-filler-spiller combination, 206, **206**
  as solo performer, 215, **215**
  as spiller plant, 167
Sweet Somethings, 203, **203**
Swiss chard
  'Bright Lights'
    in small-area thriller-filler-spiller combination, 195, **195**
  in large-pot thriller-filler-spiller combination, 176, **176**
  in medium-pot thriller-filler-spiller combination, 187, **187**
  succession planting and, 78
Syrphid flies (hoverflies), 105

Tarragon, French
  in medium-pot thriller-filler-spiller combination, 190, **190**
Tea Time, 209, **209**
Temperatures
  protecting plants from low in fall, 109
  for transplanting seedlings, 80
Tempting Tripod, 181, **181**
Terra-cotta (clay) containers, 2, **2**
  characteristics of, 12–13
  drilling holes in, 11
  weather and, 14
"Three sisters" method of planting, 170
Thriller-filler-spiller design concept, 163–64, 164
  companion planting and, 170–71
  fillers, 163–64, 166–67, 166, 166
  large-pot combinations
    Cucumber Lovers Only, 174, **174**
    Low Rider, 175, **175**
    Nutrition Station, 183, **183**
    Potluck, 176, **176**
    Sophisticate, The, 177, **177**
    Southern Sprawler, 178, **178**
    Summer Delights, 179, **179**
    Summery Sides, 180, **180**
    Tempting Tripod, 181, **181**
    Vampire Repellent, 182, **182**
  layouts considerations
    in containers, 169–70
    in raised beds, 168–69
    salad greens and, 169
  maintenance of plantings in, 171–72
  medium-pot combinations
    Bean Scene, 185, **185**
    Bold Statement, 186, **186**
    Leafy Glade, 187, **187**
    Lunar Landing, 188, **188**
    Pepper Party, 189, **189**
    Provence Provenance, 190, **190**
    Spring Greens, 191, **191**
  solo performers
    Beans on a Tripod, 213, **213**
    Heirloom Tomatoes, 213, **213**

    Jerusalem artichoke, 214, **214**
    rhubarb, 214, **214**
    sweet potato, 215, **215**
  spillers, 164, 167–68, 167, 167
  thrillers, 163, 165, **165**
  two-plant combinations, 192
    Basil Blowout, 193, **193**
    The Bitter End, 194, **194**
    To Boldly Grow, 211, **211**
    Bollywood Bowl, 195, **195**
    Box of Crayons, 201, **201**
    Cheerful Companions, 196, **196**
    Chive Talk, 204, **204**
    Dinner Bell, 197, **197**
    Green Lanterns, 198, **198**
    In a Pickle, 199, **199**
    Rhapsody in White, 205, **205**
    Roman Holiday, 200, **200**
    Sage Advice, 206, **206**
    Seasonal Salad, 207, **207**
    Silver Sophistication, 210, **210**
    Sow Easy, 202, **202**
    Sweet and Golden, 208, **208**
    Sweet Somethings, 203, **203**
    Tea Time, 209, **209**
Thrillers, 163
  plants useful as, 165
Thyme (*Thymus vulgaris*), 275, **275**, 284–85
  golden
    in medium-pot thriller-filler-spiller combination, 191, **191**
  as spiller plant, 167
  variegated
    in large-pot thriller-filler-spiller combination, 177, **177**
    in small-area thriller-filler-spiller combination, 205, **205**
To Boldly Grow, 211, **211**
Tomatillo, in small-area thriller-filler-spiller combination, 198, **198**
Tomatoes (*Solanum lycopersicum*), 254–57, 254, **255**, 256, **257**
  black walnuts and, 46
  cherry
    in large-pot thriller-filler-spiller combination, 179, **179**

fertilizing, 93
heirloom, 254
    as solo performer, 213, **213**
purple or black
    in small-area thriller-filler-
        spiller combination, 200,
        **200**
saving seeds of, 81
Summer Braised Vegetables,
    171
supports for, 143–45, **144**, 145,
    256
as thriller plant, 165, **165**
training, 256
transplanting temperature for,
    80
'Tumbling Tom'
    in large-pot thriller-filler-
        spiller combination, 176,
        **176**
    in medium-pot thriller-filler-
        spiller combination, 188,
        **188**
    as spiller plant, 167
upside-down planter and, 5
Tomato Ring, 143–45, **144**, 145
Tools
    for container gardening, 26–27,
        **26, 27**
    for hand watering, **83**, 87–88
    for leaf pruning, 100
    for raised bed gardening, 63,
        63
Topsoil. *See also* Soil
    buying for raised beds, 70,
        70
    filling raised beds with, 71
Transplanting
    handling plants during, 81
    planting depth for seedlings,
        81–82
    protecting plant roots during,
        82
    supporting transplanted
        seedlings, 82
    temperature and, 80
    watering, 40, 82, **83**
Transplants, **74**
    hardening off, 80
    keeping healthy, 78–79
    light requirements of, 79–80
    shopping for, 74

temperature requirements of,
    79
watering, 82
Trellises, 98–99, **99**
    Bamboo Ladder Trellis, 116–17,
        **117**
    Copper Trellis, 137–39, **138**,
        **139**
    Fence Net, 149–50, **150**
    Window-frame Trellis, 160–61,
        161, **161**
Tripods, 122–23, **123**
*Tropaeolum majus* (nasturtium),
    272, **272**, 282–83. *See also*
    Nasturtiums (*Tropaeolum
    majus*)
Try a Tripod, 122–23, **123**
Turnips
    substitute for in container
        gardens, 28
    succession planting and, 78

## U

Untalan Family garden, 46–47,
    **46, 47**
Urban Roots Community
        Garden Center, 84–85,
        **84, 85**

## V

Vampire Repellent, 182, **182**
Vegetables
    annual, 219
    crop rotation and, 67, 104–5
    enjoying the harvest, 172
    fast-growing, 239
    overwintering
        containers for, 15, **15**
    perennial, 258
    in raised beds, 67–68
    self-sowing, 64
    tips for growing in containers,
        41
    with two or more edible parts,
        247
Vermiculite, as potting soil
        component, 34–35
*Viola tricolor* (Johnny-jump-up),
    210, **210**, 270, **270**,
    278–79

## W

Walnuts, black
    juglone and, 46, 47, 171
Water, site selection and access to,
    17
Watering, 41, 82–83, **83**, 86–92, 86,
        **87, 88, 89**, 91, **92**. *See also*
        Water-saving strategies
    dipstick test for, 86
    drip irrigation, 86, 88–90, **89**
        drawbacks of, 89–90
        in seedbeds, 78
        as water-saving strategy,
            88–90, **89**
    equipment for, 77, 87–90, **88, 89**
    hand-watering tools, 26, 77, **83**,
        87–88
    how to, 86–87, 87
    newly sown seeds and, 77–78
    powdery mildew and, 102–3
    raised beds and, 60, 156, **157**
    seedlings, 78, 79
    self-watering systems, 8–9, 9,
        12–13, 90
        homemade in Palamuso/
            Siracuse roof garden,
            22–23
    soaker hoses, 86, 88, **88**
    time of day for, 82–83
    during vacations, 86
    vacations and
        tricks that don't work, 91
    where to water, 86–87
Watermelons, substitute for in
        container gardens, 28
Water-retaining crystals
        (hydrogels)
    as potting soil component,
        34–35, 91
Water-saving strategies, 90, 91, 92.
        *See also* Watering
    collecting rainwater, 90, 92, **92**
    drip irrigation as, 88–90, **89**, 90
    mulch, 90
    recycling water, 92
    selecting drought-tolerant
        varieties, 92
    self-watering containers, 8–9, 9,
        12–13, 90
    water-retaining crystals
        (hydrogels) and, 91

Water sprays, for insect pest
    control, 107
Weather
    choosing containers for
        prevailing local, 11, 12–13,
        14–15
    clay containers and, 14
    degree days, 103
    frost
        protecting plants from, 109
    glazed ceramic containers and,
        14
    spring frost-free date
        seed sowing and, 77
Whiskey barrels
    characteristics of, 12–13
    as containers, 6–7
Wilting
    moving containers as remedy
        for, 86
    as physiological reaction to heat
        or light, 83, 86
    shading plants as remedy for,
        86
Window boxes, 4
    characteristics of, 12–13
    filling with soil, 37

Window-frame Trellis, 160–61, 161,
    161
Wine boxes, as containers, 7–8
Wood. *See also* Wood projects
    chips (bark) as potting medium,
        32, 34–35
    drilling holes in, 11
    for raised beds, 48–49, 49, 51–53,
        52, 52
        durability of, 53
        framing kits for, 51
        maintenance of, 53
        reusing old, 53
        sealers for, 53
        size of, 61
    rounds for paths, 65
    shavings (sawdust) as potting
        medium, 32, 34–35
    treated and raised beds, 49,
        51–52
Wood chips (bark)
    as potting soil component,
        34–35
Wood pallets, as containers, 8
Wood planter boxes
    characteristics of, 12–13
    weather and, 15

Wood projects
    Deck Corner Shelf, 147–48,
        148
    Fence Net, 149–50, 150
    Pot Caddy, 151–52, 151
    Raised Beds, 153–57, 154, 156–
        57, 157
    Stacked Pot Planter, 158–59,
        159
    Window-frame Trellis, 160–61,
        161, 161
    working with wood in, 146
Wood rounds, as paths for raised
    beds, 65
Wood shavings (sawdust), as
    potting soil component,
    32, 34–35
Wood stakes, 97
Wreath forms, 144, 145

# Z
*Zea mays* (corn), 229–31, 229. *See
    also* Corn (*Zea mays*)
Zucchini
    powdery mildew and, 102–3
    Summer Braised Vegetables, 171